HISTORY
OF
BERKS COUNTY,
PENNSYLVANIA,
IN THE
REVOLUTION,
FROM
1774 to 1783,
BY
MORTON L. MONTGOMERY,

MEMBER OF THE BAR OF BERKS COUNTY,

Author of " Political Hand Book of Berks County" (1883), "History of Berks County" (1886), "School History of Berks County" (1889), and " Life and Times of Conrad Weiser " (1893).

VOLUME ARRANGED IN TWO BOOKS:

BOOK I.—Revolution.
BOOK II.—Biographical Sketches.

Southern Historical Press, Inc.
Greenville, South Carolina

This volume was reproduced from
a personal copy located in the
Publisher's private Library

All rights reserved. No part of this publication may be reproduced,
stored in a retrieval system, transmitted in any form, posted
on to the web in any form or by any means without
the prior written permission of the publisher.

Please direct all correspondence and orders to:

www.southernhistoricalpress.com
or
SOUTHERN HISTORICAL PRESS, Inc.
PO BOX 1267
375 West Broad Street
Greenville, SC   29601
southernhistoricalpress@gmail.com

Originally published: Reading, PA. 1894
ISBN #978-1-63914-015-2
All rights Reserved.
Printed in the United States of America

PREFACE.

THE first attempt at the compilation of local history in Berks County was made in 1841 by William Stahle, a storekeeper at Reading. He published a small volume of 68 pages in the English and German languages, in separate editions, which related chiefly to the business affairs of Reading, and was entitled, "A Description of the Borough of Reading." It was prepared by a promising young lawyer, Jackson H. Sherman, who had shortly before been admitted to practice in the courts of Berks County. He was a man of considerable talent, but the result of his labor shows that he lacked the real spirit of research and the true love of authorship. The facts collected by him fall far short of what might have been gathered at that time with ordinary pains. The opportunity was afforded for collecting important data that was truly enviable. Many persons were still living who could have supplied numerous particulars, either of their own knowledge or from hearsay; and various documents of an historical nature were still in existence, which could have been consulted and made the basis of a most exhaustive and reliable history.

As to the Revolution, the nine survivors (whose names are mentioned) could have been easily interrogated. All of them were over seventy-five years old. When the struggle for independence was going on, they were young men. By their assistance, the compiler could have collected sufficient materials to have enabled him to write a satisfactory story of the part that Berks County took in the war; and by patient inquiry and determination he could have obtained almost every important fact worth mentioning. But this opportunity was neglected; and this neglect is surprising to me, for the reason that there were then at Reading at least a dozen men who were highly qualified to compile an interesting and correct history, not only by their education, but also by their social position and their ample means, which would have enabled them to go ahead earnestly and successfully, without the fear of embarrassment or failure.

The next attempt was made by I. Daniel Rupp, of Lancaster, in 1844. For some years before, he had been gathering information relating to a number of counties in Pennsylvania that lay to the east and west of the Susquehanna River, and the result of his persevering industry was published in separate volumes, entitled after the several counties. One of them was the "History of Berks and Lebanon Counties," an octavo volume of 504 pages. His local information does not show much research. Beyond the taxables and the descriptive nature of the work, his effort is not to be classed above that of Stahle's. The joining of Lebanon County to Berks was a misconception, because there was no just reason for doing so. He should have joined Schuylkill County, for which there were many good reasons.

The disconnected portions about the Revolution are of the most ordinary nature. With the ability and experience that he apparently possessed to guide and encourage him, he should have been particularly successful, because he was looking up so many counties at the same time and for the same purpose. His chief aim must have been personal rather than general. He gave considerable space to two prominent political characters of Berks County (Weiser and Hiester), and also several ministers, without even a reference to others. Joseph Hiester, it is true, acted his part well in the Revolution; but there were other men who were his superiors in various ways, and yet Rupp did not regard them as worth looking after at all. I allude to such active and influential men as Edward Biddle, George Nagel, Henry Haller, Jacob Morgan, Nicholas Lotz, Mark Bird, Bodo Otto, Jonathan Potts, Daniel Udree, Daniel Hunter, Daniel Brodhead, Valentine Eckert, John Lesher and John Patton. These men were so prominent that he could not have failed to learn much about them while making his inquiries, if he had directed his efforts in the proper way.

Until then, the natural and inevitable changes from the lapse of time were not numerous nor great. Many of the older buildings, erected before 1776, still remained. Hence documents and correspondence of all kinds could have been found in the different counties that would have proven of incalculable value. But during the lapse of forty years more, the changes were both numerous and great, and matters and things had not only come to be disturbed very much, but many valuable links connecting the past with the present, that is to say, the times of 1776 with those of 1826, and particularly with 1876, were absolutely gone.

When I came to interest myself earnestly in historical subjects after 1880, I was not only surprised but very much disappointed to find available materials about the Revolution so limited at Reading; and personal inquiries at Harrisburg, Lancaster, Philadelphia and Washington were next to fruitless. The men at Reading, from 1830 to 1850, who were highly qualified for literary work, with leisure to accomplish it, are inexcusable for this gross neglect respecting a topic of such general value and importance. Even the proprietors of newspapers of that interesting period did not regard such information as worthy of preservation. The people seemed to turn constantly towards distant countries for knowledge relating to general history, government, &c.; and it never occurred to them that local matters were more important in the daily affairs of life. The Revolution was a subject that was particularly valuable, for the reason that it concerned their own personal freedom, unrestricted enterprise and local government; and a discussion of its causes, its merits and its successes would have given the two succeeding generations a higher conception of these elevating and ennobling ideas. This notion has been transmitted even until now, making it apparent that progress in this respect could not be expected to reach a plane above that occupied then.

In 1859, Amos K. Strunk, of Boyertown, published a small and useful book of 124 pages that contains the names of officers of the county who officiated from 1752 to 1860. He caused it to be printed in two editions, one in the English language and the other in the German. He gave much labor to its compilation, but he received only a little praise for his pains and enterprise. In 1883, I published the "Political Hand-Book of Berks County" (octavo volume of 104 pages), an enlargement of Strunk's idea as a book of reference. These two publications did not make any pretensions beyond the subject treated, and nothing else should be looked for in them.

In 1886, I completed the "History of Berks County," a royal octavo volume of 1204 pages. In it I devoted thirty-one pages (double column) to the Revolution. That was something on this line of inquiry, a good start; but a comparison of the matters therein contained with the contents of this volume will show that I had made only a feeble attempt at portraying the part Berks County accomplished in that important crisis of our history. In the short time that has elapsed since 1886, a considerable new information about the Revolution has come to light. The State of Pennsylvania published several additional volumes of *Archives* which were devoted entirely to that topic. Yet with this information as to Berks County added, and the whole narrative reconstructed, I still find this compilation imperfect and short of what it should be.

The patriots from Berks County in the war for personal liberty and free government had a right to expect succeeding generations to appreciate their sacrifices and to preserve a record of their actions. In doing their part well, they were not only prompted by selfish considerations for the enjoyment of privileges and advantages in their day, but by noble impulses for justice, and by the hope that their children would have the blessings of self-government, equality and peace. Such a record, however, was neglected by the next generation after them, and even by the second generation. What would those heroes, as colonels and captains and committeemen have said to their sons and grandsons if, by some mysterious power, they should have appeared in 1826, more especially in 1876, and seen naught done by way of recognizing or appreciating their services for freedom? The third generation is also rapidly passing away. Shall it be said of the great-grandsons that they, too, have not shown a proper spirit of appreciation?

My great-grandfather, John Spohn, was one of the captains of the year 1776. As a great-grandson of one of the heroes of that momentous struggle, I have endeavored to do my part towards building up a record worthy of their courage in the destructive ordeal of war for the right of self-government, and I hope it will be the means of awakening a proper spirit of inquiry by other descendants, looking to a completion of the undertaking herein attempted.

This volume is arranged in two books. The first is devoted to show the public support given by the people of Berks County to the Revolution; and the second to historical sketches of the more prominent men from the county who were engaged in active service. The former required much labor, research and study; but numerous facts in the latter were far more tedious to obtain.

The zinc etchings, published in connection with the biographical sketches, were made by John E. Heinly and William Diener, of the Reading Wood Cut and Photo-Engraving Company. The names are *fac-similes* of signatures, which I copied from the last wills of the respective persons on file in the Register's office, or from the entry of satisfaction of mortgages in the Recorder's office.

I have not given any references, showing the sources of my information, because a great many pages would have been marred by numerous repetitions of the same book; and also because the general reader is not interested in foot notes. The greater part of my information in the first book was obtained from the valuable publications issued by the State of Pennsylvania, namely, the *Colonial Records* and *Pennsylvania Archives*, first and second series; and in the second book from the papers on file, and also from the records in the offices of the Register and Recorder of Berks County. Besides the publications mentioned, the more prominent books consulted are the following :

Rupp's History of Berks and Lebanon Counties.
Scharf & Wescott's History of Philadelphia County.
Futhey & Cope's History of Chester County.
Bean's History of Montgomery County.
Rupp's History of Lancaster County.
Mombert's History of Lancaster County.
Egle's History of Dauphin and Lancaster Counties.
American Archives (Penn'a Historical Society).
Irving's Life of Washington.
Autobiography of Charles Biddle.
Bancroft's History of the United States.
Ramsey's History of the United States.
Johnson's Campaign of 1776 Around Brooklyn and New York.

I acknowledge the kindly attentions of Dr. William H. Egle (State Librarian of Pennsylvania), and Mr. Frederick D. Stone (Librarian of Pennsylvania Historical Society), to me at various times during the course of my researches for this compilation.

I cannot conclude this preface without expressing my appreciation of the co-operation and indulgence of Mr. Charles F. Haage, the printer, in the satisfactory production of this volume as to its arrangement, appearance, etc., for they contributed a great deal of encouragement to me in the completion of my arduous undertaking.

M. L. Montgomery.

READING, PA., June 1, 1894.

CONTENTS.

BOOK I.—REVOLUTION.

INTRODUCTION..................................... 17-18

CHAPTER I.
CAUSE OF THE REVOLUTION.................... 19-21

CHAPTER II.
PATRIOTIC SPIRIT OF THE COUNTY............ 23-38

> Public Meeting at Reading, July 2, 1774; Resolutions Adopted; Committee Appointed—Provincial Conference, July 15, 1774—Congress of Deputies, Sept. 4, 1774—Committee of Observation Chosen at Public Meeting, Dec. 5, 1774—Delegates to Provincial Convention Appointed, Jan. 2, 1775—Letters to Lancaster Committee—Circular Letter as to Wool—Resolutions of Provincial Convention—Battle at Lexington Awakens County—Conscientious Scruples Against War—First Officers Selected from County by Council of Safety—Germans to the Rescue—Population and Districts of County in 1776.

CHAPTER III.
ASSOCIATORS....................................... 39-42

> Counties of Pennsylvania in 1775—Recommendation of Congress—County Colonels of Associators—Preamble to Articles of Association—County Committee Recommends Articles.

CHAPTER IV.

INDEPENDENCE OF THE PROVINCE 43–55

Suppression of British Authority—Support of Civil Authority by the County—Provincial Conference, June, 1776; Deputies from County; Address; Declaration of Independence; Address for Flying Camp—Declaration of Independence by Congress; Read in County, July 8, 1776—Constitutional Convention of the Province; County Delegates Elected; Preamble to Constitution: Declaration of Rights.

CHAPTER V.

MILITIA SYSTEM................................ 56–74

System Provided by General Assembly—County Returns for 1775—County Returns for 1776; Delegates from County to Lancaster Convention, July 4, 1776—County Returns for 1777—New System Provided, June 13, 1777; Oath of Allegiance Required; County Districts Established; Battalions, Companies and Classes; Pay and Rations; Days of Drill; Fines; Pensions; Persons Exempted from Service; Oaths Administered in the County—County Returns for 1778—County Returns for 1780—County Returns for 1783.

CHAPTER VI.

COMPANIES FROM COUNTY IN THE REVOLUTION 75–150

In 1775.

Nagel's Company at Cambridge; Roll of Company; Services of Company.

In 1776.

Jones's Company in Canada Campaign; Roll of Company; Services of Company—Companies at New York: Of Captains John Spohn, Peter Decker and Henry Christ; Services of Companies—Lotz's Battalion in Flying Camp; Field and Commissioned Officers; Letter of Standing Committee to Con-

CONTENTS.

gress; Intentions of Congress Explained; County Troops at Bethlehem; Marching Order to Capt Daniel DeTurck; Roll of Company; Order to Organize; Battle of Long Island; Incidents of Hiester's Company—Weiser's Company in the German Regiment; Roll of Company; Services of Company; Other Men from County in the Regiment—County Troops at South Amboy; Battalion of Col. John Patton; Field Officers of Battalion; Companies of Captains John Lesher, Michael Wolf, George Miller and Michael Furrer; Battalion of Col. Mark Bird; Letter to Council of Safety; Resolution of Congress—Haller's Battalion near Trenton; Letter to Council of Safety; Resolution of Council of Safety.

In 1777.

Hunter's Battalion in New Jersey; Letter of Col. Daniel Brodhead; Resolution of Council of Safety; Letter from Gen'l Israel Putnam—Three Companies at Newtown; Letter of Gen'l Thomas Mifflin; Companies of Captains George Will, John Diehl and Nicholas Scheffer—County Men in Continental Line; Companies of Captains Jacob Moser and Jacob Bower; Sundry Enlistments: Captains, Subalterns and Privates—Two Battalions at Chester, Commanded by Hunter and Udree—Spyker's Battalion at White Marsh; Lieutenant Whitman Wounded at Germantown—Washington's Army near the County—Troops Encamped at Kutztown—No British Invasion of County.

In 1778.

Dragoons from the County in Provost Guard; Company of Capt. Bartholomew Von Heer—Lindemuth's Battalion on the Frontiers.

In 1780.

Hiester's Battalion with Reed's Army; Field Officers; Companies of Captains Charles Gobin, Ferdinand Ritter, Conrad Sherman, John Ludwig, Jacob Baldy and Henry Strouch; Selections from the 3rd Battalion—Two Companies of Ely's Battalion in the Frontier Service; Inhabitants Killed by the Indians.

In 1781.

Class of Lindemuth's Battalion on the Frontiers—Ely's Battalion at Newtown; Company of Capt. John Robinson—Capt. Jacob Livingood's Company.

In 1782.

County Troops on the Frontiers; Robinson's Company in Northumberland County; Sundry Troops Supplied.

Other Enlistments from the County; Names of Men Ascertained—Army Surgeons from the County; Hospitals at Reading—Reports of Men Supplied from the County—Payments for County Militia.

CHAPTER VII.

PRISONERS OF WAR AT READING............... 151–167

English Prisoners; Letter from Committee to Delegates in Congress; Conduct of Prisoners; Letter from James Read to Council of Safety; Quaker Prisoners from Philadelphia; Company of Capt. Conrad Geist on Guard Duty—Hessian Prisoners; Letter by Council of Safety about Removal of Prisoners to Reading; Camp Located on Commons; Camp Surprised by Militia in Disguise of Indians; Officer Drowned; Sickness and Burial of Hessians—German Prisoners; Company of Capt. Charles Krause on Guard Duty; Additional Men as Guard; Continental Troops as Guard; County Militia as Guard; Order of Council of Safety; Company of Capt. Peter Nagel on Guard Duty.

CHAPTER VIII.

ESTIMATE OF MEN IN SERVICE................ 168–173

For the Years 1775, 1776, 1777, 1778, 1780, 1781 and 1782—Recapitulation—Names of Captains Ascertained—Names of Colonels Ascertained.

CHAPTER IX.

ARMY SUPPLIES FROM THE COUNTY........... 174–189

Store House at Reading—Reports of Supplies Manufactured—Reports of Supplies Collected—Supplies taken in Oley in 1778—Masts for the United States Navy—Receipt Book of Col. Nicholas Lotz—Prominent Industries; Names and Location of Furnaces and Forges; Iron Masters; Other Industries—Prices during the Revolution—Pay of Men in Service—Continental Paper Money.

CHAPTER X.

PROCLAMATIONS FOR THE FAVOR OF GOD.... 190–193

First Recommendation of Congress for Prayer—Appeal for Support in Warfare—Proclamation Issued by Executive Council—Observance by County.

CHAPTER XI.

COUNTY INCUMBENTS OF POSITIONS........... 194–197

National Positions—State Positions—County Positions.

CHAPTER XII.

AFFAIRS AT READING...................... 198–204

Public Papers Removed from Philadelphia—Social Condition in 1777—Conway-Cabal supposed at Reading—Duel at Reading—Pre-Revolutionary Buildings at Reading.

CHAPTER XIII.

CONCLUSION 205–208

Independence and Peace—Return of the Soldiers—Revolutionary Survivors in 1823; in 1840; in 1846.

BOOK II.—BIOGRAPHICAL SKETCHES.

Edward Biddle	209	John Ludwig	246
Mark Bird	212	Jacob Morgan	247
Jacob Bower	214	Jacob Morgan, Jr	250
Michael Bright	215	David Morgan	253
Daniel Brodhead	216	George Nagel	254
Edward Burd	218	Peter Nagel	255
Henry Christ	219	Bodo Otto	258
Peter Decker	220	John A. Otto	261
George Douglass	220	John Patton	262
Thomas Dundas	221	Jonathan Potts	263
Valentine Eckert	223	Collinson Read	264
Conrad Eckert	224	James Read	265
George Ege	225	William Reeser	266
Balser Geehr	227	Christopher Schultz	267
Alexander Graydon	230	Edward Scull	268
Henry Haller	230	Peter Scull	268
Gabriel Hiester	232	Charles Shoemaker	269
Joseph Hiester	233	Jacob Shoemaker	271
Daniel Hunter	235	John Soder	271
Thomas Jones, Jr.	236	John Spohn	272
John Lesher	237	Benjamin Spyker	274
Daniel Levan	238	Peter Spyker	275
Sebastian Levan	238	Henry Spyker	276
Abraham Lincoln	239	Daniel Udree	277
Jacob Livingood	241	Henry Vanderslice	280
Nicholas Lotz	242	Benjamin Weiser	281
Christian Lower	245	Christopher Witman	282

BERKS COUNTY IN THE REVOLUTION.

BOOK I.—REVOLUTION.

INTRODUCTION.

The American Revolution was carried on from 1774 to 1783 against Great Britain by the thirteen Colonies that constituted the prominent settlements along the Atlantic coast from New Hampshire to Georgia, and existed under organized forms of government. The direct cause was the attempted imposition of increased taxes by parliament upon the inhabitants without representation or without their consent. The great majority of the people were distinguished for their steadfast determination and inflexible resolution in such an important matter as concerned their personal welfare, more especially the leaders of public thought and action in the several colonies, and this widely-prevailing sentiment developed amongst them a spirit of opposition that was earnest, persistent and courageous.

This sentiment, however, was not created in 1774. It had its origin thirty, even forty, if not fifty, years before. Without a steady growth through a number of years, it could not have become substantial. Looking at the situation and qualification of the people in this manner, we can not fail to give great credit and honor to the men of sound discrimination who lived several decades before that time and exerted a strong influence over them in establishing correct notions of social freedom, political equality, and local rights.

The County of Berks was erected in 1752 as a separate political body in Pennsylvania. For over thirty years, the taxpayers had been practically interested in public business that related to the laying out of roads for facilitating intercourse of one community with another, and to the erection of townships for administering local affairs. Afterward, in quick succession, numerous things of general concern were conducted in their midst to keep them interested in public progress, the more important having been the "Indian Invasion," the erection of the "District of Reading," the proposed change of government, and the building of the Court House and County Prison, together with many township improvements and private enterprises. In this way they were gradually and unconsciously prepared for a more serious undertaking, and when the crisis came that required them to show real appreciation of personal rights and local welfare, they manifested such a wonderful degree of social energy and co-operative resistance as to enable them to carry burdensome taxation, and endure trying and costly warfare for over eight years, until they finally realized the establishment of free government.

CHAPTER I.

CAUSE OF THE REVOLUTION.

The Parliament of Great Britain passed an Act on March 22, 1765, which required all instruments of writing, such as deeds, bonds and promissory notes, to be written on parchment or paper and stamped with a specific duty, otherwise they were to have no legal effect; but this measure met with such general opposition in Great Britain and throughout the American colonies, and was found to be so unpopular, that the act was repealed in the following year, February 17, 1766. The cheapest stamp was of the value of one shilling. The stamps on documents increased in value according to their importance. All the colonists manifested unbounded joy over the repeal of this odious law.

This opposition, however, led Parliament to pass a declaratory Act—which accompanied the repealing Act—asserting the power over the colonies "in all cases whatsoever." And in 1767 an Act was passed imposing certain duties on tea, glass, paper, and painters' colors that were imported into the Colonies. There was no representation in Parliament from the several Colonies, and regarding taxation of this kind as unjust and tyrannical, they held public meetings, formed associations to discourage and even to prevent the importation of British goods, and passed appropriate resolutions, which they forwarded to the King. His ministers, believing that a reduction of the tax would restore tranquillity, ordered this law also to be repealed, saving only a tax of three pence per pound on tea; and in 1770 an Act was passed accordingly. But even this was not satisfactory to them, and their recommendations to one another not to receive any tea were strictly carried out.

In the meantime, the East India Company had accumulated 17,000,000 pounds of this article on hand, and fearing great losses, they led Parliament to authorize the exportation of tea to any part of the world free of duty. With such encouragement, the company in 1774 loaded several ships with tea and sent them to the American Colonies; but the colonists were firm in their resolution and determined to obstruct the sale of it and to refuse to pay even so slight a tax as three pence per pound. When the ships arrived near Philadelphia and New York, the captains were warned not to land, and, fearing this warning, they returned to England. The tea sent to Charleston was landed, but it could not be sold, and after having been stored for a while in damp cellars it became a total loss to the company. And at Boston, while efforts were being made to land the tea, certain men in the disguise of Indians stole their way upon the vessels, broke open 342 chests of tea and threw the contents overboard. When Parliament heard of these proceedings, an Act was passed, called the "Boston Port Bill," directing the Port of Boston to be closed and the Custom House to be removed to Salem; and other humiliating Acts were also passed which were particularly offensive to the people of Boston, indeed of all Massachusetts.

Information about these Acts reached Boston on May the 10th, and on the 13th, at a town meeting, the inhabitants resolved:

> "That, if the other Colonies would unite with them to stop all importations from Great Britain and the West Indies until those Acts should be repealed, it would prove the salvation of North America and her liberties; but if they should continue their exports and imports, there was reason to fear that fraud, power and the most odious oppression would triumph over justice, right, social happiness and freedom."

Copies of this resolution were transmitted to all the other Colonies. It awakened not only a feeling of sympathy but a strong spirit of co-operation, and led them to concur in the propriety of calling a Provincial Congress.

Public meetings were held at different places, such as county towns, and, besides discussing topics so important to liberty and general welfare, committees of correspondence were appointed to communicate the actions of the several meetings to one another throughout the Colonies. In this way it was discovered that the same feeling prevailed everywhere, and naturally there came to be united efforts towards accomplishing a common result for the benefit of all.

About this time the terms "Whigs" and "Tories" were introduced to designate either those who were arrayed on the side of the Colonies in sympathy with Boston, or those who were in sympathy with the policy of the British government.

COURT HOUSE, PENN SQUARE, READING.

CHAPTER II.

PATRIOTIC SPIRIT OF THE COUNTY.

PUBLIC MEETING AT READING IN 1774.

When the news reached Reading, in Berks County, the citizens manifested great excitement and meetings were held at which the action of the British government was condemned. These meetings were called by notices headed "Boston Port Bill," and posted throughout the town. A report of one of these meetings has been preserved, and is presented in this connection to show what action the people of Reading and vicinity were inspired to take, and what expressions they were led to make in the matter.

RESOLUTIONS ADOPTED

At a meeting of a very respectable body of freeholders and others, inhabitants of the County of Berks, held in the Court House at Reading, the 2d of July, 1774, Edward Biddle, Esq., in the chair, the following resolutions were adopted:

"This assembly, taking into their very serious consideration the present critical situation of American affairs, do unanimously resolve as follows, viz.:

"1. That the inhabitants of this county do owe, and will pay due allegiance to our rightful Sovereign, King George the Third.

"2. That the powers claimed, and now attempted to be put into execution by the British Parliament, are fundamentally wrong, and cannot be admitted without the utter destruction of the liberties of America.

"3. That the Boston Port Bill is unjust and tyrannical in the extreme. And that the measures pursued against Boston are intended to operate equally against the rights and liberties of the other colonies.

"4. That this assembly doth concur in opinion with their respective brethren of Philadelphia, that there is an absolute necessity for an immediate congress of the deputies of the several advices, in order to deliberate upon and pursue such measures as may radically heal our present unhappy disturbances, and settle with precision the rights and liberties of America.

"5. That the inhabitants of this county, confiding in the prudence and ability of the deputies intended to be chosen for the general congress, will cheerfully submit to any measures which may be found by the said congress best adapted for the restoration of harmony between the mother-country and the colonies, and for the security and firm establishment of the rights of America.

"6. That, as the people of Boston are now suffering in the grand and common cause of American liberty,

"*Resolved*, That it is the duty of all the inhabitants to contribute to the support of the said sufferers, and that the committee hereafter named do open subscriptions for their relief. And further, that the said committee do lay out the amount of such subscriptions in purchasing flour and other provisions, to be sent by them to our said suffering brethren.

"7. That Edward Biddle, James Read, Daniel Brodhead, Henry Christ, Esqs., Christopher Schultz, Thomas Dundas and Jonathan Potts, gentlemen, be, and they are hereby appointed a committee to meet and correspond with the committees from the other counties of the Province."

The thanks of the assembly were unanimously voted to the chairman for the spirited manner in which he pointed out the dangerous situation of all the American colonies. He expressed at the same time the greatest loyalty to King George, notwithstanding he had the highest regard for the liberties of America.

There was great unanimity of sentiment as to the resolutions, and all cordially agreed to sacrifice every temporary advantage for the purpose of securing freedom to themselves and to their posterity.

The committee doubtless raised money and forwarded flour and provisions to the suffering brethren at Boston soon after the meeting, but I have not been able to ascertain the quantity. Reading was a prominent centre of trade in 1774, and the country roundabout possessed an abundance of grain and provisions. There were numerous grist mills within a radius of ten miles, and the collection of many barrels of flour was a comparatively easy matter for such a worthy cause, especially under the appeal of such men as composed the committee. All were capable, influential men. Biddle and Read were attorneys, Christ an innkeeper, Potts a physician, Dundas a merchant, Brodhead a large miller of Heidelberg, and Schultz a prosperous farmer of Hereford.

Similar meetings were held in the other counties during June and July, and committees were also appointed to act for and represent the respective counties.

From this meeting to the close of the Revolution, the people of Reading and of the county participated actively in all the affairs of the province which were conducted towards the establishment of independence. They were represented by delegates at the several conferences; and they contributed their quota of men, money and supplies in the successful prosecution of the war.

PROVINCIAL CONFERENCE.

The delegates from the several counties of the Province were called to meet at Philadelphia on July 15, 1774. This meeting was attended by the committee named as representatives from Berks County. The notice for the meeting was issued by the committee of Philadelphia City in the following form:

"The Governor declining to call the Assembly, renders it necessary to take the sentiments of the inhabitants; and for that purpose it is agreed to call a meeting of the inhabitants of this city and county at the State House on Wednesday the 15th instant [July.] And we would wish to have the sentiments and concurrence of our brethren in the several counties who are equally interested with us in the General Cause. We earnestly desire you to call together the principal inhabitants of your county and to take their sentiments. We shall forward to you, by every occasion, any matters of consequence that come to our knowledge and we should be glad if you would choose and appoint a committee to correspond with us."

The first action of the meeting was the reading of the letters from Boston, dated May 13, 1774, and a statement of the steps taken in consequence thereof, and of the measures pursued in this and the adjoining provinces. Then a series of sixteen appropriate resolutions were adopted, which are remarkable for earnestness and courage in behalf of local rights and independence; and a committee was appointed to prepare and bring in a draught of instructions. On this committee was Daniel Brodhead, from Berks County. The committee performed its duty in an admirable manner, and the result of its deliberations was a document truly distinguished for its devotion to the King, but also to the political and social welfare of the people. Upon its adoption, the committee was directed to present the same to the General Assembly (which was then in session at Philadelphia), and this the committee accordingly did, in a body, on the 21st of July.

CONGRESS OF DEPUTIES.

Among other things in the instructions, they asked the Assembly "to appoint a proper number of persons to attend a Congress of Deputies from the several Colonies at such time and place as may be agreed upon to effect a general plan of conduct;" and the Assembly accordingly appointed eight Deputies from the representatives of the eleven counties in the State. Edward Biddle, Esq., from Berks County, was selected as one of them. The other Colonies also appointed Deputies. All of them, numbering fifty-five, assembled at Philadelphia on September 4, 1774, and effected an organization in Carpenter's Hall on the 5th, with Peyton Randolph, of Virginia, as president. The sessions of this Congress were continued until the 25th of October following. Though a desire for conciliation was manifested, the opposition of Massachusetts to the Parliamentary legislation was approved and the declaration was made that, if the British government should attempt to carry out its provisions, all America ought to unite in sustaining the sister colony in her opposition. The delegates agreed upon a declaration of rights, a determination to stop imports from and exports to Great Britain and a discontinuance of the slave trade; and they also prepared a petition to the King and an address to the British people. Then they adjourned to meet again at the same place on May 10, 1775, unless redress should be afforded in the meantime.

Besides the matters mentioned, this Congress also adopted Articles of Association, and one of the articles provided that a Committee of Observation should be chosen in every county, city and town by the qualified electors.

COUNTY COMMITTEE OF OBSERVATION.

Pursuant to advertisements scattered throughout Berks County, a respectable number of the inhabitants met on December 5th, 1774, at the court-house, in Reading, and proceeded by ballot to the election of a committee, as recommended by Congress, when the following gentlemen were duly chosen:

Edward Biddle,	Michael Bright,	Sebastian Levan,
Christopher Schultz,	John Patton,	George Nagel,
Dr. Jonathan Potts,	Mark Bird,	Christopher Witman,
William Reeser,	John Jones,	Jacob Shoemaker,
Baltzer Geehr,	John Old,	James Lewis.

In the latter part of December, the Committee received a communication from the Committee of Philadelphia, dated December 22, 1774, which read as follows:

"Gentlemen: By order of the Committee of the City and Liberties of Philadelphia, we have the pleasure to transmit you the following resolves, passed this day with great unanimity, viz:

"That this Committee think it absolutely necessary that the Committees of the Counties of this province, or such deputies as they may appoint for this purpose, be requested to meet together in provincial convention as soon as convenient; and that it be recommended to the County Committees to meet in said convention on Monday, the 23d day of January next, in the City of Philadelphia."

"From a view of the present situation of public affairs, the Committee have been induced to propose this convention that the sense of the province may be obtained; and that the measures to be taken thereupon may be the result of the united wisdom of the Colony.

"The obvious necessity of giving an immediate consideration to many matters of the greatest importance to the general welfare will, we hope, sufficiently apologize to you for naming so early a day as the 23d of January."

DELEGATES TO PROVINCIAL CONVENTION.

In pursuance of this letter, the Committee met at Reading on January 2, 1775, and unanimously agreed to the proposed Provincial Convention, and they appointed the following delegates to represent the county at the convention:

Edward Biddle,	Sebastian Levan,	Jonathan Potts,
Mark Bird,	John Patton,	Christopher Schultz.
Baltzer Geehr,		

They also then appointed a Committee of Correspondence for the county:

Edward Biddle,	Jonathan Potts,	Christopher Witman.
Mark Bird,	William Reeser,	

This Committee selected Dr. Jonathan Potts to act as secretary.

LETTERS TO LANCASTER COMMITTEE.

On the same day, Dr. Potts addressed a letter to the Committee of Correspondence for the County of Lancaster, stating therein that they had received a letter from the Committee of Correspondence of the City and Liberties of Philadelphia, in which it was proposed that a Provincial Convention be held at Philadelphia on the 23d instant, and adding that they had considered the proposition, unanimously agreed to the convention, and appointed the delegates named to attend the proposed convention in behalf of Berks County. He concluded his letter by informing them also of the selection of a Committee of Correspondence, and adding the five names of the Committee.

Another letter from the same Committee was addressed to the Committee of Lancaster on January 5, 1775. It was as follows:

"Gentlemen: Enclosed is an extract from the proceedings of the Committee of this County, by which you will see that deputies are appointed to attend the proposed Provincial Convention.

"When we consider that our disputes are drawing fast to a crisis, and that the most cordial unanimity is absolutely necessary for our preservation, we cannot doubt but that your respectable committee will without hesitation appoint deputies to attend the Provincial Congress. The neglect of any one County may have the most fatal consequences. And we well know the pleasure it would give our enemies to see even the appearance of a disunion at this very important time. The great consequence of this subject will, we hope, apologize for this freedom."

CIRCULAR LETTER AS TO WOOL.

The following letter, in reference to sheep and wool in the county, was circulated throughout the county during the latter part of January, 1775:

"READING, January 16th, 1775.
"*To the Farmers of Berks County:*

"The Committee of the County of Berks having considered the association of the butchers of this town not to kill any sheep whatsoever till the first day of May next, take the liberty earnestly to recommend to the inhabitants of this county not to sell any sheep whatsoever to any butcher from Philadelphia or elsewhere till the first day of May. The preserving of wool being an object of the greatest consequence, the committee flatter themselves that the farmers will cheerfully observe this recommendation, and as the committee will meet in Reading on Tuesday, the 14th day of February, if any inhabitants have any objections to make to the measure hereby recommended, such inhabitants are requested to attend the committee to make their objections, that the same may be maturely considered.

"Any person having wool which he cannot dispose of in the country, may bring it to the house of Mr. Mark Bird, in Reading, who will give fourteen pence per pound for any quantity.

"By Order of the Committee,

"JONATHAN POTTS, *Secretary.*"

From the patriotic spirit that prevailed, this recommendation was doubtless observed, but I could not find any notice of a meeting of the Committee on February 14, 1775.

RESOLUTIONS OF PROVINCIAL CONVENTION.

The delegates from the several counties accordingly assembled at Philadelphia on January 23, 1775, and adopted the following resolutions:

That this Convention most heartily approve of the conduct and proceedings of the Continental Congress.

That we will faithfully endeavor to carry into execution the measures of the Association entered into and recommended by them.

That, as it was necessary to lay a restraint on importation and supply of articles necessary for subsistence, and clothing and defense must be provided, no person should use, sell or kill for market any sheep under four years old, and it was recommended that woolen manufactories be set up, especially for coating, flannel, blankets, rags, coverlids, hosiery and coarse cloths.

That flax and hemp be raised, and mills be erected for breaking, swinging and softening them; salt made in the manner used in other countries, and saltpetre; gunpowder manufactured as largely as possible; nails, wire and steel made, and also different kinds of paper from the old linen and rags preserved for that purpose; that houses be set up for glass, wool combs and cards, tin plates, copper sheets, bottoms and kettles, grindstones and fulling mills; and as the brewing of malt liquors would tend to render the consumption of foreign liquors less necessary, that proper attention be given to the cultivation of barley.

That all the inhabitants of the province promise themselves to use our own manufactures, and those of the other colonies in preference to all others.

That societies be established and premiums be granted in the several counties to persons who may excel in the several branches of manufacturing.

That any manufacturer or vender of goods, who shall take advantage of the necessities of his country by selling his merchandise at an unusual or extravagant profit, shall be considered an enemy to his country and be advertised as such by the committee.

That printers use the types made by an ingenious artist in Germantown in preference to any which may be hereafter imported.

That the Committee of Correspondence of Philadelphia be a standing Committee for the several counties, but to give notice to them whenever a Provincial Council becomes necessary."

While preparations were being made for this Conference, the House of Lords met in London on January 20th, and it was on that occasion that Chatham made his brilliant defense o the American Colonies and appealed most eloquently for reconciliation. But his appeal was in vain, for his motion was rejected by a vote of 68 against 18, almost four to one.

BATTLE AT LEXINGTON AWAKENS COUNTY.

The battle of Lexington was fought on April 19, 1775. When the news of the battle reached Reading, about a week afterward, a company of men was formed, who wore crape for a cockade in token of the sorrow for the slaughter of their brethren. Each township in Berks County resolved to raise and discipline its company. On the 25th of April, a town meeting was called at Philadelphia, when thousands of the inhabitants assembled, and agreed to associate for the purpose of defending with arms their lives, their property and their liberty.

This patriotic feeling prevailed also at Reading and in the county. The following extract of a letter from Reading, dated April 26, 1775, presents it forcibly:

"We have raised in this town two companies of foot under proper officers; and such is the spirit of the people of this free county, that in three weeks time there is not a township in it that will not have a company raised and disciplined, ready to assert at the risk of their lives the freedom of America."

The companies mentioned were those commanded by Capt. George Nagel and Capt. John Spohn.

Conscientious Scruples against War.—A meeting of deputies of divers inhabitants of the county, who were conscientiously scrupulous against bearing arms, was held at Reading on September 1, 1775. They passed certain resolutions, which, briefly stated, were as follows:

1. Agreeing to voluntary subscriptions for the uses pointed out by the recommendations of the Assembly on June 30, 1775, and of the Continental Congress on July 18, 1775.
2. Ordering accounts of moneys received and expended to be kept by a treasurer.
3. Submitting the moneys to the disposal of the Committee of Safety as a part of the share to be accounted for by Berks County.
4. Agreeing to answer requisitions on them by the Committee of Safety.

These resolutions were signed by Wm. Reeser, as president of the meeting. On September 11, 1775, he sent a copy of them to the Committee of Safety, stating in his accompanying letter that they were conscientiously scrupulous of taking up arms, though fully sensible of the justice of the cause, but that they were willing to contribute to its support. He acknowledged to have received in hands the sum of £152 for the Committee of Safety, and assured the Committee that they would ever cheerfully contribute their proportion towards the safety and welfare of the public.

FIRST OFFICERS SELECTED FROM THE COUNTY.

The first meeting of the Committee of Safety at Philadelphia, which Edward Biddle, Esq., attended, was on January 2, 1776. Congress had recommended that Pennsylvania furnish four battalions of troops, and at this meeting the Committee were to agree upon the four colonels who were to be placed in command. Biddle evidently attended to favor Daniel Brodhead, of Heidelberg township, but he could not control a sufficient number of votes. On the next day they voted for Lieutenant Colonels. Brodhead's name was again presented with seven others, but he was not selected. On the 4th of January, they selected field officers; George Nagel, of Reading, was one of them. On the following day, he was commissioned as Major of the Third Battalion; and then they also selected 31 Captains for the four Battalions. Among those chosen were John Spohn, Peter Scull and Peter

Decker, all of Reading. On January 6th, they selected 32 Lieutenants. Among them was Daniel Brodhead, of Reading. It appears that Biddle did not attend any meetings after the 6th of January. His absence was doubtless caused by sickness.

GERMANS TO THE RESCUE.

By looking over the names of the numerous men in Berks county who participated in the movement for independence, it will be found that they are almost entirely German. The population of the county was largely German and of German descent, and this preponderance of names over those of all other nationalities was to be expected. The proportion was fully nine-tenths. They used the German language in their daily affairs, excepting the transfer of title to real estate which was required to be in the English language by a provincial law. The location of the English people in 1775 was mostly at Reading, and in Robeson, Caernarvon, Union, Exeter, Oley, Maidencreek and Richmond townships, or eight districts out of twenty-nine, but the major part of the people in these districts also was German, excepting the southern section of the county. It can be stated that Berks county was then distinctively the most German county of the eleven counties in the Province.

It was natural for the electors of the county to show a most positive sympathy for this movement, because it was in accordance with their notions of political life and social existence. They had a firm belief in local government and desired to carry it on successfully without unnecessary restrictions or burdens. Taxation without representation was to them a most unreasonable and unjust doctrine, and they were not disposed to tolerate its continued enforcement. Either they or their fathers had emigrated from Germany and settled in the county during the previous fifty years for the express purpose of enjoying civil rights, and of conducting their business, social and political affairs with as little foreign interference as possible ; and finding that extra taxes were to be imposed upon and exacted from them without their consent for the benefit of the King of Great Britain, and not for their own improvement or convenience, they felt impelled to express a decided opposition to such a proceeding.

The system of militia, which had been provided for by the Assembly, was appreciated by them, and they co-operated sincerely in its establishment throughout the county. They effected an organization and responded to the call for troops in a willing and prompt manner. Their promptness gave them such public distinction that Bancroft, the historian, makes especial mention of it in that part of his History of the United States which relates to the Revolution. This action was shown soon after the Battle of Lexington had been fought, not simply at Reading where there was a considerable population in a small area of territory covering less than a square mile, but in every township of the county whose inhabitants were widely scattered over an extended area embracing fully twelve hundred square miles. The militia returns of the county for 1775 show the organization of seven battalions, and by July, 1775, there were at least forty companies ready to answer the call for practical military duty in actual warfare. Their zeal will be more fully appreciated when we understand that there was not a single post office in the county, and that the only means of dispatching communications was by express riders.

Some opposition to this movement was shown in the county, but it did not presume to effect an organization in behalf of preventing the development of the sentiment for indepencence. The people who manifested this feeling were confined to the districts where the English language was used, and on that account they were called "Tories." The property of some of these was confiscated and converted to the uses of the government in prosecuting the war.

A small number of inhabitants in the county had conscientious scruples against war, and though they succeeded in holding a public meeting and forming an organization, they did not constitute a factor of any importance in creating public opinion.

A slight inclination was also manifested by some men in the county to discourage the continental currency. Two men were arrested for doing this, but they were discharged after having publicly acknowledged their error at Reading on January 30, 1776, begged the pardon of the community, and promised to conform thereafter to the rules and regulations that existed.

It is evident that the Germans were too numerous and their sympathies for independence too strong to permit any feelings or sentiments contrary to their own to become of any recognized public influence.

POPULATION AND DISTRICTS OF THE COUNTY.

In 1776, the territory of Berks County included not only that part which lies within the present boundary lines to the south of the Blue Mountains, but also nearly the entire area of Schuylkill County to the north, the excepted portion being about one-sixth part at the eastern end. But that section beyond the mountains was sparsely settled, the resident taxables numbering about 150, and the population about 600. The total population—as near as I can estimate it—was about 20,000, and the taxables numbered about 4000, the same number as those subject to military duty between the ages of 18 and 53 years.

The estimated population of Pennsylvania then was 300,000 white people and 2000 black.

The townships or districts established in the county numbered 29. They were distributed as follows:

East of the Schuylkill River—18.

Manatawny Section:
Alsace, Douglass, Reading,
Amity, Exeter, Rockland,
Colebrookdale, Hereford, Ruscombmanor.
District, Oley,

Ontelaunee Section:
Albany, Maidencreek, Richmond,
Greenwich, Maxatawny, Windsor.
Longswamp,

West of the Schuylkill River—9.

Schuylkill Section:
Brecknock, Cumru, Union.
Caernarvon, Robeson,

Tulpehocken Section:
Bern, Heidelberg, Tulpehocken.
Bethel,

Beyond the Blue Mountains—2.
Brunswick and Pine Grove.

CHAPTER III.

ASSOCIATORS.

At the inception of the Revolution, there were eleven counties in the Province of Pennsylvania. They were:

Philadelphia,	York,	Bedford,
Bucks,	Cumberland,	Northumberland,
Chester,	Berks,	Westmoreland.
Lancaster,	Northampton,	

On June 30, 1775, the General Assembly approved of "the Association entered into by the good people of this colony (Pennsylvania) for the defense of their lives, liberties and properties;" decided to pay the necessary expenses of the officers and soldiers while in active service, repelling any hostile invasion of British or other troops; and recommended the county commissioners of the several counties to "immediately provide a proper number of good, new firelocks with bayonets fitted to them, cartridge boxes with 23 rounds of cartridges in every box, and knapsacks." The allotted number for Berks County was 400. Edward Biddle and Henry Christ were then the representatives from Berks County, and Biddle was selected by the Assembly as one of the Committee of Safety "for calling forth such and so many of the Associators into actual service when necessity requires." The committee consisted of 25 members.

RECOMMENDATION OF CONGRESS.

On July 28, 1775, the Assembly approved of the resolution of Congress, passed July 18th, which recommended:

"That all able-bodied men between 16 and 60 years of age in each colony immediately form themselves into regular companies to consist of one captain, two lieutenants, one ensign, four sergeants, four corporals, a clerk, drummer and fifer, and 68 privates.

"That the officers of each company be chosen by the respective companies.

"That the companies be formed into Battalions, officered with a Colonel, Lieutenant-Colonel, two Majors, and an Adjutant or Quartermaster.

"That the officers above captain be appointed by the Assembly or by the Committee of Safety.

"And that each soldier be furnished with a good musket that will carry an ounce ball, with a bayonet, steel ram-rod, worm priming wire with brush fitted thereto, a cutting sword or tomahawk, a cartridge box that will contain 23 rounds of cartridges, 12 flints, and a knapsack."

The musket barrels were 3 ft. 8 in. long, and the bayonets 16 in. long; the bore of the barrels of sufficient size to carry 17 balls to the pound.

COUNTY COLONELS OF ASSOCIATORS.

Delegates from the eleven named counties, numbering altogether fifty-three, assembled at Philadelphia on August 19, 1775, for the purpose of adopting Articles of Association. They were Colonels of the Associated Battalions. The representatives from Berks County were:

Edward Biddle,	Daniel Brodhead,	Christian Lower.
Mark Bird,	Baltzer Geehr,	

Preamble to Articles of Association.—The preamble to the Articles of Association read as follows:

"We, the officers and soldiers, engaged in the present association for the defense of American liberty, being fully sensible that the strength and security of any body of men acting together, consists in just regularity, due subordination, and exact obedience to command, without which no individual can have that confidence in the support of those about him, that is so necessary to give firmness and resolution to the whole, do voluntarily and freely, after consideration of the following articles, adopt the same as the rules by which we agree and resolve to be governed in all our military concerns and operations, until the same or any of them, shall be changed or dissolved by the Assembly or Provincial Convention, or in their recess, by the Committee of Safety, or a happy reconciliation shall take place between Great Britain and the Colonies."

There were thirty-two articles which provided for the regulation of military affairs, and these articles the Associators were expected to sign.

County Committee Recommends Articles.—The Committee of Safety in Berks County recommended the adoption of the Articles of Association, as will appear by the following letter:

READING, January 20, 1776.

At a meeting of the Standing Committee for Berks County, held this day, Mark Bird, Esq., in the chair,

The Committee taking into their consideration the present state of the Association in this County, and being persuaded of the pressing necessity of being prepared for defence, do earnestly recommend it to their brethren to sign the Articles of Association formed by the House of Assembly at their last meeting; this Committee trusting that such amendments will be made at the next sitting of Assembly as will make the Association not only more effectual but more consonant to the principles of justice and equality. And afterward, at a meeting of the Committee, on the 30th of the same month,

Resolved, unanimously, that it is the opinion of this Committee that it will be highly requisite, in case the Assembly should not think proper to make the necessary amendments in the said Association, that a Provincial Convention be held for that purpose; and they do accordingly appoint—

Edward Biddle,	Daniel Brodhead,	Valentine Eckert,
Mark Bird,	Baltzer Geehr,	Nicholas Lotz,
Jonathan Potts,	Collinson Read,	Sebastian Levan,
Richard Tea,		

to attend the said Convention in behalf of this county.

By order of the Committee,

COLLINSON READ, *Secretary*.

CHAPTER IV.

INDEPENDENCE OF THE PROVINCE.

Suppression of British Authority.—On May 15, 1776, the Continental Congress adopted a resolution that recommended the total suppression of all authority under the King of Great Britain. It was as follows :

Whereas, his Brittanic majesty, in conjunction with the Lords and Commons of Great Britain, has by a late Act of Parliament, excluded the inhabitants of these United Colonies from the protection of his crown.

And Whereas, no answer whatever, to the humble petitions of the colonies for redress of grievances and reconciliation with Great Britain, has been, or is likely to be given, but the whole force of that kingdom, aided by foreign mercenaries, is to be exerted for the destruction of the good people of these colonies.

And Whereas, it appears absolutely irreconcilable to reason and good conscience, for the people of these colonies, now to take the oaths and affirmations necessary for the support of any government, under the crown of Great Britain; and it is necessary, that the exercise of every kind of authority, under the said crown should be totally suppressed, and all the powers of government exerted, under the authority of the people of the colonies, for the preservation of internal peace, virtue and good order, as well as for the defense of their lives, liberties and properties, against the hostile invasions and cruel depredations of their enemies; therefore,

Resolved, That it be recommended to the respective assemblies and conventions of the United Colonies, where no government sufficient to the exigencies of their affairs has been hitherto established, to adopt such government as shall, in the opinion of the representatives of the people, best conduce to the happiness and safety of their constituents in particular, and America in general.

Support of Civil Authority by the County.—A copy of this resolution having been received at Reading shortly afterward, and the people taking its importance into serious consideration, the Standing Committee of the county determined that the existing civil authority should nevertheless be supported until a new government should be provided, and accordingly passed the following resolution:

READING, June 8, 1776.

At a meeting of the Standing Committee of the County of Berks held this day, Mark Bird in the chair,

Resolved, That as some people have declared that no obedience ought to be paid to the civil authority, because a government will shortly be founded on the authority of the people in the room of the present government; and as such a conduct will only serve to introduce confusion and disorder, and endanger the lives and properties of every individual in society, it is the opinion of this committee, and they are determined to support the same to the utmost of their abilities, that the same obedience should be paid to the civil authority as used to be paid to it, till a new Constitution shall be formed by a Provincial Convention, and commissions shall be issued by virtue of the new legislative authority for the appointment of courts and magistrates, to preserve the peace and administer justice to the people; and then the authority of the present courts and magistrates will cease of course.

By order of the Committee,

COLLINSON READ, *Secretary.*

PROVINCIAL CONFERENCE.

Pursuant to the foregoing resolution of Congress, a Provincial Conference was held in Carpenters' Hall, at Philadelphia, from June 18th to June 25th, 1776, which was composed of deputies from the several counties of the Province. The deputies from Philadelphia had issued a circular letter to the Committees of the several counties, fixing a time and place for the proposed meeting, and suggesting the appointment of deputies.

Deputies from the County.—The representatives from Berks County were :

Col. Jocob Morgan,   Dr. Bodo Otto,   Col. Valentine Eckert,
Col. Henry Haller,   Mr. Benjamin Spyker,   Col. Nicholas Lotz,
Col. Mark Bird,   Col. Daniel Hunter,   Capt. Joseph Hiester,
                     Mr. Charles Shoemaker.

The Conference determined that a Convention should be called for the purpose of forming a new government in this province on the authority of the people only, fixed the qualifications of Associators and of the members of the Convention, and asked each county to send eight delegates. The election of the delegates was ordered to be held on Monday, July 8, 1776, and the delegates were directed to assemble at Philadelphia on Monday, July 15, 1776.

Address of Conference.—The following Address was then issued :

To the people of Pennsylvania :

Friends and Countrymen : In obedience to the power we derived from you, we have fixed upon a mode of electing a convention, to form a government for the Province of Pennsylvania, under the authority of the people.

Divine Providence is about to grant you a favor, which few people have ever enjoyed before, the privilege of choosing deputies to form a government under which you are to live. We need not inform you of the importance of the trust you are about to commit to them ; your liberty, safety, happiness and everything that posterity will hold dear to them to the end of time, will depend upon their deliberations. It becomes you, therefore, to choose such persons only, to act for you in the ensuing convention, as are distinguished for wisdom, integrity and a firm attachment to the liberties of this province, as well as to the liberties of the United Colonies in general.

In order that your deputies may know your sentiments as fully as possible, upon the subject of government, we beg that you would convey to them your wishes and opinions upon that head immediately after their election.

We have experienced an unexpected unanimity in our councils and we have the pleasure of observing a growing unanimity among the people of the province. We beg, that this brotherly spirit may be cultivated, and that you would remember that the present unsettled state of the province, requires that you should show forbearance, charity and moderation to each other. We beg that you would endeavor to remove the prejudices of the weak and ignorant, respecting the proposed change in our government, and assure them that it is absolutely necessary to secure property, liberty, and the sacred rights of conscience, to every individual in the province.

The season of the year, and the exigencies of our colony, require dispatch in the formation of a regular government. You will not therefore be surprised at our fixing the day for the election of deputies so early as the 8th of next July.

We wish you success in your attempts to establish and perpetuate your liberties, and pray God to take you under his special protection. Signed by unanimous order of the Conference,

THOMAS M'KEAN, *President.*

Declaration of Independence.—And the following Declaration of Independence of the Province was agreed to:

Whereas, George the Third, King of Great Britain, etc., in violation of the principles of the British constitution, and of the laws of justice and humanity, hath by an accumulation of oppressions, unparalleled in history, excluded the inhabitants of this, with other American Colonies, from his protection.

And Whereas, he hath paid no regard to any of our numerous and dutiful petitions for a redress of our complicated grievances, but hath lately purchased foreign troops to assist in enslaving us;

and hath excited the savages of this country to carry on a war against us, as also the negroes to imbrue their hands in the blood of their masters, in a manner unpracticed by civilized nations, and hath lately insulted our calamities, by declaring that he will show us no mercy until he has reduced us.

And Whereas, the obligations of allegiance, (being reciprocal between a king and his subjects) are now dissolved, on the side of the colonists, by the despotism of the king, insomuch that it now appears that loyalty to him is treason against the good people of this country.

And Whereas, not only the parliament, but there is reason to believe too many of the people of Great Britain, have concurred in the aforesaid arbitrary and unjust proceedings against us.

And Whereas, the public virtue of this colony, (so essential to its liberty and happiness,) must be endangered by a future political union with, or dependence upon a crown, and nation so lost to justice, patriotism and magnanimity.

We, the deputies of the people of Pennsylvania, assembled in full Provincial Conference, for forming a plan for executing the resolve of congress, of the 15th May last, for suppressing all Authority in this province, derived from the crown of Great Britain, and for establishing a government upon the authority of the people only, now in this public manner, in behalf of ourselves, and with the approbation, consent and authority of our constituents, unanimously declare our willingness to concur in a vote of the congress, declaring the United Colonies free and independent states; providing the forming the government, and the regulation of the internal police of this colony, be always reserved to the people of the said colony; and we do further call upon the nations of Europe, and appeal to the great arbiter and governor of the empires of the world, to witness for us, that this declaration did not originate in ambition, or in an impatience of lawful authority; but that we were driven to it in obedience to the first principles of nature, by the oppressions and cruelties of the aforesaid king and parliament of Great Britain; as the only possible measure that was left us, to preserve and establish our liberties, and to transmit them inviolate to posterity.

Address for Flying Camp.—In obedience to the resolutions of Congress of the 3d and 4th of June, 1776, this Conference also made provisions for raising

4500 militia towards establishing a "flying camp" of 10,000 men in the Middle Colonies, and caused the following remarkable address to the Associators to be issued:

To the Associators of Pennsylvania:

"Gentlemen: The only design of our meeting together was to put an end to our own power in the province, by fixing upon a plan for calling a convention, to form a government under the authority of the people. But the sudden and unexpected separation of the late Assembly has compelled us to undertake the execution of a resolve of Congress for calling forth 4500 of the militia of this province, to join the militia of the neighboring colonies, to form a camp for our immediate protection. We presume only to recommend the plan we have formed to you, trusting that, in a case of so much consequence, your love of virtue and zeal for liberty will supply the want of authority delegated to us expressly for that purpose.

"We need not remind you that you are now furnished with new motives to animate and support your courage. You are not about to contend against the power of Great Britain, in order to displace one set of villains to make room for another. Your arms will not be enervated in the day of battle with the reflection that you are to risk your lives or shed your blood for a British tyrant; or that your posterity will have your work to do over again. You are about to contend for permanent freedom, to be supported by a government which will be derived from yourselves and which will have for its object, not the emolument of one man or class of men only, but the safety, liberty and happiness of every individual in the community. We call upon you, therefore, by the respect and obedience which are due to the authority of the United Colonies, to concur in this important measure. The present campaign will probably decide the fate of America. It is now in your power to immortalize your names by mingling your achievements with the events of the year 1776—a year which, we hope, will be famed in the annals of history to the end of time, for establishing upon a lasting foundation the liberties of one-quarter of the globe.

"Remember the honor of our colony is at stake. Should you desert the common cause at the present juncture, the glory you have acquired by your former exertions of strength and virtue will be tarnished; and our friends and brethren, who are now acquiring laurels in the most remote parts of America, will reproach us and blush to own themselves natives or inhabitants of Pennsylvania.

"But there are other motives before you. Your houses, your fields, the legacies of your ancestors, or the dear-bought fruits of your own industry, and your liberty, now urge you to the field. These cannot plead with you in vain, or we might point out to you, further, your wives, your children, your aged fathers and mothers, who now look up to you for aid, and hope for salvation in this day of calamity only from the instrumentality of your swords.

"Remember the name of Pennsylvania—Think of your ancestors and of your posterity.

"Signed by an unanimous order of the conference,

"THOMAS M'KEAN, *President.*
"June 25, 1776."

DECLARATION OF INDEPENDENCE BY CONGRESS.

The "Declaration of Independence" was passed by the Continental Congress late on the afternoon of July 4, 1776, and ordered to be printed. A resolution was adopted at the same time, directing copies to be sent to the several Assemblies and Committees of Safety, and to the several commanding officers of the Continental troops, and that it be proclaimed in each of the United States and at the head of the army.

There were seventy representatives accredited from the several Colonies to the Continental Congress. Of these, twenty-two did not sign the Declaration of Independence for various reasons. Among this number was Edward Biddle, and the reason explaining the omission is given as follows in the *History of Philadelphia*, (1884):

"Edward Biddle, of Philadelphia, died during the session of a lingering disease, which probably disabled him at the time of the Declaration."

This statement is erroneous in two particulars. Biddle was not of Philadelphia, and though he had met with an accident before 1776, which culminated in serious illness, he did not die until 1779. He attended the meetings of the Committee of Safety of Pennsylvania during January, 1776. In 1778, he was one of the Representatives from the county to the Assembly, and that body selected him as one of seven members to Congress.

Declaration Read in the County.—In pursuance of the resolution of Congress, the State Board of Safety addressed a letter to the Committee of Berks County on the 6th of July, 1776, enclosing a copy of the Declaration of Independence, and directing it to be read on Monday, July 8th, at 12 o'clock noon, at the place where the election of delegates was to be held. This was done by Henry Vanderslice, the sheriff of the county, on that day at the Court House on Penn Square, the bell having been rung earnestly beforehand, as elsewhere, to call the people together so that they should learn the comprehensive significance of that important and courageous public document in behalf of political freedom and representative government.

CONSTITUTIONAL CONVENTION OF THE PROVINCE.

Delegates from the County.—According to the direction of the Provincial Conference, the electors of

Berks County held an election on Monday, July 8, 1776, at the Court House, in Reading, and chose as their representatives the following eight prominent men :

Jacob Morgan,	Benjamin Spyker,	Charles Shoemaker,
Gabriel Hiester,	Daniel Hunter,	Thomas Jones.
John Lesher,	Valentine Eckert,	

On July 15, following, they attended the Convention at Philadelphia and participated in the formation of a Constitution for the government of the Province.

The labors of the Convention were concluded on September 28, 1776, and then all the delegates present subscribed the Constitution which they had adopted. All the delegates from Berks County subscribed their names, excepting John Lesher and Daniel Hunter.

On July 23, 1776, the Constitutional Convention elected a Council of Safety to discharge the executive duties of the State government, dissolving in this manner the Committee of Safety. This Council was composed of twenty-five members, among them Daniel Hunter, of Berks County.

The Preamble and Declaration of Rights being so elevated in sentiment and so admirable in construction, I introduce them in this connection. John Lesher represented Berks County in the committee of eleven, (one from each county) who were appointed to draft the frame of government.

Preamble.

Whereas, all government ought to be instituted and supported for the security and protection of the community as such, and to enable the individuals who compose it to enjoy their natural rights, and the other blessings which the author of existence has bestowed upon man; and whenever these great ends of government are not obtained, the people have a right by common consent to change it, and take such measures as to them may appear necessary, to promote their safety and happiness.

And Whereas, the inhabitants of this commonwealth have, in consideration of protection only, heretofore acknowledged allegiance to the king of Great Britain, and the said king has not only withdrawn that protection, but commenced and still continues to carry on with unabated vengeance, a most cruel and unjust war against them, employing therein not only the troops of Great Britain, but foreign mercenaries, savages and slaves, for the avowed purpose of reducing them to a total and abject submission to the despotic domination of the British Parliament, (with many other acts of tyranny more fully set forth in the declaration of congress) whereby all allegiance and fealty to the said king and his successors are dissolved and at an end, and all power and authority derived from him ceased in these colonies.

And Whereas, it is absolutely necessary for the welfare and safety of the inhabitants of said colonies, that they be henceforth free and independent states, and that just, permanent and proper forms of government exist in every part of them, derived from, and founded on the authority of the people only, agreeable to the direction of the honorable American Congress.

We, the representatives of the freemen of Pennsylvania, in general convention met, for the express purpose of framing such a government, confessing the goodness of the great governor of the universe, (who alone knows to what degree of earthly happiness mankind may attain by perfecting the arts of government) in permitting the people of this state, by common consent and without violence, deliberately to form for themselves, such just rules as they shall think best for governing their future society; and being fully convinced, that it is our indispensible duty to establish such original principles of government, as will best promote the general happiness of the people of this state and their posterity, and provide for future improvements, without partiality for, or prejudice against, any particular class, sect or denomination of men whatsoever, do, by virtue of the authority vested in us by our constituents, ordain, declare and establish the following declaration of rights, and frame of government, to be the constitution of this commonwealth, and to remain in force therein for ever unaltered, except in such articles as shall hereafter, on experience, be found to require improvements, and which shall by the same authority of the people, fairly delegated, as this frame of government directs, be amended or improved for the more effectual obtaining and securing the great end and design of all government, herein before mentioned.

Declaration of Rights.

1. That all men are born equally free and independent, and have certain natural, inherent and unalienable rights, amongst which are the enjoying and defending life and liberty, acquiring, possessing, and protecting property, and pursuing and obtaining happiness and safety.

2. That all men have a natural and unalienable right to worship Almighty God, according to the dictates of their own consciences and understanding, and that no man ought, or of right can be compelled to attend any religious worship, or erect or support any place of worship, or maintain any ministry, contrary to, or against his own free will and consent; nor can any man who acknowledges the being of a God, be justly deprived or abridged of any civil right as a citizen, on account of his religious sentiments, or peculiar mode of religious worship; and that no authority can, or ought to be vested in, or assumed by any power whatever, that shall in any case interfere with, or in any manner control the right of conscience in the free exercise of religious worship.

3. That the people of this state have the sole, exclusive and inherent right of governing and regulating the internal police of the same.

4. That all power being originally inherent in, and consequently derived from the people; therefore all officers of government, whether legislative or executive, are their trustees and servants, and at all times accountable to them.

5. That government is, or ought to be, instituted for the common benefit, protection and security of the people, nation or community; and not for the particular emolument or advantage of any single man, family or set of men, who are a part only of that community; and that the community hath an indubitable, unalienable and indefeasible right to reform, alter or abolish government, in such manner as shall be by that community judged, most conducive to the public weal.

6. That those who are employed in the legislative and executive business of the state, may be restrained from oppression, the people have a right, at such periods as they may think proper, to reduce their public officers to a private station, and supply the vacancies by certain and regular elections.

7. That all elections ought to be free and that all free men, having a sufficient evident common interest with and attachment to the community, have a right to elect officers or to be elected into office.

8. That every member of society hath a right to be protected in the enjoyment of life, liberty and property; and therefore is bound to contribute his proportion towards the expense of that protection, and yield his personal service when necessary, or an equivalent thereto; but no part of a man's property can be justly taken from him or applied to public uses, without his own consent or that of his legal representatives; nor can any man who is conscientiously scrupulous of bearing arms be justly compelled thereto if he will pay such equivalent, nor are the people bound by any laws but such as they have in like manner assented to, for their common good.

9. That in all prosecutions for criminal offenses, a man hath a right to be heard by himself and his council; to demand the cause and nature of his accusation; to be confronted with the witnesses, to call for evidence in his favor, and a speedy public trial by an impartial jury of the country, without the unanimous consent of which jury he cannot be found guilty; nor can he be compelled to give evidence against himself; nor can any man be justly deprived of his liberty, except by the laws of the land or the judgment of his peers.

10. That the people have a right to hold themselves, their houses, papers and possessions free from search and seizure; and therefore warrants, without oaths or affirmations first made affording a sufficient foundation for them, and whereby any officer or messenger may be commanded or required to search suspected places, or to seize any person or persons, his or their property not particularly described, are contrary to that right, and ought not to be granted.

11. That in controversies respecting property, and in suits between man and man, the parties have a right to trial by jury, which ought to be held sacred.

12. That the people have a right to freedom of speech and of writing and publishing their sentiments; therefore the freedom of the press ought not to be restrained.

13. That the people have a right to bear arms for the defense of themselves, and the state; and as standing armies in the time of peace are dangerous to liberty, they ought not to be kept up, and that the military should be kept under strict subordination to, and governed by the civil power.

14. That a frequent recurrence to fundamental principles and a firm adherence to justice, moderation, temperance, industry and frugality, are absolutely necessary to preserve the blessings of liberty and keep a government. The people ought therefore to pay particular attention to these points in the choice of officers and representatives, and have a right to exact a due and constant regard to them from their legislatures and magistrates, in the making and executing such laws as are necessary for the good government of the state.

15. That all men have a natural and inherent right to emigrate from one state to another that will receive them, or to form a new state in vacant countries, or in such countries as they can purchase, whenever they think that thereby they may promote their own happiness.

16. That the people have a right to assemble together to consult for their common good, to instruct their representatives, and to apply to the legislature for redress of grievances by address, petition or remonstrance.

It were well if the foregoing sentiments could be impressed upon the people, so as to lead them to fully appreciate their excellence and adaptation for the general welfare. Their preservation is dependent upon the uniform elevation of the people through industry, education and equality, under the guidance of a fraternal spirit. Manhood, citizenship and patriotism, with social impulses towards the prosperity and peace of the people, are superior to mechanical progress and the riches, envy and strife which it develops in certain channels and classes, and they are therefore worthy of serious public consideration.

CHAPTER V.

MILITIA SYSTEM.

The Convention of 1776, in framing the first Constitution of Pennsylvania, made the following provision for the establishment of a military system:

"The freemen of this commonwealth and their sons shall be trained and armed for its defense under such regulations, restrictions and exceptions as the General Assembly shall by law direct, preserving always to the people the right of choosing their Colonels and all commissioned officers under that rank."

In pursuance of this provision, the General Assembly established the necessary regulations, and through them the county of Berks, under the direction of the officer designated thereby, called a "Lieutenant," with the assistance of "Sub-Lieutenants," was enabled to supply promptly and successfully all the orders made by the State government for troops during the progress of the Revolution.

Previous to this system, the military affairs were governed by Articles of Association. The men who associated together for purposes of defence were commonly known as "Associators," and those who acted in opposition, either openly or secretly, were called "Non-Associators."

By the following returns, it is apparent that the men in the county, subject to military duty, appreciated the necessity of organization and co-operated earnestly with the Executive Council in making the law effective. The persons chosen for lieutenant-colonels and majors of the seven battalions for 1775, at the beginning of the Revolution, represent the best class of taxpayers that the county possessed. They were all prominent men and stood at the head of business, political and social affairs. This selection exhibits, not only the discrimination which the people exercised, but also the respect which they had for qualification and influence. The subsequent returns until 1783 show a similar selection of men.

COUNTY RETURNS FOR 1775.

The following officers were chosen for the several battalions of the Associators of Berks County for the year 1775-76. It is the earliest military record of this county that I could find relating to the Revolution. The company rosters were not published in that connection:

1st Battalion—Central Section.
Lieut.-Col., Henry Haller. Maj., Gabriel Hiester.

2nd Battalion—Southern Section.
Lieut.-Col., Mark Bird. Maj., John Jones.

3rd Battalion—Central Section.
Lieut.-Col., Nicholas Lotz. Maj., John Old.

4th Battalion—Northern Section.
Lieut.-Col., Balser Geehr. Maj., Michael Lindemuth.

5th Battalion—Western Section.
Lieut.-Col., John Patton. Maj., John Thornburgh.

6th Battalion—Eastern Section.
Lieut.-Col., Daniel Hunter. Maj., Conrad Leffler.

7th Battalion—Northeastern Section.
Lieut.-Col., Sebastian Levan. Maj., Samuel Ely.

COUNTY RETURNS FOR 1776.

Seven battalions were organized in the county, as will appear by the delegates sent to the election at Lancaster, July 4, 1776, for two brigadier-generals, but the complete returns for 1776 have not yet been discovered.

Eight companies of the County Militia were paid for subsistence during the Summer of 1776. They were as follows:

Captains.	£.	sh.	d.	Captains.	£.	sh.	d.
Daniel Deturk,	1	3	6	George Will,	1	18	8
Jacob Moser,	16	15	5	John Old,	2	4	
Nicholas Scheffer,	1	3	4	—— Moyer,	1	13	4
John Soder,	2	2	8	Stephen Crumrine,		15	

Three companies were on duty at South Amboy, in New Jersey, in August, 1776, commanded by Michael Wolf, George Miller and Michael Furrer.

These eleven companies are all that I could find for this year, of which any mention was made.

County Delegates to Lancaster Convention.—A public meeting was held at Lancaster on July 4, 1776, for the purpose of electing two brigadier-generals to command the battalions and forces in Pennsylvania. The meeting consisted of the officers and privates of fifty-three battalions of the Associators. A full ratio of men was sent by the militia of Berks County. The following delegates represented the county at the meeting:

1st Battalion: Officers—Major, Gabriel Hiester; Lieut., Philip Cremer; privates, John Hartman, Peter Filbert.

2nd Battalion: Officers—Col., Mark Bird; Major, John Jones; privates, David Morgan, Benjamin Tolbert.

3rd Battalion: Officers—Lieut.-Col., Nicholas Lotz; Captain, George Riehm; privates, Henry Spohn, Matthias Wenrich.

4th Battalion: Officers—Major, Michael Lindemuth; Captain, George May; private, Michael Moser.

5th Battalion: Officers—Col., John Patton; Lieut.-Col., John Rice; privates, Jacob Seltzer, Christian Winter.

6th Battalion: Officers—Major, Conrad Leffler; Lieut., John Miller; privates, John Hill, Henry Lark.

7th Battalion: Officers—Col., Sebastian Levan; Adj., Samuel Ely; privates, Philip Wisters, Casper Smeck.

Colonel Mark Bird, of the 2nd Battalion, was one of the judges of the election. Daniel Roberdeau was elected the first brigadier-general, and James Ewing, the second. Mark Bird received seven votes. Eight candidates were placed in nomination.

COUNTY RETURNS FOR 1777.

Colonel Jacob Morgan and his sub-lieutenants met at Reading on April 25, 1777, for the purpose of receiving returns of the inhabitants of Berks County, between the ages of 18 and 53 years. The number then returned was about 4000. These were arranged in six districts, and meetings were ordered to be held on the 5th and 6th of May following, for the purpose of electing officers and forming companies. Morgan reported that he had forwarded to the Executive Council an exact list of the field officers, captains, subalterns and court-martial men, comprising the six battalions of the Berks County militia, or one battalion for each district. This list appears in the *Pennsylvania Associators*, vol. 2, pp. 257 to 276. The several battalions were returned on May 16, 1777. I have added the sections of the county showing where the companies were organized.

1st Battalion—Eastern Section.

Col., Daniel Hunter, Oley.
Lt.-Col., John Guldin, Oley.
Maj., John Cunius, Oley.
Adj., Philip Bertolet, Oley.
Chaplain, Jacob Michael.
Q. M., Isaac Feather, Reading.
Surgeon, Daniel Welcher.

1st Co.—Hereford.

Mathias Wick,	Captain.
Christopher Folk,	1st Lieut.
Charles Geiger,	2nd Lieut.
Henry Reiff,	Ensign.
John Pott,	Court Martial
Jacob Heffner.	men.

5th Co.—Colebrookdale.

Jacob Hill,
George Schall,
John Betz,
Joseph Delaplane,
Philip Mathias,
Jacob Antey.

2nd Co.—Colebrookdale.

Stephen Crumrine,	Captain.
Henry Knouse,	1st Lieut.
Isaiah Davis,	2nd Lieut.
Jacob Gerver,	Ensign.
Mathias Rhoads,	Court Martial
Baltzer Trout.	men.

6th Co.—Ruscombmanor.

Peter Wanner,
Henry Strauch,
Adam Hamscher,
Henry Schurtz,
Elias Wagner,
Henry Hess.

3rd Co.—District.

Sebastian Lentz,	Captain.
Jacob Rhoads,	1st Lieut.
Adam Heiter,	2nd Lieut.
Henry Hess,	Ensign.
Baltzer Beam,	Court Martial
Peter Gabel.	men.

7th Co.—Oley.

Daniel Reiff.
Daniel Leinbach,
Philip Reiff,
Peter Scheffer,
Daniel Schneider,
John Scheffer.

4th Co.—Oley.

George Focht,	Captain.
John Stapleton,	1st Lieut.
Jacob Griesemer,	2nd Lieut.
John Yoder,	Ensign.
Daniel Levan,	Court Martial
George Yoder.	men.

8th Co.—Hereford.

David Strause,
Jacob Rickstein,
John Miller,
John Roeder,
Henry Rauch,
George Moll.

2nd Battalion—Northeastern Section.

Col., Daniel Udree, Oley.
Lt.-Col., Jacob Boyer, Oley. Surgeon, John Umstead, Union.
Maj., John Huy. Surg. Mate, Thos. Kerlin, Amity.
Adj., George Riehm, Cumru. Q. M., Conrad Foose, Reading.

1st Co.—Longswamp.

Charles Crouse,	Captain.
Philip Mertz,	1st Lieut.
Nicholas Mertz,	2nd Lieut.
Christian Kercher,	Ensign,
Casper Seibert,	Court Martial
Adam Helwig.	men.

5th Co.—Maxatawny.

Casper Smeck,
Jacob Grim,
Jacob Zimmerman,
Jacob Sigfried,
Joseph Gross,
John Beaver.

2nd Co.—Rockland.

Peter Smith,	Captain.
George Roap,	1st Lieut.
Michael Eayre,	2nd Lieut.
John Kreamer,	Ensign.
Henry George,	Court Martial
George Leye.	men.

6th Co.—Richmond.

Michael Voyge,
Henry Adam,
John Fegley,
John Lesher,
Frederick Leiby,
Valentine Hoffman.

3d Co.—Richmond.

Jacob Rothermel,	Captain.
Jacob Dreibelbis,	1st Lieut.
Christopher Denn,	2nd Lieut.
Daniel Ely,	Ensign.
Jacob Wanner,	Court Martial
George Kelchner.	men.

7th Co.—Maidencreek.

Abraham Huy,
Christian Bearringstein,
John Weidenhammer,
Christian Burkhart,
Jacob Stein,
Jacob Rhaun,

4th Co.—Maxatawny.

George Kemp,	Captain.
Jacob Levan,	1st Lieut.
Michael Peifer,	2nd Lieut.
Jacob Schweyer,	Ensign.
Philip Geehr,	Court Martial
Peter Scherer.	men.

8th Co.—Longswamp.

Henry Egner,
Henry Fegley,
John Trice,
Martin Royer,
Philip Deal,
Jacob Collman.

3rd Battalion—Northern Section.

Col., Michael Lindemuth, Bern.
Lt.-Col., George May, Windsor.
Maj., Martin Kercher, Windsor.

1st Co.—Pine Grove.

Jacob Wetstein,	Captain.
George Brouch,	1st Lieut.
Ludwig Herring,	2nd Lieut.
Henry Wetstein,	Ensign.
Conrad Sheffer,	Court Martial
Rudolph Buzzard.	men.

2nd Co.—Brunswick.

Conrad Minich,	Captain.
John Graul,	1st Lieut.
John Stout,	2nd Lieut.
Philip Boning,	Ensign.
Gideon Moyer,	Court Martial
John Crawford.	men.

3d Co.—Bern.

Jacob Shraedel,	Captain.
George Albright,	1st Lieut.
George Kaufman,	2nd Lieut.
Adam Klauser,	Ensign.
Christian Albright,	Court Martial
John Knevel.	men.

4th Co.—Bern.

Sebastian Emrich,	Captain.
Francis Umbehacker,	1st Lieut.
George Ludwig,	2nd Lieut.
George Moyer,	Ensign.
George Belleman,	Court Martial
Anthony Kershner.	men.

5th Co.—Bern.

John Soder,
Jacob Frantz,
John Epler,
Philip Fox,
Jacob Freyberger,
John Epler, Sr.

6th Co.—Windsor.

Jacob Shadle,
Charles Siegfried,
William Williamson,
George Reber,
George Hower,
Eberhard Shappel.

7th Co.—Bern.

Daniel Will,
Jacob Meicksel,
Henry Kalbach,
Abraham Luckenbill,
Peter Focht,
Peter Baldy.

8th Co.—Windsor.

Ferdinand Ritter,
Michael Smith,
George Adam,
Jacob Stapleton,
Jacob Tenant,
John Brobst.

REVOLUTION. 63

4th Battalion—Central Section.

Col., Nicholas Lotz, Reading.
Lt.-Col., Joseph Hiester, Reading.
Maj., Peter Decker, Reading.

1st Co.—Reading.

Conrad Geist,
Philip Ruppert,
Charles Gobin,
John Kidd,
Peter Feather,
George Gardner.

Captain.
1st Lieut.
2nd Lieut.
Ensign.
Court Martial
men.

5th Co.—Reading.

George Riehm,
Henry Focht,
Thomas Atkinson,
John Wentzel,
Jacob Koch,
William Hottenstein.

2nd Co.—Reading.

John Reitmyer,
Michael Bush,
Christian Grouse,
John Burkhard,
Jacob Groff,
Nicholas Scherer.

Captain.
1st Lieut.
2nd Lieut.
Ensign.
Court Martial
men.

6th Co.—Heidelberg.

Conrad Eckert,
Adam Hain,
Peter Young,
Mathias Wenrich,
Peter Kuhl,
Simpson Hain.

3d Co.—Alsace.

Daniel DeTurck,
Paul Feger,
Jacob Kissinger,
Henry Schneider,
Isaac Levan,
John Baum.

Captain.
1st Lieut.
2nd Lieut.
Ensign.
Court Martial
men.

7th Co.—Cumru.

Sebastian Miller,
Adam Ruth,
John Gernant,
John Ruth,
Michael Ruth,
Peter Fisher.

4th Co.—Reading.

Peter Nagel,
Paul Kerper,
Daniel Grove,
Joseph Colier,
Baltzer Fornewalt,
Henry Wolf.

Captain.
1st Lieut.
2nd Lieut.
Ensign.
Court Martial
men.

8th Co.—Cumru.

Philip Krick,
Philip Spohn,
Michael Moyer,
John Bullman,
Henry Spohn,
Joshua Evans.

5th Battalion—Southern Section.

Col., Jacob Weaver, Amity.
Lt.-Col., Mathias Rhoads, Amity.
Maj., George Lorah, Amity.

1st Co.—Union.

Thomas Parry,	Captain.
William Hays,	1st Lieut.
George Kerston,	2nd Lieut.
George Ax,	Ensign.
John Umstead,	Court Martial
John Wagner.	men.

2nd Co.—Robeson.

William Lewis,	Captain.
Adam Beard,	1st Lieut.
Richard Millard,	2nd Lieut.
John Hahn,	Ensign.
Adam Scheirer,	Court Martial
Herman Umstead.	men.

3rd Co.—Exeter.

John Bishop,	Captain.
Mathias Herner,	1st Lieut.
John Ludwig,	2nd Lieut.
John Thompson,	Ensign.
Adam Young,	Court Martial
Nicholas Herner.	men.

4th Co.—Alsace.

Adam Alstatt,	Captain.
John Wagner,	1st Lieut.
Mathias Patterner,	2nd Lieut.
Paul Derst,	Ensign.
Abraham Levan,	Court Martial
John Hartman,	men.

5th Co.—Amity.

Jacob Rhoads,
Joseph Sands,
Jacob Weaver,
Daniel Ludwig,
Daniel Winder,
Henry Haffa.

6th Co.—Douglass.

George Bucher,
Solomon Mathews,
Michael Stophlet,
Jacob Keely,
Peter Meffert,
John Swineheart.

7th Co.—Robeson.

Joseph Davis,
Thomas Hamilton,
David Edwards,
George Glass,
Paul Geiger,
Casper Straub.

8th Co.—Caernarvon.

David Morgan,
John Robinson,
Joseph Talbot,
Jacob Finfrock,
James Ross,
Henry Menges.

6th Battalion—Western Section.

Col., Henry Spyker, Tul'hock'n.   Adj., Fred'k Ernst, Tul'hock'n.
Lt.-Col., George Miller,   "   Q. M., George Lechner,   "
Maj., Michael Furrer,   "   Surgeon, Philip Finkel,   "

1st Co.—Heidelberg.

John Lesher,	Captain.
Isaac Depuy,	1st Lieut.
John Anspach,	2nd Lieut.
Valentine Reed,	Ensign.
Martin Stupp,	Court Martial
Jacob Weiser.	men.

5th Co.—Tulpehocken.

Michael Bretz,
Bernhard Zimmerman,
Peter Bressler,
Peter Smith,
John Stone,
Peter Smith,

2nd Co.—Bethel.

George Batdorff,	Captain.
Henry Batdorff,	1st Lieut.
Jacob Rehrer,	2nd Lieut.
Tobias Rheam,	Ensign.
Leonard Swartz,	Court Martial
Nicholas Ketner.	men.

6th Co.—Tulpehocken.

Henry Weaver,
John Scheffer,
Henry Koch,
Jacob Knoll,
Adam Emrich,
Valentine Moyer.

3rd Co.—Tulpehocken.

Henry Shepler,	Captain.
Christopher Kern,	1st Lieut.
John Riegel,	2nd Lieut.
George Loos,	Ensign.
Nicholas Hawk,	Court Martial
John Foust,	men.

7th Co.—Tulpehocken.

Jacob Kremer,
Jacob Rehrer,
Daniel Hoffman,
George Stout,
Michael Kehl,
George Berger.

4th Co.—Heidelberg.

Conrad Weiser,	Captain.
Daniel Womelsdorf,	1st Lieut.
Henry Walter,	2nd Lieut.
George Gensemer,	Ensign.
Jacob Seltzer,	Court Martial
George Brown.	men.

8th Co.—Heidelberg.

Philip Filbert,
Philip Moyer,
Francis Artellia,
Leonard Zerbe,
Henry Knopp,
Samuel Boyer.

Commissions were forwarded to Col. Jacob Morgan for the foregoing six battalions June 14, 1777, by Timothy Matlack, Secretary of the Executive Council.

NEW MILITIA SYSTEM PROVIDED.

After the foregoing returns had been made, the Assembly deemed it necessary to provide a new militia system, because the "Associators" had lost their effectiveness. Shortly after the Battle of Princeton whole companies deserted. In this behalf a law was passed on June 13, 1777.

Oath of Allegiance.—One of the first requirements was the taking of an oath of allegiance which had to be done before July 1, 1777. This was allowing only seventeen days, but in this time its provisions had become thoroughly known in Berks County. The time for deliberation or hesitation had passed, and prompt action was necessary.

The preamble and oath, provided by the said Act, were as follows :

"*Whereas*, From sordid or mercenary motives, or other causes inconsistent with the happiness of a free and independent people, sundry persons have withheld, or may yet be induced to withhold, their service or allegiance from the Commonwealth of Pennsylvania as a free and independent State, as declared by Congress.

"*And Whereas*, Sundry other persons in their several capacities have, at the risk of their lives and fortunes, or both, rendered great and eminent services in defence and support of the said independence, and may yet continue to do the same, and as both these sorts of persons remain at this time mixed, and in some measure undistinguished from each other, and the disaffected deriving undeserved service from the faithful and well-affected.

"*And Whereas*, Allegiance and protection are reciprocal, and those who will not bear the former are not or ought not to be entitled to the benefits of the latter.

"*Therefore, be it enacted, etc.*, That all white male inhabitants of the State, except of the counties of Bedford and Westmoreland, above the age of eighteen years, shall, before the 1st day of the ensuing July, and in the excepted counties before the 1st day of August, take and subscribe before some justice of the peace an oath in the following form :

"I, ———, do swear, (or affirm,) that I renounce and refuse all allegiance to George the Third, King of Great Britain, his heirs and successors; and that I will be faithful and bear true allegiance to the Commonwealth of Pennsylvania, as a free and independent State, and that I will not at any time do, or cause to be done, any matter or thing that will be prejudicial or injurious to the freedom and independence thereof, as declared by Congress; and also, that I will discover and make known to some justice of the peace of said State all treasons or traitorous conspiracies which I now know or hereafter shall know to be formed against this or any of the United States of America."

Persons, who neglected or refused to take this oath, were declared to be incapable of holding any office; serving as jurors; suing for debts; electing or being elected; buying, selling, or transferring real estate; and they were liable to be disarmed by the County Lieutenants and Deputies. If they were not provided with passes, they were liable to be arrested as spies, upon being found out of the city or county away from their immediate residence; and forgery of a certificate was punishable with a flogging and a fine of £50.

County Districts Established.—This law directed the counties to be divided into districts, and each district was to contain not less than 440 men, nor more than 680, fit for duty, to be arranged in eight companies. The officer in charge of a county was called a "Lieutenant," and of each district, a "Sub-Lieutenant." It was the duty of the "Lieutenant" to enlist the people, collect the fines, and execute the details of the law.

Battalions, Companies and Classes.—Each district was subdivided into eight parts with due regard to the convenience of the inhabitants, and each district elected its officers, from lieutenant-colonel down to sub-alterns. The term of service was three years. A company was set apart for each subdivision, and this was also divided by lot into eight parts, called classes, as nearly equal as possible, and the several classes were numbered from one to eight in numerical order. Berks County was divided into six districts. Accordingly, the county had six battalions, or forty-eight companies.

The rank of the battalions and their officers, also of the captains and sub-alterns, was determined by lot. The precedence of the officers of the several counties, as to rank, was arranged according to the seniority of the counties, Philadelphia being first.

In case of invasion, or assistance were asked by Congress, the militia was called out by classes. The first draft consisted of class one of each company, and if insufficient, then class two, and so on as occasion required. Each class was liable to serve two months, and it was relieved by the next class in numerical order.

Pay and Rations.—The pay and rations were the same as Continental troops. They were to commence two days before marching, and to be allowed at the rate of twenty miles a day till the men returned home.

Days of Drill.—Days of drill were set apart in the Spring and Fall for military exercise; *in companies*, on the last Monday of April, and first three Mondays of May; also, on the last two Mondays of August, the last two Mondays of September, and the third Monday of October; and *in battalions*, on the fourth Mondays of May and October.

Fines.—Enrolled men who refused to parade were fined 7sh. 6d. per diem; absent officers, 10sh.; non-commissioned officers and privates, 5sh. On field days, the fine for non-attendance was £5, and for non-commissioned officers and privates, 15sh.

Pensions.—Pensions were allowed for incapacitating injuries not exceeding one-half the pay received; and for persons who died from wounds, or were killed, in service, the Orphans' Court was authorized to allow support to the families in amounts not to exceed one-half the pay of such persons.

Persons Exempted from Service.—The excepted persons from bearing arms were Delegates in Congress, Members of the Executive Council, Judges of the Supreme Court, Masters and Faculty of Colleges, Ministers, and servants purchased *bona fide*.

Oaths Administered in the County.—In pursuance of said Act, over forty-nine hundred men took the oath of allegiance in Berks County during the years 1777 and 1778, before the Justices of the Peace in the several sections of the county. The greater number was taken from June to October in 1777.

The Justices, who administered the oaths, and the number taken by each Justice, were as follows:

Henry Christ, Reading	943
Jacob Shoemaker, Central Section	1149
John Ludwig, Central Section	287
Peter Spyker, Western Section	779
Charles Shoemaker, Northern Section	300
Samuel Ely, Northeastern Section	497
Daniel Rothermel, Eastern Section	315
John Old, Southeastern Section	228
Jacob Weaver, Southern Section	385
Jacob Morgan, Southern Section	37
Total	4920

This number would indicate how many men were in Berks County at that time over the age of eighteen years. It exceeds the number of those who were subject to military duty, but many of the men were, of course, over sixty years of age.

The several Justices presented certified lists of the names of the persons, who had "taken and subscribed the oath of allegiance and fidelity," to Henry Christ, Esq., (the Recorder of the County,) and he recorded them in a book provided for that purpose, which was entitled "Book D, volume 1."

COUNTY RETURNS FOR 1778.

The militia returns for the year 1778 were as follows. Total number of men enrolled was 4058:

1st Battalion—Lower Eastern Section.

Colonel, Daniel Hunter.
CAPTAINS.

Christopher Foulk,	George Focht,	Daniel Reiff,
Stephen Crumrine,	Jacob Hill,	David Stause,
Sebastian Lentz,	Peter Wanner,	

Number of men enrolled, 642.

2nd Battalion—Upper Eastern Section.

Colonel, Daniel Udree.
CAPTAINS.

Charles Krouse,	George Kemp,	Abraham Huy,
Peter Smith,	Casper Smeck,	Henry Egner.
Jacob Rothermel,	Michael Voyge,	

Number of men enrolled, 565.

3rd Battalion—Upper Western Section.

Colonel, Michael Lindemuth.
CAPTAINS.

Jacob Whetstone,   Sebastian Emrich,   Daniel Will,
Conrad Minnich,   George Souter,   Ferdinand Ritter.
Jacob Schraedle,   Jacob Shable,

Number of men enrolled, 722.

4th Battalion—Central Section.

Colonel, Joseph Hiester.
CAPTAINS.

Conrad Geist,   Peter Nagel,   Sebastian Miller,
John Reitunger,   George Riehm,   Philip Krick.
George Ax,   Conrad Eckert,

Number of men enrolled, 756.

5th Battalion—Lower Western Section.

Colonel, Jacob Weaver.
CAPTAINS.

Joseph McMurray,   Jacob Graul,   John Keim.
———— Harris,   Joseph Sands,   David Morgan.
John Bishop,

Number of men enrolled, 645.

6th Battalion—Western Section.

Colonel, Henry Spyker.
CAPTAINS.

John Lesher,   Conrad Weiser,   Jacob Kreamer,
George Batdorff,   Michael Bretz,   Philip Filbert.
Henry Shepler,   Henry Weaver,

Number of men enrolled, 728.

ADDITIONAL CAPTAINS.

Daniel Deturk,   George Grant,   Jacob Rhoads.
George Beaver,

COUNTY RETURNS FOR 1780.

A return of the Field Officers, Captains, and Subalterns of the county militia was certified to by Col. Jacob Morgan, the Lieutenant of the county on May 10, 1780, when he issued commissions and delivered them to Col. Jacob Morgan, Jr. It is published in the *Pennsylvania Associators*, 2nd vol., pp. 278 to 292. The Field Officers and Captains were as follows:

1st Battalion—North-Eastern Section.

Lt.-Col., Samuel Ely. Maj., Abraham Betz.

CAPTAINS.

Charles Crouse,	Jacob Mourer,	Leonard Stone,
Jacob Ledich,	George Beaver,	Jacob Rickstein.
Jacob Rothermel,	Jacob Balty,	

2nd Battalion—Western Section.

Lt.-Col., Henry Spyker. Maj., John Lesher.

CAPTAINS.

Henry Shepler,	Michael Wolf,	John Sheffer,
Daniel Groff,	Philip Hetrich,	John Fulmer.
John Anspach,	Philip Filbert,	

3rd Battalion—Southern Section.

Lt.-Col., Jonathan Jones. Maj., Jacob Kirlin.

CAPTAINS.

David Weidner,	Michael Stophel,	John Ludwig,
Thomas Hamilton,	George Graul,	David Morgan.
Adam Beard,	George Ax,	

4th Battalion—Northern Section.

Lt.-Col., Michael Lindemuth. Maj., Martin Kercher.

CAPTAINS.

Jacob Frantz,	Daniel Will,	Ferdinand Ritter,
Jacob Weston,	Jacob Shartel,	Francis Umbenhacker.
Christian Balty,	Jacob Strabel,	

5th Battalion—Eastern Section.

Lt.-Col., John Cunius.   Maj., Michael Mullin.

CAPTAINS.

Abraham Kiefer,	Jacob Griesemer,	Daniel Leinbach,
Henry Knause,	Jacob Hill,	David Strause.
Anthony Schroeder,	Henry Strouch,	

6th Battalion—Central Section.

Lt.-Col., Joseph Hiester.   Maj., Edward Scull.

CAPTAINS.

Sebastian Miller,	Paul Feger,	George Riehm,
Conrad Geist,	Peter Nagel,	John Spohn.
Conrad Eckert,	Charles Gobin,	

COUNTY RETURNS FOR 1783.

A similar return was made by Col. Valentine Eckert, the Lieutenant of the county for the year 1783, and he issued commissions to the officers elected in April of that year. It is published in *Pennsylvania Archives*, vol. 10, pp. 190 and 331. The number of men in the 1st Battalion, commanded by Lt.-Col. Nicholas Lotz, was about 840; and of the 6th Battalion, commanded by Lt.-Col. John Cunius, was 643.

The number of men in the several companies of the other Battalions was not given.

The Battalion officers were as follows:

1st Battalion—Centre.
Lt.-Col., Nicholas Lotz.
Major, Jacob Bower.

2nd Battalion—North.
Lt.-Col., Balser Geehr.
Major, Martin Kercher.

3rd Battalion—Northeast.
Lt.-Col., Samuel Ely.
Major, Stephen Balty.

4th Battalion—South.
Lt.-Col., George Ax.
Major, Benjamin Talbert.

5th Battalion—West.
Lt.-Col., Henry Spyker.
Major, Christian Lower, Jr.,

6th Battalion—East.
Lt.-Col., John Cunnius.
Major, Nicholas Hunter.

NOTE.—By way of getting at the returns of the companies for the year 1776, it has been stated on page 58 that only eleven companies were found of which any mention was made. I overlooked the following thirteen companies :

Jonathan Jones.	Joseph Hiester,	John Ludwig,
John Spohn.	Jacob Maurer,	Benjamin Weiser,
Peter Decker.	George May,	John Lesher,
Henry Christ,	George Douglass,	Conrad Geist.
Jacob Graul,		

Besides Lotz's Battalion, and part of Patton's, three other battalions were in service—Geehr's, Bird's and Haller's—but their respective companies were not obtainable. (See Chap. VI.)

Capt. George Riehm is mentioned as a delegate to the Lancaster Convention for the 3rd Battalion. He also had a company organized. I have thus identified twenty-five companies out of forty-two estimated for the seven battalions. Thirteen of them were from the central section of the county, and five from the western.

CHAPTER VI.

COMPANIES FROM THE COUNTY IN THE REVOLUTION.

After much research and study, I am enabled to present the following companies and battalions of men from Berks County which were engaged in the Revolution during the period extending from 1775 to 1782. The evidence relating to them was taken almost entirely from the publications issued by the Commonwealth of Pennsylvania, comprising the *Colonial Records, Pennsylvania Archives*, (first and second series,) and *Pennsylvania Associators*.

I made diligent and persistent inquiry in the several county offices in the Court House at Reading, but I found only a single record that related to this important event in our history. In locating the several battalions, companies and leading men at the head of affairs, I had recourse to the public records. Occasionally I found private manuscripts in different parts of the county, but they were few in number and limited in character.

NAGEL'S COMPANY AT CAMBRIDGE.

On June 14, 1775, the Continental Congress passed resolutions requiring twelve companies of expert riflemen to be raised for the purpose of joining the army near Boston. Eight of these companies were to be raised in Pennsylvania, formed into a battalion, and commanded by officers recommended by the Assembly. The command formed of these companies was called "Colonel Thompson's Battalion of Riflemen." Each company consisted of one captain, three lieutenants, four sergeants, four corporals, a drummer or trumpeter and sixty-eight privates. The pay was as follows: Captain, $20 a month; lieutenant, $13⅓; sergeant, $8; corporal, $7⅓; drummer, $7⅓; private, $6⅔. They supplied their own arms and clothes. The term of enlistment was one year. The form of enlistment was as follows :

> "I have this day voluntarily enlisted myself as a soldier in the American Continental Army, for one year, unless sooner discharged, and do bind myself to conform in all instances to such rules and regulations as are or shall be established for the government of the said army."

One company in this battalion was from Reading. It was commanded by Capt. George Nagel.

By the "Journal of Capt. Wm. Hendricks" in *Penna. Archives*, vol. 15, p. 26, it appears that three companies, commanded by Captains Patterson, Smith and Lowden were at Reading, with the company of a Capt. "Noggle," awaiting the arrival of two companies from Carlisle, commanded by Captains Wm. Hendrick and John Chambers, all destined for Cambridge. The latter two companies remained at Reading from July 17th to 22nd. All the companies started in a body on the 22nd. The Capt. "Noggle" mentioned can not have been George Nagel, because his company was then at Cambridge.

Roll of Company.

Captains.

George Nagel, com. June 25, 1775; prom. major of the 5th Batt., Col. Robert Magaw, Jan. 5, 1776; to Lt.-Col. 9th Regt., Continental Line, Oct. 25, 1776, to rank from Aug. 21, 1776; to Col. of 10th Regt. Feb., 1778, and became a Supernumerary July 1, 1778.

Morgan Conner, com. Jan. 5, 1776; March 9th called from camp by Congress, and sent into the Southern Department; afterwards Lt.-Col. of Col. Hartley's Regiment.

First Lieutenants.

Morgan Conner, com. dated July 17, 1775; prom. capt.
David Harris, appointed Jan. 5, 1776.

Second Lieutenants.

Peter Scull, com. July 17, 1775; prom. capt. in 3rd Penn. Batt., Col. John Shee, Jan. 5, 1776.
Benjamin Chambers, Sr., from private in Capt. Chambers' Co., Jan. 5, 1776; subsequently first lieut., 1st Pa. Regt.

Third Lieutenants.

Peter Grubb, com. July 17, 1775; app. to Miles' rifle regt.
Peter Weiser, app. Jan. 5, 1776.

Sergeants.

Jacob Bower, app. Q. M.
Hananiah Lincoln.
John McKinty.
Alexander Brannon.
Philip Gibbons.

Corporals.

James Williams.
Hugh Hughes.
Henry Snevely.
Casper Heiner.

Surgeon.

Dr. Jonathan Potts.

Drummer.

John Maloy.

Privates.

Thomas Bain.
Christopher Balty.
Yost Berger.
Conrad Bourke.
Peter Bowman.
Peter Brough.
James Brown.
John Bermeter.
Michael Ceney.
Casper Cool, or Kool.
John Cox.
Robert Creed.
William Crowley.
Henry Deckert.
Christian Derr, re-enlisted in old 11th regt.
Hugh Dennison.
John Dombaugh.
Jacob Duck.
Jacob Elgerts.
Jacob Ebright.
Andrew Engel.
Peter Felix.
George Fisher.
Christian Fought.
Michael Foust.
Lewis Franklinberry.
George Gearhart.
Charles Gordon.
Daniel Gorman.
Daniel Graff.
John Grant.

Abraham Griffith.
John Grow.
Timothy Harris.
John Huber.
William Jones.
George Kemmerling.
John Kerner, wounded at Lechmere Pond, Nov. 9, 1775; re-enlisted in 6th Pa. regt. in 1777.
Charles Kleckner, prom. ensign of German Regt.
Nicholas Leasure.
John Leaman.
Casper Leib.
Harmon Leitheiser, ensign 6th Pa. Reg.
John Lewis.
Samuel McFarland.
Christopher Martin.
Michael Miller.
Peter Mingle.
Alexander Mogey [McGee.]
Adam Moyer.
Christian Moyer, or Christopher Myer.
Michael Moyer.
Ernst Nibber [Lawrence.]
Frederick Nipple.
Henry Orwig.
Samuel Parks.
Adam Pickle.
Elias Rieger.
Thomas Reilly.
John Rewalt.
William Robinson.
Christian Rone.
Nicholas Shanefelt.
Andrew Shirk.
Joseph Smith.
Henry Snevely, Sr.
George Spotts.
John Stone.
John Strecker.
Frederick Tueo.
Abraham Umstead.
Philip Waggoner.
Nicholas Waltman.
Christian Wander.
John Weiser.
Isaac Willey.

A return of March, 1776, states the strength of the company present, as follows: 1 captain, 3 lieutenants, 4 sergeants, 4 corporals, 1 drummer and 65 privates.

Within three weeks from the time of their enlistment, some of the companies took up their line of march to the Hudson River on their way to the army at Cambridge, Mass. During July and August, 1775, they passed through New Windsor, (on the Hudson several miles above West Point.) Nagel's company reported at headquarters, at Cambridge, on the 18th of July. The last of the battalion arrived on the 18th of August. The appearance of the men was described as follows:

"They are remarkably stout and hardy men, many of them exceeding six feet in height. They are dressed in white frocks or rifle-shirts and round hats. These men are remarkable for the accuracy of their aim, striking a mark with great certainty at two hundred yards distance. At a review, while on a quick advance, a company of them fired their balls into objects of seven inches diameter at the distance of two hundred and fifty yards. They are now stationed in our lines, and their shot have frequently proved fatal to British officers and soldiers who expose themselves to view even at more than double the distance of common musket-shot. Each man bore a rifle-barreled gun, a tomahawk or small ax and a long knife, usually called a 'scalping-knife,' which served for all purposes in the woods. His underdress—by no means in military style—was covered by a deep ash-colored hunting-shirt, leggins and moccasins—if the latter could be procured. It was the silly fashion of those times for riflemen to ape the manners of savages."

The battalion was first actually engaged and sustained its first loss in killed and wounded on the 27th of August, while covering an entrenching party.

Services of Company.

The services of this company were in connection with Thompson's Battalion at and about Cambridge, and are detailed in 10 *Penna. Archives*, (2nd series), pp. 3 to 13. No losses in the company were reported. The battalion received orders about March 11, 1776, to march from Cambridge to New York. The men went by way of Hartford, and New York was reached on March 28th. On April 22nd, Gen'l Washington, while at New York, said in a letter addressed to the President of Congress :

"The time for which the riflemen enlisted, will expire on the 1st of July next, and as the loss of such a valuable and brave body of men will be of great injury to the service, I would submit it to the consideration of Congress whether it would not be best to adopt some method to induce them to continue. They are indeed a very useful corps ; but I need not mention this, as their importance is already well known to the Congress."

It was stated in a letter of June 30th, by Col. Hand, that "almost all the men discharged to-day declare that they will stay to know what the fleet will do." On July 1st, the battalion entered upon another term of service as the 1st Regiment of the Continental Line.

A number of gentlemen went along in the march to Cambridge as independent volunteers. Their names were not entered on the rolls, and they claimed the privilege of paying their own expenses and returning at pleasure. Among these was Edward Burd, then a practicing attorney-at-law of Reading, who, in August, 1776, participated in the Battle of Long Island as a Major under Lieut.-Col. Nicholas Lotz, and there became a prisoner of war.

JONES'S COMPANY IN THE CANADA CAMPAIGN.

The news from Lexington and Concord reached Berks County in the latter part of April, 1775, and Jonathan Jones, of Caernarvon township raised a company of men in that township and vicinity. Six companies of riflemen were ordered to be raised in Pennsylvania in June, but it was not until the following October that the first regular regiment was called out by Congress. On the 25th of that month, the captains were appointed, and among them was Captain Jones. In December, Congress ordered four additional regiments to be raised in Pennsylvania, and in January, 1776, still another. These six regiments then composed the Pennsylvania Line, and the 1st, 2nd, 4th and 6th participated in the movements against Canada. The company of Capt. Jones was the first named in the 1st Regiment, commanded by Col. John Philip DeHaas. The roll was complete at the time of enlistment, but the following names are all that were obtainable:

Roll of Company.

Captain.
Jonathan Jones.

Corporals.

—— Bean.   Jacob Candy.
—— Kelly.   Matthew Clark.

Privates.

George Alexander.	John McGregor.	James Murphy.
John Brown.	Robert McKillup.	Albert Pearson.
James Dagley.	Joseph McMullen.	Ezra Shea.
Brice Dunlap.	Patrick McLaughlin.	Joseph Skelton.
Joseph Fullerton.	Clement Merls.	William Tennent.
Robert Gouger.	Philip O. Miller.	William Walker.
Daniel Leary.	Robert Murdock.	Thomas Walters.
James McCorley.		

Services of Company.

On January 23, 1776, Capt. Jones began a long march from Philadelphia to Canada with his company. The weather was intensely cold, that Winter having been one of great severity. They had one baggage wagon but no tents, depending upon such lodgings and provisions as their quarter-master could procure for them on the way. The roads were in a bad condition and the greater part of the journey extended through a wilderness. Even the best parts of the country were but sparsely settled, and limited accommodations were afforded for so large a body of men. The company proceeded by way of Germantown, Bethlehem and Easton to the Hudson river, and were then transported on boats at the public expense to Albany. It took eleven days to cover this distance. By that time their mittens and shoes were worn out and their muskets were useless from constant exposure. After a detention of several days in obtaining the necessary supplies, they continued up the Hudson and over Lakes George and Champlain to St. John and Montreal, partly by boats but mostly on foot. They remained at Montreal two weeks and then marched to Quebec, where they halted the latter part of March. The weather was still very cold, the snow at some places six feet deep, and the situation of affairs extremely discouraging. The campaign was unsuccessful and the American Army was obliged to retreat to Ticonderoga, where the men were entrenched and remained for some time on the defensive. The British, not succeeding in their mission, returned to Canada, and General Gates then ordered the regiment with certain other troops to embark for Pennsylvania. They started November 15th, and while marching homeward, Washington sent pressing orders to them to join his army at Trenton; but before reaching that place they were ordered to halt thirty miles to the North. After the defeat of the British at Trenton, they marched to Philadelphia and were discharged on January 10, 1777. It is not known how many returned with the company. The roll, as presented, numbers only twenty-seven men.

COMPANIES AT NEW YORK.

Three companies from Berks County were in service at New York and in that vicinity in 1776. Two of them formed part of the 5th Battalion of Pennsylvania troops, which was under the command of Col. Robert Magaw, of Carlisle. The captains were John Spohn and Peter Decker, both residents of Reading. The men of Spohn's company were also from Reading, but those of Decker's were mostly from the districts surrounding Reading.

The third company constituted part of the Pennsylvania Rifle Regiment, of which Samuel Miles was appointed Colonel. It was commanded by Capt. Henry Christ, who was also from Reading.

The company rolls are incomplete.

Roll of Spohn's Company.

Captain.

John Spohn, com'd Jan. 5, 1776; resigned Nov. 4, 1776.

First Lieutenant.

John Morgan, Philadelphia, com'd Jan. 6, 1776; taken August 16, 1776; same day prom. capt., *vice* Miller, killed; June 1, 1778, became supernumerary; exch. Aug. 26, 1778.

Second Lieutenant.

William Stanley, com'd Jan. 8, 1776; taken Aug. 16th; same day prom. 1st lieut.; exch. Aug. 25, 1780.

Ensign.

John Gansel, com'd Jan. 8, 1776.

Sergeant-Major.

Enoch Wright, app'd Nov. 16, 1776.

Sergeants.

Jacob Vanderslice.
Adam Ruth.

Corporals.

Henry Vanderslice.
Henry Goodheart.
James Campbell.

Privates.

Jacob Albert.
John Allison, sergt.-maj. of 4th Pa.
John Barnhest.
Richard Barington.
Anthony Bishop.
George Cole.
William Collins.
Timothy Carney.
Dennis Calaghan.
Valentine Dengler.
Peter Duck.
William Fletcher.
Henry Goodhart.
Christopher Havener.
George Heilman.
Christian Holick.
Jacob Hausknecht.

George Hoffner.
Martin Link.
Nicholas Mann.
George Marshal.
Jacob Miller; re-enlisted in Col. Hartley's regt.; disch. 1781.
Peter Miller.
John Nair.
John Rangler.
Michael Raume.
John Rheam.
Michael Selser.
John Shelson.
Michael Whitmer.
George Whitmire; died in New York two days before exchange.
Benjamin Ziegler.
Michael Zurn.

Roll of Decker's Company.

Captain.
Peter Decker, com'd Jan. 5, 1776; resigned Feb. 2, 1777.

First Lieutenant.
Charles Phile, com'd Jan. 6, 1776; prom. capt. Feb. 1, 1777; exch. Aug. 26, 1778.

Second Lieutenant.
John Rudolph, com'd Jan. 8, 1776; prom. capt. Feb. 1, 1777; exch. Oct. 25, 1780.

Ensign.
James Mulloy, com'd Jan. 8 1776.

Sergeants.
James Forsythe.
Michael Gabby.
Christopher Weiser.

Corporal.
Philip Duck.

Privates.
Abraham Brosius.
Michael Burkhart; died in prison.
Jacob Churchner (Kerchner); died in prison.
Andrew Cook.
Leonard Dell.
James Finerty.
Robert Fry.
George Huber.
Anthony Lehman.
Peter Moyer; exch. 1778; re-enlisted in Bankson's Co.
Matthias Spang.
Leonard Strow.
Edward Welsh.
Jacob Young.
Michael Zeller.
John Zuier, died in prison.

Services of Companies.

On June 11, 1776, Magaw's Battalion, and that of Col. John Shee, (a merchant of Philadelphia) were ordered to march to New York. They started on the 15th and reached their destination from the 20th to the 25th, and on the 29th they were placed under the command of Gen. Thomas Mifflin. They encamped where Fort Washington was erected—being employed in its construction under Col. Israel Putnam, and remained there until the fighting of the Battle of Long Island August 27th, when they marched back to New York, reaching that place after the battle was over. On the 28th, they went to Brooklyn, where, annoyed by continual rains, without tents, they lay upon their arms and kept up incessant firing with the British. On the 30th, they were ordered to retire, and on the 31st, came to re-occupy Fort Washington. These battalions then remained five weeks on the Harlem Heights. On November 16th, the fort was invested by Gen. Howe's army and captured. Then Magaw's battalion, with others, mostly from Pennsylvania, were posted in the lower lines of Harlem Heights. The superiority of the British drove all finally into the fort, when they surrendered, and the battalions of Shaw and Shee became prisoners almost entirely. Many of them were paroled in December following. The men were retained as prisoners until in January, 1777, by which time their term of enlistment had expired. Most of the officers did not secure their release for years afterward.

A return of May 28, 1776, showed that Spohn's company had 78 men, including officers, of whom 15 were absent on account of sickness; and Decker's company had 86, of whom 9 were absent, also on account of sickness. On the day before the surrender, (Nov. 15, 1776) the companies were as follows:

Spohn's company—45 men, comprising the first and second lieutenants, 4 sergeants, 20 men fit for duty, and 19 unfit.

Decker's company—52 men, comprising captain, first and second lieutenants, 4 sergeants, drummer and fifer, 37 men fit for duty, and 6 unfit.

In Shee's Battalion, Daniel Brodhead, of Reading, was commissioned as Lt.-Col. on October 25, 1776; and Peter Scull, also of Reading, as a Capt. January 5, 1776. Scull was appointed Brigade Major on March 23, 1776.

Capt. Peter Decker has been included with the Regiment commanded by Lt.-Col. Nicholas Lotz in the "Flying Camp," in the returns and publications that relate to this regiment; but the services of his company are identified entirely with Col. Magaw's Regiment as detailed.

Roll of Christ's Company.

Captain.

Henry Christ, Jr.; resigned March 19, 1777.

First Lieutenant.

Daniel Topham; captured Aug. 27, 1776; exch. April 20, 1778.

Second Lieutenant.

Jacob Maess.

Third Lieutenants.

Abner Davis; resigned Oct. 19, 1776.

George Gyger, from sergt. Oct. 24, 1776.

Sergeants.

George Gyger, April 1, 1776.

Matthew Whitlow, April 20, 1776; missing since the battle, Aug. 27, 1776.

Sergeants.

Jeremiah Geiss, March 29, 1776; missing since the battle, Aug. 27, 1776.

Adam Christ, from private; wounded, ball passing through his breast at Brandywine.

Joseph Starke.

Drum and Fife.

Samuel Keiser,
Nathan Hinkel.
Matthias Rehrer.

Privates.

William Albert.
Henry Alter.
Michael Arnold.
William Butler; re-enlisted in 2nd Pa.
Adam Christ.
Melcher Close.
Godfry Dering.

John English.
Francis Fisher.
Henry Fisher.
Godfrey Fister.
Henry Frederick.
Paul Frederick; missing since battle of Aug. 27, '76.

Yost Fuchs (Fox); missing since the battle.
Herman Geiss.
John Green.
Peter Groff.
Michael Groff.
Valentine Gyger.

John Hambright.
Nicholas Hamm.
William Herbert.
Jacob Heckman.
Yost Heck.
George Heffner.
John Herman.
Michael Hinterleiter.
Henry Hill.
Nathan Hinkel.
Dan'l Hausknecht,
John Hummel.
George Jones.
Francis Keehl.
Christian Kemmerer.
George Kettner.
Christian Kraemer.
Simon Kreisher.
Abraham Lantsert.
Henry Leffler.
George Lehnig.
Isaac Linwill.
Emanuel Lippert.
John Long.
Philip Lott.
John Lutz.
Gotlieb Mack.
Simon Madeira.
George Mengel.
Henry Mertz.
Philip Miller.
Joseph Muffly.
Daniel Nitterhaus.
John Nordstein.
Frederick Poust.
Charles Reichard.
Jacob Reiff.
Jacob Riegle.
David Siebold.
Yost Seyler.
Adam Shaffer.
Joseph Stark.
Adam Streckdefinger.
Frederick Struble.
Peter Treher.
Christian Walk.
John Weaver.
John Weidman.
Henry Weiss.
George Whitman.
Michael Wissler.
Henry Wolf,
George Zenig.
Philip Zott.

Services of Company.

The Pennsylvania Rifle Regiment was embodied strictly for the defense of the Province, at the suggestion of the Committee of Safety, on February 20, 1776, when they passed a resolution praying that the House of Representatives order the raising of 2000 men for that purpose. The House acted promptly and on March 4th appointed a committee to estimate the expense of levying a body of 1500 men, victualing and paying them for one year. On March 5th the estimate was reported, and on the same day the levy was made and the men were ordered to be enlisted to serve until January 1, 1778, subject to be discharged at any time. The first two captains were appointed on March 7, 1776; the others on the 9th.

Daniel Brodhead of Reading was appointed Lieut.-Colonel of the 2nd Battalion on March 13, 1776, and Ennion Williams, of Bethel township, was appointed Major of the 1st Battalion on the same day, both of whom afterward became prominent in the Revolution.

The regiment was raised in about six weeks and rendezvoused at Marcus Hook. On July 2nd it was ordered to Philadelphia, when the number of officers and men in Christ's company reported on duty were 62; on the 4th to Bordentown, on the 5th to Trenton, and thence to Amboy under orders to join General Mercer, which it accomplished by the 16th. On August 1st, a report of the company showed 64 on duty. On August 10th, the regiment was ordered to New York under the command of Brig.-Gen'l Lord Sterling. According to a general return on the 24th, 867 officers and men of this rifle regiment were present.

The regiment was engaged in the Battle of Long Island on Aug. 27, 1776, where it was stated that the Pennsylvanians got a "drubbing" and were "prettily taken in." The army of about 5000 men was surrounded by 15,000 English and Hessians. The number of killed of the latter was large, but of the Continentals very trifling. About 700 Continentals were taken prisoners and among them "more officers than perhaps was ever known in a like number of men." Among the killed was Col. Miles. In this battle the rifle regiment was so badly broken up that Gen'l Washington ordered the three battalions to be considered as a regiment, and to be placed under the command of Brodhead until further orders.

On September 27, 1776, these battalions were in Gen'l Mifflin's brigade and stationed at Mount Washington. By a rearrangement of October 5th, Christ's company became the 7th in the regiment, which was afterward known as the "Regiment of Foot." At that time the situation of the company was 4 sergeants, 1 drummer and 41 privates, with 11 men absent. Thence it followed the fortunes of the Continental army. It was engaged in the capture of the Hessians at Trenton on December 26, 1776; also in the battle of Princeton on January 3, 1777; and then lay part of the winter at Philadelphia. The remaining service until Jan. 1, 1778, has not been ascertained.

LOTZ'S BATTALION IN FLYING CAMP.

In pursuance of the address to the Associators, Col. Nicholas Lotz, chairman of the Standing Committee, on Thursday, June 27, 1776, issued the following notice for a meeting of the Committee on July 2nd:

"*Resolved*, That notice be immediately given to the members of the General Committee of this county to meet at the Court House in Reading, on Tuesday next, the second day of July, on affairs of public importance and very interesting at this critical time, especially to choose officers for 666 men; and that the several members be desired to enquire what officers now in the Association are willing to go into immediate service on call."

This meeting was held at the time appointed, and from the published record in the *Pennsylvania Associators*, vol. 2, p. 776, the following officers were then chosen:

Col., Henry Haller.
Lt.-Col., Nicholas Lotz.
Maj., Edward Burd.

Captains.

Jacob Graul, Reading.
Joseph Heister, Reading.

Jacob Maurer, Maidencreek.
John Ludwig, Exeter.

John Old, Amity.
George Douglass, Amity.
Peter Decker, Reading

The rosters of the several companies have not as yet been found, nor have the names of all the officers of the battalion been ascertained. But a letter, which the Committee of Correspondence addressed to Congress on July 13, 1776, indicates that one company more than the quota of the county had been raised. By the notice it would appear that this quota of the 4500 men from the whole Province was 666. The letter was as follows:

Committee Letter to Congress.

READING, July 13, 1776.

Sir: We have received your letter, containing a resolve of Congress for the removal of the privates, who are prisoners in this town, to Lancaster, which we shall carry into execution with all the despatch in our power.

We received a letter from the honorable the Delegates of this Province, mentioning that we should be informed by express, or by the gentlemen from our County, then at Lancaster, that all the Militia that could possibly be equipped and armed should be called forth. We also received a letter from the Committee of Lancaster, enclosing copies of letters from a Committee of Congress, and from the Committee of the City of Philadelphia; in the former of which it is mentioned that the forces from the several Counties should be collected and marched to Brunswick; in the latter it is mentioned that only the 4500 men ordered to be raised in the Province, as a part of the Flying Camp, were meant by the letter of the Committee of Congress. We, therefore, continued our plan of raising our quota for the Flying Camp, and, indeed, added a company more, to complete the battalion, hoping for the approbation of Congress in so doing; since which we have seen in the public prints the proceedings of the Conference of the Delegates of the several Counties, and of the Committee of Safety of the City and Liberties. But as we had nearly raised several companies to compose the Flying Camp, (the place of which this Militia is intended to supply) and the others were proceeding with great success, considering the great scarcity of every kind of tolerable arms among the people to arm such a multitude, we hope our completing the original plan will be approved of, as the men will be more quickly raised and better equipped than if we were to take down the whole Militia. Our conduct is dictated by the warmest attachment to the cause of our country, and we trust it will be considered in that light by the honorable Congress.

We are, with great respect, sir, your most obedient and very humble servants,

    Henry Haller, John Whitman, Jun., Collinson Read.
    Edward Burd, Paul Kerper,

To the Honorable John Hancock, Esq.

INTENTIONS OF CONGRESS EXPLAINED.

Notwithstanding the promptness of the county in responding to the call for a "Flying Camp," it seems that some misrepresentation of the intentions of Congress had arisen amongst the Associators of the county and the officers who were appointed to form the "Flying Camp." It was in respect to the march and arrangement of the Associators and militia who were to compose the said camp, and the Standing Committee on that account addressed a letter to the Constitutional Convention on July 22, 1776; to which the following reply was made on the 24th:

"Your letter, 22d Inst., to the Hon'ble B. Franklin Esq'r, Presid't of the Convention, was refered by the Hon. Convention to the Council of Safety. They must acknowledge the Laudable zeal with which your Committee has, at all times, carried into execution the recommendation of such powers as acted under the People; But, particularly, your ready & cheerful Obedience to the ordinance of Convention for disarming of non-Associators.

"The embarrassments you Labor under in consequence of Resolves of Congress and others, which, from the confused state of the times, appeared somewhat Contradictory, appears to us excusable. In order to render the intentions of Congress more plain & Comprehensive and to their expectations, The Council of Safety have inclosed you their resolution upon the matter, requesting that you will take such Measures to publish it through your district as will be most Effectual & Expeditious, and that you would encourage the Associators to turn out on this very important Immergency."

The resolution alluded to in the letter was as follows :

"*Resolved*, That all the Militia who may be furnished and equip'd agreeable to the Resolve of Congress do march to such place as they have been respectively ordered by Congress, and that the persons who have been appointed Captains in the Flying Camp and have not enlisted 25 men for that service, do return them to their respective Corps of Associators to which they formerly belonged, and continue with them; the appointment of the officers for the Flying Camp still to continue, and the men already enlisted to be considered as bound by their enlistment, and to be continued in service when the militia may be permitted to return, and subject to further orders of the Convention or this Board. And it is further recommended that those Companies which have been raised to form the Flying Camp, which already consists of 25 privates and upwards, do immedialely proceed to Trenton or Brunswick, as heretofore directed.

"*Resolved*, That this Board will allow the Officers who were appointed to command the Flying Camp all such reasonable expenses as have accrued in the recruiting service."

COUNTY TROOPS AT BETHLEHEM.

The following extracts were taken from the *Pennsylvania Magazine of History*, vol. 12, pps. 390-91, having reference particularly to troops from Berks County at Bethlehem in August, 1776:

Capt. Old's company, on the way from Reading to New York arrived at Bethlehem on Aug. 4, 1776, at 9 a. m. He asked the Moravian minister to preach to his men, and came with them to the chapel where the Rev. Ettwein discoursed both in the English and German languages.

On Aug. 16th, four companies of militia from Tulpehocken, with flying colors, drums and fifes, arrived at the same place *en route* for the Flying Camp at New Brunswick. They lodged over night at the Sun Tavern.

On Aug. 23rd, a company from Reading under Capt. Will, *en route* for the Jerseys arrived at Bethlehem and lodged over night. They attended evening service.

On Aug. 26th, two companies arrived. One was from Oley, under Capt. Daniel DeTurk, and the men attended evening service; and on Aug. 28th, a company from Reading, under Capt. George May arrived.

On Sept. 1st, the 4th Battalion of Berks County Militia, under the command of Col. Balser Geehr arrived at Bethlehem at noon; and at four o'clock in the afternoon, Rev. Ettwein preached to them in the chapel.

The companies of Capt. Old and Capt. May are mentioned in connection with Lotz's Battalion, but they evidently were not with Lotz and the battalion in their march to Long Island. The others named are additional to those that were engaged in that battle.

The four companies from Tulpehocken must have been part of the 5th Battalion of County Militia, commanded by Col. John Patton. They were from the Western section of the county. The 4th Battalion, under Col. Geehr, was from the Northern section, and, from the extract given, it would seem that the entire battalion was in actual service.

Marching Order to Capt. DeTurck.

The following order was issued by Col. Henry Haller to Capt. Daniel DeTurck, directing him to march his company to Amboy:

By Henry Haller, Esq., Colonel of the Regiment raising in Berks County, to compose part of the quota of the troops which is to be furnished by Pennsylvania for the Flying Camp.

To Daniel Turck, Esq., Captain of a Company in the said Battalion:

You are directed to march your company the nearest and best way to Amboy in the Jerseys with all expedition that lies in your power, where you are to join the Pennsylvania forces and then to apply to the Commander in Chief for the time being for further orders.

You are to place guards over the baggage wagons, who are to be furnished with powder and ball, but must not load without necessity. The Guards always to be accountable and must deliver over the Ammunition which they have received to the succeeding guard.

The men to be restrained as much as possible from drinking too much strong liquor or committing the least insult on the inhabitants of the places through which they march.

Given under my Hand and Seal at Reading ye 23rd August, 1776.

{ SEAL.
  S. & P. L. }   HENRY HALLER.

In pursuance of this order, Capt. DeTurck proceeded with his company from Reading on August 24, 1776. The roll of the company was as follows:

Roll of DeTurck's Company.

Captain.
Daniel DeTurck.

First Lieutenant.	*Second Lieutenant.*
Paul Kerber.	Charles Gobin.

Sergeants.

Henry Yeager.
Henry Wax.
John Phillippi.
Jacob Briner.

Corporals.

John Dippery.
John Heebner.
Conrad Krafft.

Fifer.

George Phillippi.

Privates.

Christ'r Rightmire.
George Brown.
Peter Baum.
Nicholas Scull.
Valentine Seahler.
Michael Rosch.
John Ernst.
Henry Baum.
Job Herbey.
Christ'r Schneider.
Frederick Fernsler.
Henry Hatt.
John Beck.
Martin Yung.
Philip Hatt.
David Fox.
John Kiehn.
Benjamin Leinbach.
Charles Zent.
Deob. Haberacker.
Michael Bleyler.

Deobald Schmidt.
George Miller.
Caspar Wecht.
Samuel Homan.
Nicholas Seitel.
Philip Hartman.
Ulrick Kissinger.
Joshua Evans.
William Lewis.
David Betz.
George Schleer.
Henry Leinbach.
Philip Wentzel.
Gabriel Gantzer.
George Wingert.
Henry Strunk.
William Goodhart.
Dieter Miller.
George Albert.
Henry Frymire.
George Lawyer.

Henry Fisher.
Henry Faust.
Henry Ruth.
John Hill.
Charles Mell.
Nicholas Eckert.
John Brown.
Joseph Billing.
Wm. Shealhiemer.
Christian Scheaffer.
Christian Waldschmidt.
Carl Schucker.
Frederick Bechtel.
Christian Ruth.
Elijah Dewees.
John Hesch.
Christian Fisher.
Paul Steph.
Nicholas Dick.

The foregoing 72 men entered the service on August 26, 1776, for two months, excepting the following: Charles Gobin, George Phillippi, Joseph Billings, John Hesch, Christian Fischer and Paul Steph, who joined the company in September. All were discharged on October 26th.

The monthly pay of the men was as follows: Captain, £15; Lieutenants, £10, 2sh., 6d.; Sergeants, £3; Corporals and Fifer, £2, 15sh.; and privates £2, 10sh.

These facts were taken from the original pay roll which I inspected. It was entitled: "A Pay Roll of Capt. Daniel DeTurck's Company of Militia of the Third Class of Berks County, commanded by Col. Michael Lindemuth." Col. Henry Spyker, the Paymaster, paid the men in 1778.

Capt. DeTurck is mentioned as of Oley, but he was from Alsace.

Order to Organize.—His company was slow in organizing, and it may be that the men misunderstood the resolution of Congress in reference to raising troops for the service. Col. Haller had issued the following order to him:

READING, July 12, 1776.

Dear Sir:—The inhabitants of Berks County being indifferent to organizing a volunteer militia, it becomes necessary that we should take similar action as the other counties, or suffer such disgrace that it will not be forgotten if it do not cause our entire ruin.

In behalf of the good name of Berks County, to avoid any further delay, and especially to serve the public welfare, we should not neglect the distinct order of the Honorable Congress any longer.

Therefore I direct you to call your company together on next Sunday without fail and then make a proper step forward. Your help in this matter will be expected without fail. An officer from here will be in attendance, but you must let me know as soon as possible the time and place where you propose to meet.

I am, my dear sir, your friend and servant,

HENRY HALLER.

To Captain Daniel Duerck.

This order was written in German. It was evidently prepared by some scrivener and issued by Col. Haller as a common form for all the captains.

DeTurck's Company having arrived at Bethlehem on August 26, and remained there over night, it is apparent that they did not reach their destination, (over 50 miles farther on) until the last of August.

Battle of Long Island.—Eight battalions of Pennsylvania troops in the "Flying Camp" were sent to the army at New York. Three of them were incomplete, and of these, one was composed of Berks County Associators, under the command of Lieut.-Col. Nicholas Lotz. The colonel, Henry Haller, did not join the army till after the opening of the campaign. The command of Lotz was said to comprise only 200 men. It was in Sterling's brigade. On August 24, 1776, Washington was in doubt as to the intentions of the enemy. He found the British 16,000 strong, but they had been estimated at only 8000. He ordered more reinforcements over on the Brooklyn side, and among these was Lotz's command. The Battle of Long Island was fought on August 27, 1776. In the engagement, part of Lotz's command, under Major Burd, was stationed at the coast-road, at and around the "Red Lion Tavern." Burd was at the lower road with Hand till he was relieved. In numbers, the British exceeded the Americans on the island three to one. The advance-guard of the British, under Grant, marched up the Narrows and struck the American pickets in the vicinity of the "Red Lion" about two o'clock in the morning. The pickets retreated before the enemy without checking their march. There was hardly more than an exchange of fire with Major Burd's detachment when he and many others—about 800—were taken prisoners. This skirmish took place on the "Narrows Road," between 38th and 40th Streets. The Americans were defeated because the British had completely outflanked and surprised them on the Jamaica road. Among the prisoners there were 91 officers. The killed were 6 officers and 50 privates, and less than 16 officers and 150 privates were wounded. The total loss of the British was reported as 367 officers and men. There was no official report of the losses in Lotz's detachment. He had 6 officers taken from him, all prisoners, none killed or wounded. The following appeared among the list of prisoners: Lieut.-Col. Nicholas Lotz, Maj. Edward Burd, Capt. Jacob Graul, Capt. Joseph Hiester and Capt. Jacob Maurer. Hiester and Maurer were exchanged in December, 1776. Lotz was admitted to parole within certain bounds on April 16, 1777, and exchanged on September 10, 1779, when he returned to his home in Reading.

The reduction of men from 666 to 200 has not been explained. The companies in the battalion were full, judging from the letter referred to, and the extra company was that of Capt. Peter Decker, which was attached to the battalion commanded by Col. Robert Magaw. Taking the notice of Col. Lotz and the letter to Congress together, I am led to say that the battalion was full when it marched to participate in the Long Island campaign, and conflicting statements in the description of the Battle of Long Island by various authors must be considered with hesitation. At least six companies accompanied the battalion, yet only three captains are mentioned as having been taken prisoners, Graul, Hiester and Maurer. What became of the remaining three, Ludwig, Old and Douglass? From the assumption that the battalion was not complete and had only 200 men in the engagement, the other three companies must have become detached from the battalion, or must not have been in the service at all. Of these three companies, Ludwig's was from Exeter, in the central section of the county, but Old's and Douglass's were, I think, from the southern section.

Incidents of Hiester's Company.—Joseph Hiester, a young man only twenty-three years old, was selected as one of the delegates from Berks County to the Provincial Conference which assembled in Carpenters' Hall at Philadelphia during June, 1776, and upon its adjournment he carried the spirit, which had been developed there, to Reading and acted promptly in behalf of the provision for troops to constitute part of the "Flying Camp." On July 10, 1776, he called together, by beat of the drum, 25 or 30 of his fellow-citizens and asked them to take into consideration the alarming state of the country. He explained the situation and said that there was a necessity for action. Having aroused their patriotism, he expressed a desire to raise a company of volunteers and march with them to the assistance of Gen'l Washington, who was then in a perilous situation in New Jersey. He was listened to with great respect, and at the conclusion of his remarks he said (laying $40 in money on a drum-head): "I will give this sum as a bounty and the appointment of a sergeant to the first man who will subscribe the articles of association to form a volunteer company to march forthwith and join the commander-in-chief."

He also pledged himself to furnish the company with blankets and necessary funds for their equipment and on the march.

Matthias Babb was the first to step forward. He took the money from the drum-head after signing the articles. This example induced 20 others to sign also. Notices were sent out into the neighborhood and meetings were held. In ten days afterward, Hiester had enrolled 96 men, and they were promptly organized, when they became a part of the "Flying Camp" in the regiment commanded by Lieut.-Col. Nicholas Lotz.

Learning at Elizabethtown that Gen'l Washington had marched to Long Island, some of his company, and the company commanded by Capt. Graul, declared their determination not to march any farther, stating that they had proceeded farther than they could have been compelled to go. He called the men into line and, addressing them in bold, impassioned, patriotic language, asked them to fall in and march forward to join Washington and fight for freedom. All responded nobly excepting three. When the drums began to beat and the men to march, these three could not resist the feeling, and they, too, marched along to Long Island. Some of them were killed in that battle, others wounded, and many taken prisoners. As prisoners they were treated with great cruelty. With other officers, Hiester was confined for six weeks on board of the prison-ship "Jersey." Thence he was removed to another prison-ship. Shortly afterward, he was confined on board of the ship "Snow Mentor," and there similar bad treatment was inflicted upon him. He became very sick with fever and very weak—so feeble, indeed, that he was compelled to crawl on hands and knees to get up and down stairs. Whilst there he was plundered of all his clothing and money. He was exchanged in December, and then he returned to Reading. During his imprisonment he was elected a major, and upon his return home he was elected a colonel. He received both commissions at the same time.

WEISER'S COMPANY IN THE GERMAN REGIMENT.

Benjamin Weiser, a merchant of Heidelberg township, (residing at Womelsdorf) and a son of Conrad Weiser—the pioneer military commander in Berks County, who rendered valuable services in the French and Indian War—commanded a company of men in the German Regiment of the Continental Line. This regiment originated from a resolution of Congress passed June 27, 1776, which directed four companies to be raised in Pennsylvania to compose the "German Battalion," and to serve for three years, unless sooner discharged.

Congress had requested the State Board of Safety "to recommend four gentlemen as suitable persons as Captains to four Companies of Germans to be raised in the Province for the Continental service." Among the four recommended on July 6, 1776, was Benjamin Weiser, and on July 12, 1776, the Board recommended the appointment of Jacob Bower, 1st Lieut., George Schaffer, 2nd Lieut., and Jacob Cramer, Ensign, for the said Company. These men were also of Berks County, from the same vicinity.

Captain.
Benjamin Weiser.

First Lieutenant.	*Corporals.*
Jacob Bower.	Nicholas Waldman.
Second Lieutenant.	George Price.
Frederick Yeiser.	Conrad Rahn.
Ensign.	*Drummer.*
Jacob Cramer.	William Marx.
Sergeants.	*Fifer.*
Charles Glichner.	Adam Bush.
Stewart Herbert.	
John Benkler.	
Joseph Miller.	

Privates.

John Barnheisell.	Jacob Mickley.	John Snyder.
John Bishop.	Baltzer Newfang.	Frederick Spire.
John Christman.	John Bortner.	Adam Stull.
John Derr.	Abr. Price.	Peter Toney.
George Fick.	John Razor.	Frederick Trester,
John Heier.	Michael Riegel.	Conrad Treywitz.
John Henry.	Martin Reiskell.	John Tudro.
Casper Kealer.	Joseph Romig.	William Wallman.
Philip Killmar.	Adam Rosemeisell.	Philip Warley.
Peter Lesher.	Peter Shiffer.	Christopher Weigle.
John Lorash.	Benj. Seryey.	Frederick Williams.
Joseph Mast.	Henry Seyfert.	Vincent Williams.
John Maurst.	Jacob Smith.	Michael Yeisley.
Eberhart Mayer.		

The men in the foregoing Company entered the service during July and August.

Services of Company.

The German Regiment was engaged at Trenton on December 26, 1776, and at Princeton on January 3, 1777. In May, 1777, it was in Sullivan's Division which conducted a campaign against the Indians. In the Spring of 1780, it was stationed on the frontiers of Northumberland County. By a resolution of Congress in October of that year, the regiment was reduced in number, and by January 1, 1781, its organization was ended.

Capt. Weiser was commissioned on July 8, 1776. He moved with his family to Selinsgrove in the latter part of 1776. On January 21, 1778, he was commissioned as a Justice of the Peace for Northumberland County.

Other Men from County in the Regiment.—The following additional privates were enlisted from Berks County in the German Regiment:

David Bloom.	James Gohoon (corporal).	John Smeltzer.
Detner Bouser.		Henry Snyder.
Jacob Botamer.	Andrew Hagar.	Henry Swetzgay.
George Funk (corporal).	Peter Meyer.	John Weidman.
	George Price.	Jacob Weisler.

COUNTY TROOPS AT SOUTH AMBOY.

The following four companies of Berks County Militia were on duty during August and September, 1776, at South Amboy, in New Jersey, at the mouth of the Raritan river, opposite the southern extremity of Staten Island. They were at that place while the Battle of Long Island was going on.

BATTALION OF COL. JOHN PATTON.

These companies were raised in the western section of Berks County, and constituted part of the Battalion commanded by Col. John Patton, a prominent iron master of Heidelberg township, who carried on the Berkshire Furnace which was situated in that township. They were collected together at Womelsdorf, and while there the battalion was supplied with 1068 rations. A record of the march from that place to Perth Amboy was published in the *Berks and Schuylkill Journal*, but the writer mentioned only the Lesher Company in that connection, doubtless because he was a survivor of that company and therefore named his company in preference to the others. From the article it would seem that the battalion was formed and marched at the same time. The march was as follows:

"At Womelsdorf, from August 1st to 9th, getting cloth for tents and making tents. August 11th, marched at 12 M. from Womelsdorf to Sinking Spring, 9 miles. August 12th, to Reading, 5 miles, and detained there by Committee, 13th and 14th. August 15th, marched to Levan's (Kutztown), 18 miles. August 16th, to Bethlehem, 24 miles. August 17th, to Straw's Tavern, 15 miles. Next day, Sunday, remained there, raining all day. August 19th, marched to South Branch of Raritan River, 20 miles. August 20th, to 'Punch Bowl,' 20 miles. August 21st, to Bonnamtown, 17 miles; and on 22d arrived at Perth Amboy, 7 miles. Total distance marched, 135 miles."

Field Officers of Battalion.

The following were the officers of the Battalion:

Colonel, John Patton.

First Major.	*Staff Adjutant.*
Joseph Thornburgh.	Henry Spyker.
Second Major.	*Quartermaster.*
Christian Lower.	George Lechner.

Paymaster, Casper Reed.

Roll of Lesher's Company.

Captain.
John Lesher.

First Lieutenant.
Jacob Rehrer.

Second Lieutenant.
John Anspach.

Ensign.
John Bortner.

Sergeants.
Valentine Beuler.
Francis Zeller.
Wm. Eichberger.
Conrad Sherman.

Corporals.
Philip Eichberger.
Henry Krum.
Peter Weis.
Jacob Read.

Fifer.
Andrew Zeller,

Drummer.
John Weis.

Privates.

Ludwig Wirtenberger.
Lorentz Wolfe.
George Fisher.
John Gebhart.
Peter Mayer.
John Reinhart.
Jacob Megant.
George Brobst.
Christian Emerich.
Baltzer Houtz.
Frederick Young.
Michael Katterman.
Nicholas Stouch.
Peter Forney.
Conrad Wentzel.
Samuel Read.
Jacob Hitzman.
Baltzer Noll.
John Teisinger.
Philip Weber.
Henry Snyder.
Jacob Brown.
Godfried Seltzer.
Nicholas Teisinger.
Hieronymus Schrift
Nicholas Smith.
Ludwig Ohrenbaum.
George Paffinger.
Leonard Emerich.
Abraham Snyder.
Peter Pontius.
Nicholas Bressler.
Henry Sterner.

This company was organized out of men from Bethel and Tulpehocken townships in the western section of the county.

Roll of Wolf's Company.

Captain.
Michael Wolf.

1st Lieutenant.
Conrad Weiser.

Second Lieutenant.
Isaac Depuy.

Ensign.
Henry Battorf.

Drummer.
Daniel Fisher.

Fifer.
Philip Werner.

Sergeants.
Michael Selser.
Wendle Seibert.

Corporals.
Rudolph Manbeck.
Weirick Selser.

Privates.

Jacob Yeglick.
John Klein.
George Nagel.
Peter Spang.
George Groff.
Philip Smith.
Nicholas Dornmayer
Nicholas Saleday.

Peter Fegh.
James Smith.
John Guld.
Moses Hofys.
Henry Rob.
Adam Mathias.
Henry Kobel.
William Daley.

Ludwig Swartz.
John Briker.
Philip Ginder.
Christopher Henly.
Henry Rost.
Philip Groff.
George Dieter.

This company was organized out of men from Bethel and Tulpehocken townships.

Roll of Miller's Company.

Captain.
George Miller.

First Lieutenant.
John Riegel.

Second Lieutenant.
David Baker.

Ensign.
Michael Fox.

Drummer.
John Reaber.

Fifer.
George Miller.

Sergeants.
George Loose.
Michael Zerben.

Corporal.
Philip Seyler.

Privates.

Jacob Wagner.
Frederick Kerger.
Mathias Smith.
Joseph Swartzhaupt.

Jacob Sauter.
Andrew Emerich.
John Hubler.
George Wert.

Adam Albert.
Jacob Loose.
Daniel Aulenbach.
Simon Lingel.

REVOLUTION.

Nicholas Riegel.
Jacob Kehl.
Nicholas Ketner.
John Long.
Daniel Kros.
Ludwig Wert.
George Souter.

Conrad Reaber.
John Derr.
John Swartz.
Lazarus Mouns.
John Fengel.
Daniel Manensmith.
John Miller.

Jacob Ney.
John Auman.
Philip Mayer.
Thomas Miller.
Christopher Winter.
Valentine Ney.

This company was organized out of men who resided in Bern and Heidelberg townships.

Roll of Furrer's Company.

Captain.
Michael Furrer.

First Lieutenant.
Nicholas Seybert.

Second Lieutenant.
John German.

Ensign.
Jacob Read.

Drummer.
William Sherman.

Fifer.
Adam Read.

Sergeants.
Adam Anspach.
Henry Spang.
Peter Leis.
Philip Anspach.

Privates.

George Wendlewolf.
Geo. Deerwechter.
Valentine Shiffler.
John Keyser,
George Winter.
Jacob Ruhl.
George Kantner.
Nicholas Read.
Frederick Sheffer.
Jonas Read.
Daniel Read.

Michael Hoffman.
John Stup.
Henry Koch.
William Feygert.
Andreas Aulenbach.
William Sheffer.
George Emerich.
Peter Smith.
Conrad Hoster.
Peter Deefenbach.
Christian Witman.

Peter Houser.
Simon Linck.
George Swartz.
Henry Miller.
Valentine Troutman.
Nicholas Lechner.
Peter Stein.
Michael Bruker.
Daniel Kuff.
Adam Schnee.
Henry Deerwechter.

This company was organized out of men who resided in Tulpehocken township and the western section of Berks County.

BATTALION OF COL. MARK BIRD.

The Battalion of Col. Mark Bird was also at South Amboy, or in that vicinity, not far off to the south, in Monmouth County. He reported to the Council of Safety on August 7, 1776, that about 300 men in his Battalion would be ready to march in several days, he having supplied them with provisions, tents and uniforms at his own expense, and marched them to that place shortly afterward. He also was a prominent iron master; indeed, of the many in the county at that time, I think the most prominent. His principal place of business was at Birdsboro, but he lived at Reading, for in the transfer of real estate he is described as of Reading. In the beginning of the Revolution, he was very active.

His letter to the Council of Safety was as follows:

BERKS COUNTY, 7th August, 1776.

Sir: I believe there was a Resolve of Convention to advance Fifty Shillings a man to the Associators that is to march to Jersey after there being mustered by the Committee. As my Battalion will not be ready for that for two days or three, it will detain us too long after to send for the cash, take this opportunity to acquaint you of it, there will be about three hundred men in the Battalion. I have provided provisions, tents, uniforms at my own expense. If you don't think proper to send me cash without the Committee's order, as the expense is chiefly paid except the advance, you'l please to send me five hundred pounds for Ball, that has been sent, and are ready to send to the Committee of Safety, they were contracted for by Mr. Owen Biddle and that will enable me to take my Battalion to the place appointed at my own expense, it can be hereafter settled at a more Lasure time, and charge to acc't.

Your Very Humble Serv't,

MARK BIRD.

To the Honorable Council of Safety of Penna.

Resolution of Congress.—These two battalions were raised in pursuance of the following resolution, passed by Congress on July 3, 1776:

"*Resolved*, That the Committee of Safety of Pennsylvania be requested to send as many of the Troops of their Colony as they can spare to Monmouth County in New Jersey, to the assistance of the Inhabitants of that Colony & to be subject to the orders of the Commander in Chief, the said Troops to be allowed the same pay and rations as the Troops in the service of the Continent from the time of their march until their Return."

HALLER'S BATTALION NEAR TRENTON.

By a letter of December 30, 1776, which Col. Henry Haller, while at Reading, addressed to the Council of Safety, it would appear that his battalion was along the Delaware River not far from Trenton. In October, 1776, Berks County was ordered to furnish 500 men for immediate defence of Pennsylvania, and in December following, Haller's Battalion was encamped at Cornell's Ferry. He was obliged to complain of the conduct of his men while stationed there, and his written complaint was forwarded from Reading to the Council by Capt. Shaffer. In the published returns of troops at Newtown, in Bucks County, in January, 1777, it would appear that three companies were from Berks County, commanded by Captains George Will, John Diehl and Nicholas Scheffer. The Capt. Shaffer, who carried the letter, was evidently a captain in his battalion, and doubtless the Captain Nicholas Scheffer who was at Newtown. The three companies named are stated as having been of Maj. Gabriel Hiester's Battalion, and Hiester was the major of the 1st Battalion, which was commanded by Col. Haller.

Newtown was then the headquarters of Gen'l Washington. This place was situated westward from Trenton about 10 miles.

Col. Haller's letter was as follows :

"Having left the Camp at Cerral's Ferry on the 16th instant, I think it my duty to inform you that the greatest number of the men of my Battalion deserted on the 13th and 14th, a thing that might, in my opinion, have been prevented had the officers taken proper steps ; but some of them were as willing as the privates to break up the Battalion ; took no pains to get their men, and this conduct encouraged others. Since that, I have been here waiting to get the pay-rolls, that money might be drawn to pay off the men, that they might be encouraged to re-enter the service. But some of the captains give me all the delay in their power. Therefore, I pray your attention to the matter. I think if a paymaster was ordered up here to pay off the Battalion, it would have a good effect."

"There is a report that the pay of the officers has been raised. Should this be the case in the Continental Army, I should be glad to know why the same should not be paid to us, who have been immediately on the same service, and have been promised the same pay as the Continental troops."

Col. Haller must have referred to the Resolution of the Council of Safety, passed December 1, 1776, which provided :

"That each man who shall, on or before Wednesday, the 11th of this month, march to join General Washington from the Counties of Berks, * * * [and four other counties named] shall receive over and besides his monthly pay advance a bounty of ten dollars, to be paid him by the Colonel of his Battalion."

"That the first 50 men in one company shall receive ten dollars additional bounty to be paid on their arrival at the Camp, and that the second 50 men shall receive a bounty of five dollars each."

From the conduct of the men, and the letter of their Colonel, I am led to infer that they thought themselves entitled to the bounty, and, not receiving it, they felt justified in leaving the service and returning home.

HUNTER'S BATTALION IN NEW JERSEY.

From certain correspondence of Col. Daniel Brodhead and of Gen'l Israel Putnam, it appears that the battalion of Berks County Militia, commanded by Col. Daniel Hunter, was in service in January, 1777. For some unexplained reason, many of the men refused to march for a time, and after having been encamped in New Jersey, several companies of the battalion ran away. It may be that they were affected in the same manner as the Haller Battalion in December.

In the letter of Col. Brodhead, which he addressed to Owen Biddle, from Reading on January 4, 1777, he stated, among other things, as follows:

> "I was also commanded by him, [General Thomas Mifflin] on my return from thence, [Lebanon] to take a company of the Northumberland County Militia, then at this place, and with them apprehend some of the disaffected, compel some of the Militia of this County, who have refused to march, which I have done, and believe the remainder to be so much alarmed that few will think of staying at home. I intend, however, to wait a day or two longer to see how they will behave and then proceed to Philadelphia"

On the 12th of January, the Board directed Col. Morgan to have the 2nd Battalion of Militia (which he was to command) to make all necessary preparations, and hold themselves in readiness to march on the shortest notice. At that time the Board was informed that a number of the militia were returning to their respective homes, disgusted at the precipitate orders they had received to march, when they were not supplied with provisions and many other necessaries, such orders having been given without the approbation of the Board. A resolution was passed that they be asked to return, with the assurance that the Board would ever be interested in their behalf, and that its authority would be exerted to the utmost to preserve their rights as freemen ; and, further, that all such as should return would be furnished with the proper equipments and would not be compelled to join the Continental Army until so supplied. On the 18th the Board took further action in the matter, and passed the following resolution :

"*Whereas*, This Council is informed that many of the principal associators of Colonel Hunter's Battalion, of Berks County, refuse to march to join General Washington's army at this Important Crisis, when so glorious an opportunity offers of crushing the enemy, and thereby have prevented and discouraged the rest, and proceeded even to dare them to enforce the resolves of this Council upon them ; therefore,

"*Resolved*, That Colonel Hunter be directed forthwith to collect all the well affected in his Battalion, and seize upon the ringleaders in this defection and send them under guard to Philadelphia, and that he do execute the Resolve. The resolve of this Council of the seventh of December last, upon all who refuse to march without favor or affection, and that they do collect blankets and other necessaries for the use of those who are to march, paying a reasonable price for the same ; and should any person refuse to deliver such necessaries as they can spare, the Colonel is directed to take and pay for the same. Those that turn out are to march the most direct road to Head Quarters."

On January 21, Gen'l Israel Putnam addressed the following letter to Council from Princeton, which related to the same subject :

"Captain Echard and Captain Fisher, of Berks County, have just informed me that their companies have run away to a man, except a Lieutenant, Sergeant and Drummer. I hope, gentlemen, no pains or cost will be spared to apprehend these men and bring them back to their duty. I think it is of the last importance that this spirit of desertion should be crushed in its infancy, and the militia taught that there is a power that can and will detain them. I wish as part of their punishment they might be obliged to remain in the service for several months, or even till next Fall. Unless timely severity is used, we shall in a few days have not a man of the militia left."

Evidently, from this letter, we can infer that the battalion had reached camp before the action of Council took place; and we can also infer that the term of service must have been short (60 days), for it was about to expire when the letter was written.

I cannot say what companies constituted the battalion; and the only known names of the captains are those mentioned by Putnam in his letter. The number of men in this service can be estimated at about 500.

THREE COMPANIES AT NEWTOWN.

Anticipating an early military encounter in New Jersey towards the close of 1776, Congress made extra efforts to collect troops, and in this behalf sent Gen. Thomas Mifflin, of Pennsylvania, throughout the State to awaken the proper spirit of patriotism. Among the places visited was Reading. The following letter was addressed by him to James Read, Esq., one of the Committee of Correspondence, giving notice of the proposed visit and fixing a time for a meeting with the officers and associators of the county:

CHESTER, 14th December, 1776.

JAMES READ, ESQ.,

Dear Sir: The Honorable Continental Congress having directed me to visit the Associators of the several counties of this State, and to endeavor with the aid of several gentlemen of the Assembly, and of the freemen at large, to stimulate and encourage them to set forth at this critical time to the support of their country, I request the favor of you to convene the committee of your county, and to inform them that we propose to meet the Officers and Associators of the several battalions in your county at the town of Reading, on Wednesday next, at 10 o'clock in the morning.

We depend much on the zeal and activity of yourself and the other gentlemen of the committee, and trust that the appearance of your inhabitants on that day will do honor to themselves and their country.

I have the honor to be your obedient servant,

THOMAS MIFFLIN, *Brig.-Gen'l.*

I am directed to pay the expense of the Expresses, etc., which may be necessary to convene the inhabitants, which I will most cheerfully do.

T. M.

It is probable that the result of this appeal and meeting was the enlistment of three companies out of the battalion commanded by Col. Henry Haller, and of which Major Gabriel Hiester was the Major.

They were stationed at Newtown, in Bucks County, during January, 1777, and were commanded by Captains George Will, John Diehl and Nicholas Scheffer.

Roll of Will's Company of Artillery.

Captain.
George Will.

First Lieutenant.
Michael Bush.

Second Lieutenant.
———— Strohecker.

Ensign.
———— Yeager.

Sergeants.
John Fasig.
John Boyer.
Casper Koch.

Corporals.
Joseph Kendall.
Henry Setley.

Privates.

William Hiester.	David Fox.	John Printz.
Nicholas Felix.	Frederick Hofner.	Conrad Shreffer.

John Shoemaker.
Martin Kisley.
Michael Fichthorn.
John Harp.

Jacob Silfires.
John Reifsnider.
Andrew Fichthorn.
Benjamin Leinbach.
Godfrey Baker.

John Barnhard.
Christopher Walker.
Nicholas Dick.
Michael Madary.

Artificers.

Valentine Fultz.
John Fulwiler.
Frederick Ropp
Balser Henritz.
Nicholas Schlichter.

Casper Madary.
Nicholas Scherrer.
Christian Bansey.

Anthony Pap.
Nicholas Seidel.
Henry Bickley.
John Burchard.

Roll of Diehl's Company.

Roll of Capt. John Diehl's Company on January 22, 1777:

Captain.
John Diehl.

Lieutenants.
Jacob Brecht.
John Kidd.

Sergeants
William Shener.
Jacob Briner.
Christian Sherrer.

Ensign.
Ernst Griss.

Corporals.
Christian Setly.
Frederick Nagle.

Drummer.
George Marks.

Privates.

George Longkammer
Christian Deim.
William Freymeyer.
George Frey.
John Seyler.
John Hess.
Peter Diem.

Anthony Schock.
Jacob Young.
Dewalt Miller.
Henry Batty.
Jacob Boyer.
Simon Boyer.

Jacob Peterick.
Henry Lebo.
Jacob Alter.
Dallet Rhein.
Paul Ege.
Dungel Buntzler.

Roll of Scheffer's Company.

Roll of Capt. Nicholas Scheffer's Company on January 20, 1777:

Captain.
Nicholas Scheffer.

First Lieutanant.
Jacob Stine.

Second Lieutenant.
John King.

Sergeants.
Christopher Balty.
Mathias Gernandt.
Christian Barranstine.

Ensign.
Abraham Huy.

Corporals.
Jacob Reeser.
Jacob Weiser.
John Grave.

Privates.

John Reeser.
Henry Fraunfelter.
Jacob Huy.
Jacob Loudenschlager.
George Medler.
George Matz.
George Schriver.
George Adam Schneider.

Christian Gernandt.
Mathias Sourmilch.
Daniel Rothermel.
Felix Frauenfelter.
Henry Reigel.
Adam Reichard.
John Klein.
Valentine Miller.
Paul Barlet.
Conrad Kerchner.

Henry Schire.
Jacob Rauhn.
William Koch.
John Dunckel.
Michael Kreat.
Adam Mingel.
Thomas Conner.

COUNTY MEN IN CONTINENTAL LINE.

Company of Capt. Jacob Moser.—The company of Capt. Jacob Moser was in the 6th Pennsylvania Regiment of the Continental Line, which was attached to a division composed chiefly of Jersey troops; but I have not been able to collect any facts showing the nature of the services rendered. In an arrangement made during the year 1778, Capt. Moser became a supernumerary. The men were enlisted to serve "during the war." The enlistments were made mostly during the Spring of 1777.

Roll of Company.

Captain.
Jacob Moser.

First Lieutenants.
George Will.
Samuel Smith.

Second Lieutenants.
Samuel Smith.
Farquhar McPherson.

REVOLUTION.

Sergeants.
Peter Sackville.
John Albright.
John Gallagher.
Dennis Carroll.

Ensign.
Ernest Greese.

Corporals.
Dennis Carroll.
Jacob Boyer.

Drummer.
Jacob Busvalt.

Fifer.
Francis Parvin.

Privates.

William Adam.	John Hawkins.	Abraham Pyke.
Martin Armfighter.	John Herman.	John Reedy.
Charles Bates.	Henry Hopper.	Daniel Reel.
John Barnhart.	John Howard.	John Roland.
Jacob Bower.	Daniel Keel.	Baltzer Sheaf.
Samuel Boyer.	Henry Kelchner.	Jacob Schrader.
John Boyd.	John Kerner.	Michael Stainer.
Edward Brown.	Casper Knorr.	Philip William Stewart.
George Camp.	Conrad Kline.	
John Casedy.	John Leslie.	Peter Ulrick.
Adam Decker.	Jacob Lemer.	Peter Wendland.
James Dietrick.	James Matthews.	Jacob Wetzel.
Jacob Dumb.	John Metz.	Jacob Welrick.
Phineas Eachey.	Adam Meyer.	James Wilson.
David Gibson.	Thomas Mitchell.	George Wright.
Jacob Glasmire.	Isaac Muller.	Jacob Young, Sr.
John Glasmire.	Jacob Oswald.	Jacob Young, Jr.
Ludwick Guthbroad.	Thomas Pickworth.	Michael Zern.

Company of Capt. Jacob Bower.—Captain Jacob Bower also commanded a company in the 6th Pennsylvania Regiment, but there is no record of the company. Previously he had been First Lieutenant in Capt. Benjamin Weiser's Company, and for a time Quarter-Master in Thompson's Battalion of Riflemen; from which he became a Captain in the "Flying Camp," and then he was transferred to the 6th Pennsylvania Line. Afterward he was transferred to the 2nd Pennsylvania Line, (January 1, 1783). A captain in Baron Von Ottendorf's Corps is spelled Jacob Bauer, and the roll of the company as there given is as follows, some of the names indicating that it was from Berks County :

Roll of Company.

Captain.
Jacob Bower.

First Lieutenant.
Lewis Aug. de Uerchtritz.

Second Lieutenant.
John Sharf.

Sergeants.
George Bamberg.
Jacob Young.

Corporals.
Andrew Hornberg,
John Mannerson.

Drummer.
Andrew Ransier.

Privates.

Charles Butner.	Jonathan Lynch.	William Roch.
George Eirich.	John Mitchell.	Jacob Shafer.
Charles Feidler.	John G. Neimrich.	Adam Syfert.
Jacob Fernecorn.	John Pattis.	John Shepherd.
John Geisel.	Andrew Rebourg.	John Walch.
John Geo. Klein.		

Sundry Enlistments.—The following additional men from Berks County were enlisted in different regiments of the Continental Line of Pennsylvania. There were doubtless others, but I could not find their names :

CAPTAINS.

Samuel Dewees, of Heidelberg.—He was a captain in the 11th Regiment; also superintendent of certain hospitals; he died at Allentown in 1777.

John Mears, of Reading.—He was a captain in the 4th Regiment, July 5, 1777; served till May 26, 1778; resided at Reading until 1785. He was wounded in the Battle of Brandywine. He died in 1810, at Catawissa (of which place he was the founder), aged 82 years.

Peter Scull, of Reading.—He was a captain in the 3rd Regiment ; commissioned January 5, 1776; appointed brigade major March 23, 1776.

Peter Withington, of Reading.—He was a captain in the 12th Regiment, October 1, 1776. He took sick at Philadelphia in December, 1776, and was sent home to Reading, where he died May 11, 1777.

SUBALTERNS AND PRIVATES.

1st Regiment.
Francis King, private.
Samuel Kline, private.
Philip Nagle, private.
Peter Weiser, 2nd lieutenant.
George Whitman, private.
Thomas Williams, private.
Michael Youse, private.

2nd Regiment.
David Edgar, private.
Jacob Glassmire, private.
Jacob Holder, private.
Abel Morris, 2nd lieutenant.

3rd Regiment.
Stephen Gilbert, private.
Conrad Smith, private.

4th Regiment.
Matthias Baughter, sergeant.
John Dongan.
Michael Wallizer.

5th Regiment.
Jacob Wertz, private.

6th Regiment.
William Adams, private.
Ernest Greese, ensign.
Ludwig Gutbreath, private.
John Hess, private.
Henry Kalkner, private.
Herman Leitheiser.
James Matthews, private.
Abraham Pike, private.
Thomas Pikeworth, private.
John Roland, private.

7th Regiment.
Michael Lenig, private.

9th Regiment.
Peter Keplinger, private.
William Witman, 2nd lieut.

10th Regiment.
Alexander McQuillon, private.

11th Regiment.
Samuel Dewees, fifer.
Jacob Hartman, private.

TWO BATTALIONS AT CHESTER.

Congress passed a Resolution on August 3, 1777, empowering Gen'l Washington to demand of the Eastern and Middle States such number of the Militia of each State as he thought necessary to assist the Army in the Northern Department, to serve until November 15, 1777, unless sooner relieved or dismissed. Gen. Gates was appointed in command of this Army, and he applied to Pennsylvania for 750 men as her proportion. To make up this proportion, the Executive Council sent a circular letter to Col. Jacob Morgan on August 15th, requesting him to supply 350 men out of the 2nd class of the County Militia, to make up the number demanded and ordered from Bucks County, all of whom were to march immediately. There were then two classes in their second month of service from Philadelphia, Bucks and Chester, and one class from York and Cumberland. One of the classes from Philadelphia marched with alacrity to New Jersey. On the 28th of July, Col. Morgan had received orders to embody one class and forward the men with proper officers forthwith to Chester, and he replied on the 30th that he would exert himself to do so.

Col. Morgan replied to the circular letter on August 17th as follows, addressing the reply to the Vice-President of the Council:

"I just now had the honor of a letter from you of the 15th inst. by express, ordering the Second Class of Militia of this county to march. It is with great pleasure I can inform you that we have already marched two classes, having understood the Order of His Excellency, the President of Council, of the 31st of last March, in a letter from him of that date to me, to intend the marching of two classes.

"It is presumed that the greater part of the twelve companies, of which those two classes consist, are by this time at Chester, as several of them went from this town the week before last, others last week, and the last company yesterday. The whole number in the two classes, officers and privates, are six hundred and fifty-six men; in the opinion of every one here hearty and able men, fit to take the field against our inveterate enemies. The two battalions are commanded by Colonels Daniel Hunter and Daniel Udree."

While the troops were rendezvousing at Chester, Council addressed a letter on August 20th to the Pennsylvania Delegates in Congress, in which they asked that a part of the militia be dismissed, if the public affairs permitted, because the men were very deficient in arms and blankets, and totally unprovided with tents, and also because the season for sowing Winter grain was at hand, on which the country greatly depended, and laborers were very scarce, on which account great distress might ensue if the militia were continued thus embodied.

Congress passed a resolution on August 22nd requesting, among other things, that Pennsylvania keep up 4000 militia to assist in repelling the threatened attack of the enemy by the way of the Chesapeake and Delaware bays; that they should rendezvous at Lancaster, Downingtown and Chester, as Council should direct; and that the militia be in the pay of the Continent until November 30th, unless sooner discharged.

On September 6th, the Council ordered the Lieutenants of the several counties to call out a class of militia and forward them to Derby with the utmost expedition and equipped in the best manner possible. The term of enlistment was for two months.

In a "Return of the Militia belonging to the State of Pennsylvania, September 6, 1777, in the Continental Service," there appear two battalions from Berks County. They were commanded by Col. Daniel Hunter and Col. Daniel Udree. The former was in Potter's Brigade, and the latter in Irvine's Brigade. This return showed the following officers and men:

	Hunter.	Udree.		Hunter.	Udree.
Colonel	1	1	Surgeon	1	1
Lieut.-Colonel	1	1	Drummers	4	6
Major	1	..	Fifers	3	4
Captains	5	5	Fit for duty	184	183
Lieutenants	7	10	Sick, present	27	21
Sergeants	17	21	Sick, absent	13	5
Ensigns	4	6	On command	47	..
Chaplain	1	..	On furlough	1	1
Adjutant	1	1	Total	272	210
Quartermaster	1	1	Deserted	2	45

The total number of the State was 2973 men.

By referring to the "Militia Returns" in this volume, it can be ascertained with reasonable certainty who the twelve (or ten) captains were that were commissioned in the First and Second Battalions. The company rolls have not been found as yet.

SPYKER'S BATTALION AT WHITE MARSH.

On October 23, 1777, the Executive Council ordered that the 5th and 6th classes of Berks County Militia should be called out immediately, and Col. Jacob Morgan was accordingly notified. On November 9th, he reported to Council that two classes of the militia were in camp near Reading, and that he would forward two or three companies on the next day, but he did not know what he should do as to arms for the other companies that were at Reading.

On November 12th, Lieut. William Coats, in camp at White Marsh, reported to Council that Col. Morgan and his men had been there for two days, showing that he had forwarded the companies mentioned ; and on the 18th, he wrote from Reading to Council that he had sent to camp about 400 of the militia, including officers, out of the 5th and 6th classes under Col. Henry Spyker, and, as those classes had not turned out as generally as was expected, he directed the commanding officers of the different battalions to call out the 7th and 8th classes also. The camp mentioned was situated several miles to the north of Chestnut Hill, then in Philadelphia County, now in Montgomery.

From these letters, I can say that there were at least 400 of the county militia in service under Col. Henry Spyker, and these were doubtless placed in the Army under the command of Gen. John Armstrong, which was engaged at various times with the British around Chestnut Hill and Germantown. Having no special returns designating the captains of the several companies, I am not certain who they were, but it is likely they were taken out of the 6th Battalion of county militia.

No company rolls of this battalion have been discovered. The term of service was short, and when Gen'l Washington's Army went into Winter quarters at Valley Forge it is probable that the men returned to their homes in Berks County.

Reading Officer Wounded at Germantown.—The following incident of the Battle of Germantown was taken from "Watson's Annals of Philadelphia," 2 vol., p. 554. I have not been able to ascertain in which company from Berks County he was an officer. His name does not appear in the Militia Returns for 1777:

"Lieutenant Whitman, of Reading, was left on the field, supposed to be killed or mortally wounded. After a while, he made out to crawl on hands and knees to the second house on the south side in Washington lane. There he was sheltered by the resident, and was visited by Doctor Witt, who soon pronounced his case incurable, but, at the earnest begging of the lieutenant, he continued to try to save his life. He recovered surprisingly for a time, when a British officer, coming to hear of him, made him and his host both prisoners. While so held, lieutenant Whitman found a chance to get to speak with Major Andre, who procured him a release. He then went to live with Mr. Hergesheimer, where he was nursed and fed till the time of the retreat or withdrawal of the British from Germantown. While he was there hiding himself, for fear of a second capture, the American horse appeared, when he claimed their help and protection. Just then, they captured a country Friend, coming in to sell butter to the British, and, as his punishment, they made him take up lieutenant Whitman in his chair to Reading He lived many years afterwards."

At the gate leading to Chew's house, a fine, large soldier from Reading was found dead. (p. 52.)

Washington's Army near the County.—In the "Itinerary of Gen'l Washington," showing his movements during 1775, 1776 and 1777, the nearest point to Berks County that he reached was on September 21, 1777, when he and his army were in Pottsgrove township, (now in Montgomery County) about four miles south-east of Pottstown, the British having moved after him up the west side of the Schuylkill River. He remained there until the 26th of September. This was twenty miles from Reading, or about six miles from the county line.

I have not been able to locate any of the Berks County companies as having been engaged in the Battle of Brandywine, or the Battle of Germantown, or even in the rigorous encampment at Valley Forge. Washington selected Valley Forge as the Winter quarters for his army. Several of his principal generals had suggested Reading as a proper place for this purpose.

Troops Encamped at Kutztown.—There is a tradition at and around Kutztown that Washington's Army was encamped in Maxatawny township, about a mile north-east of Kutztown in 1777, and that Washington and his wife were along. This is not correct. Washington's movements throughout the Revolution are known, and from his "Itinerary" it can be stated that he was not in the county during that entire period.

Colonel Lotz's regiment in the "Flying Camp," in marching from Reading to New York in August, 1776, went by way of Kutztown, Allentown and Easton, and it is likely that the men were halted there at the end of the first day, after a tramp of over sixteen miles, which may be considered a good day's march in hot weather, especially as an introductory experience; and on August 15th the Battalion of Col. John Patton was also there on its way to New York.

In conducting the Hessian prisoners, that were taken at the Battle of Trenton, to Reading, it is not at all probable that they were marched out of the way first to Kutztown. Trenton is almost directly east of Reading, and they were marched to the Trappe and over the Philadelphia road either by way of the Swamp or the Pine Iron Works. But if they were obliged to ascend the Delaware River some miles in fording it, then it is possible that they reached Reading by way of Kutztown, and the tradition that they were there may be correct.

No British Invasion of the County.—King George III and his advisers were unwise to attempt the subjugation of the American Colonies after they had effected a Confederation in which they were all equally interested, and had shown a determinad spirit of combined resistance; but the British Army, having crossed the Atlantic Ocean for that purpose, three thousand miles from the place of supplies, and requiring from thirty to forty days to accomplish the journey, the general in command was prudent in not venturing too far away from the coast in prosecuting the war. He did not presume to give battle far from Philadelphia in his maneuvers after the American Army under Gen'l Washington. He marched up the Schuylkill Valley about fifteen miles, but did not venture to go beyond Valley Forge, even though he was desirous of capturing the valuable stores at Reading, thirty-five miles farther on.

The Battle of Brandywine occurred in Chester County on September 11, 1777, and the Battle of Germantown in Philadelphia County on October 4, 1777, in both of which the American Army was unsuccessful. But there was no battle in the adjoining county of Berks, not even a skirmish of any kind. Not a single detachment of the British Army crossed her boundary lines anywhere, or in any direction whilst carrying on military movements from one Colony to another. Hence, I have no losses nor incidents of any kind to describe as resulting from such a source. Geographically, the county was fortunately situated, and the inhabitants were highly gratified to know that their families and properties were exempt from the cruelties and sufferings of war in their midst. They, however, realized the possibility of great losses from an invasion, and, appreciating the perilous situation of the neighboring counties of Chester and Philadelphia, they responded promptly to the numerous calls for troops and furnished willingly large quantities of supplies of all kinds towards sustaining the Continental Army. This is made apparent by the complimentary expressions of the Executive Council in letters to the Lieutenant of the county, and also to the Commissioner of Forage for the successful manner in which they complied with the demands upon them.

DRAGOONS FROM THE COUNTY IN PROVOST GUARD.

Von Heer's Troop was organized under a resolution of Congress of May 27, 1778, establishing a Provost, to consist of a captain, four lieutenants, one clerk, quartermaster sergeant, two trumpeters, two sergeants, five corporals, forty-three provosts or privates, and four ex-carboniers. They were mounted and accoutred as light dragoons, and were to apprehend deserters, rioters and stragglers. In battle, they were posted in the rear, to secure fugitives. Their duties were those of a provost guard. The corps was styled the Troop of Marechausse.

Capt. Bartholomew Von Heer resigned from Proctor's Artillery to take this command, and in some papers he is styled "Provost Marshall of the Continental Army." The men were all recruited in Pennsylvania, and the following were from Reading :

Roll of the Troop.
Captain.
Bartholomew Von Heer—In Thomas Proctor's battery of artillery, March 3, 1777; resigned June 1, 1778, and then appointed captain of provost. On September 16, 1780, he was captain of troop of light dragoons at Tappan, New York. His residence was at Reading. In the Spring of 1785 he removed with his family from Berks County to near the Falls of Schuylkill, Philadelphia County.

Trumpeters.
John George Hiller. David Fox.

Privates.
Peter Cryolich. Peter Fricker. Charles Shumann.
Sebastian Cunitz. Frederick Graff. Frederick Tecius.
Andrew Fox. Frederick Mueller. Henry Willhausen.
Jacob Fox. Daniel Rightmyer. Henry Ziegler.
George Fricker. Jacob Ruppert.

LINDEMUTH'S BATTALION ON FRONTIERS.

An attack having been made by Indians and others on the frontiers, Council determined on July 14, 1778, that Berks County should supply 300 men, one-half to be sent to Sunbury, and the other half to Easton, out of the 1st, 2nd and 3rd classes of militia, even the 4th if necessary, and issued orders to Col. Morgan for that purpose. Morgan replied on August 16th that he had sent 180 men to Sunbury and 123 to Easton, doubtless having called the four classes from all the battalions in the county.

These men, particularly the number sent to Sunbury, were taken possibly from the battalion of Col. Michael Lindemuth, in the northern section of the county. I could not ascertain how many companies they were organized into, probably three at Sunbury, and two at Easton. On August 10th, Col. Hartley reported from Sunbury that Berks County had furnished her quota of militia, but Lancaster was far short.

By the following action of the Supreme Executive Council, on December 31, 1778, it would appear that Col. Michael Lindemuth and his battalion were in active service out of Berks County:

"*Ordered,* That the secretary write to the Lieutenant of Berks County to call upon Col. Lindemuth, or his Lieut.-Colonel, stationed last Summer at Fort Jenkins in Northumberland, for five rifles taken from one Webb, charged with disaffection."

Subsequently, December 13, 1780, the Council, in ordering Col. Morgan to "pay off the militia who had marched on a late tour of duty," directed that no money be issued to Col. Lindemuth without the particular direction of the Board. On June 9, 1789, Michael Moser was paid £7, 10sh. for 30 bushels of rye furnished to Col. Lindemuth's detachment of militia while in service on the frontiers in 1780.

HIESTER'S BATTALION WITH REED'S ARMY.

On July 28, 1780, Col. Morgan was directed to call out immediately three classes of the county militia, provided they numbered 600 men, exclusive of officers, and, if not, then to call out also the fourth class. This was the quota of the county towards supplying 4000 militia from Pennsylvania which Gen'l Washington required in order to co-operate with the main army, in anticipation of the movements of the British Army again to Philadelphia. The Battle of Camden was fought on August 15, 1780, and the British were victorious. Col. Morgan forwarded the men that were ordered, and the greater part comprised the Hiester Battalion, the 6th of the county militia. It may have been under General Joseph Reed, in New Jersey. It is known to have been in service for thirty days from August 10th to September 9th, but the particular duty performed I could not ascertain.

Field Officers.

Lieutenant-Colonel, Joseph Hiester.

Major.	*Surgeon.*
Edward Scull.	Dr. Andrew Forrest.
Adjutant.	*Quartermaster.*
Benjamin Morgan.	John Witman.

CAPTAINS.

Charles Gobin.	Conrad Sherman.	Jacob Baldy.
Ferdinand Ritter.	John Ludwig.	Henry Strouch.

Roll of Gobin's Company.

Captain.
Charles Gobin.

Lieutenant.	*Corporals.*
George Fister.	George Brown.
Ensign.	Peter Daubert.
Casper Heiner.	Isaac Ermel.
	James Simpson.
Sergeants.	*Drummer.*
John Burkhard.	Samuel Keyser.
Christian Deringer.	
Henry Christ, Jr.	*Fifer.*
Abraham Witman.	John Fister.

Privates.

Bastian Allgaier.	George Brown.	Joseph Collier.
Ellick Bickham.	Casper Brownwell.	Daniel Davis.
William Bohanan.	Jacob Burkhard.	Martin Eckert.
George Bower.	Gottlieb Christian.	George Engelhard.
Jacob Briner.	Thomas Clark.	John English.

Stephen Fedry.
Nicholas Felix.
Peter Fesig.
Jacob Fleisher.
George Freeman.
Nicholas Garrison.
Christian Good-
 knecht.
John Harff.
Abraham Hartman.
Moses Hays.
Abraham Hehn.
John Heimer.
George Heinlein.
George Heist.
Benjamin Heven.
Jacob Heyer.
George Jaeger.
Jacob Joder.
Michael Keller.

Barny Kepler.
Francis Krick.
Jacob Lang.
Jacob Leitheiser.
Benjamin Love.
John Miller.
John Rapp.
George Reder.
Jacob Reeser.
Peter Ritner.
Fred'k Reifsnyder.
George Seitz.
Nicholas Seitzinger.
Jacob Setley.
William Shoener.
John Shenfelder.
George Shultz.
John Shultz.
Peter Smith.
George Snell.

John Spengler.
William Spero.
Peter Stichter.
John Stect.
Ellis Thomas.
William Thomas.
John Tippery.
John Vanhorn.
Philip Wagner.
Casper Wecht.
Philip Weis.
Michael Witmyer.
Charles Witz,
John Witz.
Daniel Wolf.
Jonathan Worrel.
Morris Worrel.
George Young.
Philip Zieber.

Roll of Ritter's Company.

Captain.
Ferdinand Ritter.

Lieutenant.
Andrew Smith.

Ensign.
Leonard Dietrich.

Sergeants.
Peter Bousher.
Jacob Conner.
Christian Minnich.

Corporals.
Joseph Conrad.
Peter Dumm.
Peter Richard.

Drummer.
John Boutcher.

Fifer.
Philip Willfl.

Privates.

Adam Albrecht.
Henry Albright.
Christian Bantzy.
John Berry.
Dewald Billner.
Tobias Boutcher.
Peter Brown.

Philip Daubens.
Jacob Dengler.
Jacob Donard.
Michael Drees.
George Fige.
Christian Fisher.
Peter Fies.

Melchior Fritz.
Jacob Gerhard.
Frederick Glick.
Gottlieb Heiser.
Thomas Johnson.
Daniel Kamp.
Philip Kauffman.

Jacob Kelchner.
John Kisling.
Matthias Laub.
Christian Lerch.
Peter Lutz.
Dewalt Miller.
Jacob New.
Jacob Nunemacher.
John Plott.
John Rangler.

Nicholas Schwenk.
John Shoman.
Joseph Shomo.
Henry Shreffler.
Stoffel Shreffler.
Philip Smith.
Henry Snyder.
Michael Snyder.
John Stear.
John Strasser.

Nicholas Strasser.
Christian Swabel.
John Umbehacker.
John Wagner.
Stoffel Wagner.
Frederick Walls.
Christian Weber.
Christian Winter.
George Zechman.

Roll of Sherman's Company.

Captain.
Conrad Sherman.

Lieutenant.
Daniel Rose.

Ensign.
Henry Crum.

Sergeants.
Peter Custard.
William Deisinger.
Martin Withington.
Christian Young.

Corporals.
Nicholas Deisinger.
Henry Piece.
Peter Thomas.

Drummer.
Jacob Gassert.

Fifer.
Leonard Ruppert.

Privates.

Nicholas Angst.
George Batz.
Christian Beringer.
Henry Bickley.
Simon Boltz.
Valentine Boltz.
Nicholas Bressler.
John Brown.
Abraham Deby.
Joseph Deby.
Nicholas Denninger.
George Emrich.
Adam Fulmer.
Conrad Geisler.
Albrecht Glick.
Phil Adam Groh.

Andreas Gross.
Daniel Gross.
Albrecht Gruber.
Peter Hetrich.
Frederick Junker.
Alexander Klinger.
John Klinger.
John Laucks.
Bastian Leatch.
Henry Leatch.
Simon Miller.
Ludwig Ohrenbaum.
John Rau.
Christian Read.
Frederick Read.
Michael Read.

Peter Read.
Peter Read, Jr.
Conrad Redman.
Andrew Riegel.
Michael Riegel.
Adam Rosmeisel.
Frederick Seybert.
Nicholas Sheffer.
Jacob Shenfelter.
Adam Shreck.
Tobias Shuker.
George Wentzel.
Christian Winter.
Philip Witmyer.

Roll of Ludwig's Company.

Captain.
John Ludwig.

Lieutenant.
Jonathan Evans.

Ensign.
Henry Styles.

Sergeants.
William Evans.
Peter Finfrock.
Christian Hawk.
Thomas Stephans.

Corporal.
Bosick Bechtold.
Jacob Lambert.
James Leiby.

Drummer.
Jacob Alter.

Privates.

George Adams.
Jacob Andrew.
Jacob Becht.
Adam Boyer.
Samuel Boyer.
Manus Brombach.
William Carrigh.
John Deal.
Laughlin Doyle.
Peter Dust.
John Egel.
Henry Eurich.
John Etrel.
Peter Fisher.
Peter Fisher, Jr.
Ludwig Frantz.
Christian Frymire.
John Gensert.

Henry Gerhart.
John Hatfield.
Ludwig Herman.
Henry Hetrich.
Ludwig Hewitt.
William Hunter.
Michael Kessler.
John Kuhn.
John Larigh.
Jacob Ludwig.
Simon Lupp.
Conrad Lutts.
George Lutts.
William McClaskey.
Jacob Miller.
Henry Orts.
Garret Rapier.
Samuel Reider.

Abel Robeson.
Conrad Sherbaum.
John Sinclair.
Peter Spotz.
Nicholas Stouch.
Jacob Swallow.
Benjamin Tolbert.
Balser Ulrich.
Isaac Waggoner.
Peter Wall.
Nicholas Wattman.
Frederick Weaver.
John Wentrell.
George Wertheim.
Thomas Wolohan.
Henry Yerger.
Peter Yerger.

Roll of Baldy's Company.

Captain.
Jacob Baldy.

Lieutenant.
Jacob Sigfried.

Ensign.
Christian Medeira.

Sergeants.
Jacob Beisel.
Adam Dietrich.
Daniel Stout.
Albrecht Wagner.

Quartermaster-Sergeant.
Nicholas Brosius.

Drummer.
Nicholas Mayer.

Corporals.
John Hummel.
Frederick Godshall.
Adam Smith.

Fifer.
Philip Altendoerffer.

Privates.

Jacob Arnold.
Michael Arnold.
Daniel Bantzler.
Dietrich Beaver.
George Beck.
Nicholas Berge.
Matthias Bruder.
Jacob Bush.
Michael Christman.
Plany Coschry.
Peter Dilbone.
Henry Frauenfelder.
George Fisher.
George Foltz.
Adam Gansel.
Alex. Gross.
Burkhard Heins.
George Heist.
Michael Hoffman.

John Kemp.
John Kemp, Jr.
Frederick Kercher.
George Kercher.
Conrad Kisling.
Samuel Klein.
Christian Kles.
Anthony Kletzgy.
John Klockner.
George Kristman.
Michael Lamb.
Abram Lantzer.
Frederick Leiby.
Samuel Leiby.
John Leslie.
Joseph Lorentz.
Henry Lotz.
Jacob May.
Felix McCarty.

Frederick Mengel.
Bernhard Merkel.
Jacob Michael.
John Raush.
Mathias Reamer.
Michael Reber.
Peter Reisdorff.
John Ressler.
Michael Roads.
Mathias Sahm.
Ludwig Shartly.
Philip Sheffer.
Mathias Sleman.
Joseph Snable.
Leonard Snyder.
Jacob Sterner.
Christian Sweyer.
John Wageman.
Martin Wagner.

Roll of Strouch's Company.

Captain.
Henry Strouch.

Lieutenant.
Jacob Kester.

Ensign.
John Eckert.

Sergeants.
Christopher Beringer.
Andrew Hass.
Frederick Miller.

Corporals.
Jacob Alstat.
Jacob Heller.
John Zimmerman.

Drummer.
Peter Hufnagel.

Fifer.
Jacob Shrider.

Privates.

Peter Angstat.	John Kroner.	David Sabold.
Jacob Barto.	Jacob Kuser.	Joseph Shaffer.
Anthony Billick.	Jacob Long.	Henry Shomo.
Bernhard Coleman.	Nicholas Long.	Jacob Snyder.
Anthony Coleman.	Lawrence Lorah.	Jacob Stitzel.
John Eberhard.	Henry Martz.	Daniel Turner.
Christopher Engel.	Philip Mattis.	George Wyant.
Cornelius Geiger.	John Michael.	John Weast.
Anthony Hagy.	John Miller.	Jacob Wedman.
Peter Harnelter.	Frederick Miller.	Jacob Weitly.
Philip Hartman.	Bernhard Moyer.	Casper Werfel.
John Hooper.	Christian Oker.	Michael Widow.
George Holshoe.	Martin Oker.	Peter William.
John Kauch.	Adam Oxheimer.	Christopher Windbigler.
John Kintz.	Conrad Reiff.	
Andrew Kirch.	Henry Rice.	Henry Yoxheimer.
George Kroner.	Mathias Road.	Rudolph Zubler.

Selections from the 3rd Battalion.—The following thirty-two men marched from the several classes of Militia in Berks County, of the eight companies named in the Third Battalion, August 11, 1780. I could not ascertain to what place they marched, nor the particular service rendered. Probably they were with Hiester's Battalion, being at the same time in service:

Manus Brombach,	Abram Miller.	William Hunter.
Samuel Boyer.	Adam Begal.	Henry Smith.
George Lutz.	John Redcay.	Liter Dust.
Adam Boyer.	Conrad Lutz.	James Whittington.
Jacob Andrew.	George Blackwell.	Samuel Rider.
James Filey.	William Carrow.	James Waggoner.
John English.	John Wensel.	Jacob Huerd.
John Kerlin, Jr.	Henry Deal.	Benjamin Tolbert.
Samuel Dehart.	Jacob Keeley.	Evan Evans.
Adam Koch,	Peter Spots.	Thomas Seevans.
Christian Hunter.	Peter Forge.	

TWO COMPANIES FOR FRONTIER SERVICE.

Owing to certain incursions by hostile Indians, at the instigation of the British government, and to barbarities inflicted by them upon the inhabitants along the frontiers of the county beyond the Blue Mountains during the year 1780, letters were addressed to the Executive Council in which the startling details were described, and assistance was asked for the protection of the inhabitants. The Council accordingly ordered two companies of the militia under the command of Col. Samuel Ely, of the 1st Battalion, for service on the frontiers, but I have not been able to ascertain when they were forwarded, or by whom they were commanded.

Inhabitants killed by the Indians.

On May 6, 1780, Col. Michael Lindemuth, (of 4th Battalion of Berks County Militia) addressed a letter to Council in reference to the murder of some of the inhabitants beyond the Blue Mountains, and to the moving of certain families to the Little Schuylkill, about 15 miles from "Gnadenhuth," nearer to Susquehanna than that the savages fell on in Northampton County, and of course more liable to invasion. He asked for arms from the stores at Reading for self defense. On the 10th President Reed replied, stating that he had directed Col. Morgan to supply the necessary arms.

Col. Valentine Eckert reported to Council on August 30, 1780, that, shortly before, a man named "John Negman, who lived at a saw mill on the road from Reading to Shamokin, about three miles above Conrad Minnich's, 33 miles from Reading, was, with his three young children, barbarously murdered by the Indians, a party of whom, five in number, had been seen on the same road near Yarnal's a few days before. The day after the murder, a house and barn on the Little Schuylkill were burned by them. No persons were killed, but a boy named Shurr was taken captive. These occurrences alarmed the people so much in that neighborhood that many left it, and wagons went up in numbers to take away their effects; and unless some speedy assistance were given them, the whole settlement over the mountain would be evacuated." Council asked the President to send two companies of the militia under Col. Eckert's command for the protection of the frontiers.

Conrad Minnich lived in Brunswick township along the Schuylkill, several miles south of the Sharp Mountain.

Capt. Dennis Leary immediately marched to the place with four men, and buried Negman and two children, whom he found dead. The third child—a little girl—was carried off by the Indians. The next day he, accompanied by ten men, went in pursuit of the Indians. He was joined by Captain Baldy, and on the following day by Col. Lindemuth with 50 men. After scouring the woods till August 30th, he and his men returned to Reading. They left 60 men there to defend the different settlements. Capt. Leary was in that section for the purpose of cutting masts for the Navy of the United States.

CLASS OF LINDEMUTH'S BATTALION ON FRONTIERS.

On May 9, 1781, Col. Valentine Eckert, Lieutenant of the county, was directed to order out one class of Col. Lindemuth's Battalion of militia for the purpose of defending the frontiers of the county, and if it should not amount to 60 men he should call out one class from the next battalion in order to make up the said number.

Col. Nicholas Lotz was directed to make suitable provision for the said militia, taking care to make his purchases in the neighborhood of the said battalion; and Col. Eckert was directed to station the said militia in such a manner as to give the most effectual protection to the inhabitants of Brunswick and Pine Grove townships.

I could not find any return showing that this order was filled, but the class of 60 men was doubtless sent for the purpose mentioned.

COUNTY TROOPS AT NEWTOWN.

Ely's Battalion.—On September 11, 1781, three classes of the county militia were directed to be immediately called into service, and to rendezvous as soon as possible at Newtown, in Bucks County, pursuant to a resolution of Congress of the 10th instant; and at the same time the whole of the light horse of the county was also ordered into service.

Pursuant to this order, Col. Valentine Eckert forwarded the battalion that was commanded by Col. Samuel Ely, from the northeastern section of the county. It was in service at Newtown from October 1st to the 18th, under the command of Gen'l Lacy, who then commanded the Pennsylvania militia. The estimated number of men in the battalion was 300.

On October 8, 1781, Col. Eckert reported to President Reed that he had sent upwards of 300 men, exclusive of officers, to Newtown. Two companies were armed and the third was not armed. He added that three more companies were gathering, which would be almost as many as the former, but he had no arms to give them, and was doubtful about forwarding them.

The estimated number may include the company of Capt. John Robinson, for it was there at the same time. It is the only company that I could find which was then in service.

Robinson's Company.—The following company of Berks County Militia was in service at Newtown, in Bucks County on October 1, 1781, but the length of time was not given, nor the particular service that was rendered. The men were from the southern section of the county. By an order in his favor on Dec. 6, 1790, for £252, 8sh., 8d., it appears that the services were rendered during October 1781.

Captain.
John Robinson.

Privates.

John Cormick.	John Gibson.	John Ems.
Isaac Hahn.	John Bower.	Jacob Vosch.
Abel Robeson.	Absalom Kern.	John Lear.

Fred'k Herbold.	Jacob Eisenhower.	Christopher Benten.
Henry Fox.	Jacob Bumm.	Charles Cramp.
John Huyett.	Philip Ludwig.	John Jones.
James Thompson.	Jacob Ludwig.	Abraham Griffith.
Peter Slifer.	Michael Kern.	Jacob Menges.
Fred'k Foreman.	Samuel Kerlin.	Philip Miller.
Jacob Mitzeholtzer.	Benj. Boone.	Samuel Harper.
George Cake.	Andrew Curtain.	Matthias Derr.
Christopher Bowser.	Philip Waggoner.	Jacob Larry.
Jacob Newkirk.	Daniel Andrew.	Peter Bolick.
Henry Thompson.	Jacob Haus.	Joseph Workman.
John Lutz.	David Mee.	Mathias Wise.
Adam Weidner.	John Barkley.	William Rapp.
Joseph Quinter.	Benj. Lincoln.	Thos. McCloskey.
Jacob Quinter.	Benj. Talbot.	
John Hiestand.	John Henkirkin.	

COMPANY OF CAPT. JACOB LIVINGOOD.

By the *Colonial Records* it appears that Jacob Livingood, of Middletown (Womelsdorf), formed a company of riflemen in Heidelberg township during the latter part of September, 1781, but I could not find the roster.

In commissioning Capt. Livingood, the Executive Council took the following action on October 3, 1781:

"*Ordered*, That Captain Jacob Livingood be appointed Captain of a Company of Riflemen, enlisted to serve until the first day of January next; that he be commissioned accordingly, the said commission to continue in force until the first day of January next, unless sooner revoked by this Council, and all emoluments, pay and perquisites of the said office to cease on the said first day of January, or when the same shall be so revoked; that the said commission bear date the twenty-first instant."

On January 16, 1782, the Council drew an order in his favor for £246, 9sh., 4d., specie, "in full for the pay and subsistence of himself and the company of riflemen under his command, raised agreeably to the orders of his Excellency, General Washington, the same to be charged to the United States of America." And on January 23rd, he was paid £15 specie in full for his services as captain of this company.

I have not been able to ascertain where the services were rendered.

COUNTY TROOPS ON THE FRONTIERS.

Robinson's Company.—On February 23, 1782, the Executive Council ordered that Capt. John Robinson, now in Reading, be directed to march with his company forthwith to Northumberland County, and there put himself under the command of the Lieutenant of that county for the defence of the frontiers.

Other Troops.—In August, 1782, the Indians invaded Berks County, and the Lieutenant of the county was required to call into service a lieutenant and ensign with 25 men for the defense of the frontiers.

Shortly afterward he was ordered to send 50 men to defend the frontiers in parts adjacent to Northumberland County, and thence to march to Sunbury, where they were to be placed under the command of Col. Samuel Hunter. And in September following he was ordered to call into service immediately 125 of the county militia, who were to march to Northumberland and rendezvous at Muncy.

OTHER ENLISTMENTS FROM THE COUNTY.

Many hundred men from Berks County were engaged in the Revolution from 1775 to 1783 at different periods, whose names I have not been able to ascertain. The following names, in addition to those hereinbefore mentioned, were collected from various sources; mostly, however, from the *Pennsylvania Archives*.

Matthias Babb, first private who enlisted in Capt. Joseph Hiester's Co. He was a tall, well-proportioned and handsome man, and a coppersmith by occupation at Reading. He died in 1825, at an advanced age.

Adam Beard, lieut. of Associators.

Nicholas Brown, ensign in Capt. Joseph Hiester's Co.

Jacob Dodridge, private in Hazen's Regt., Continental Line. Discharged at end of war, June 20, 1783, with two wounds in his arm. He resided in Berks County in 1835, aged 90 years.

Michael Engle, sergeant in Capt. Noah Nicholas's Co., of Col. Benjamin Flowers's Battery of Artillery Artificers.

George Fry, veteran, who fought under Gen Wolfe at Quebec. He lived at Reading, where he died at an advanced age, on January 28, 1805.

John Gonter, farrier in 1st Partisan Legion.

Adam Gramley, private in Artillery Artificers.

John Herman, private in Hazen's Regt.

Samuel Holmes, private in Van Etten's Co., Stroud's Regt. He was wounded in Battle with Indians on the Frontiers.

William James, of Reading, survivor of the Revolution; died on February 24, 1850, aged 93 years.

John Keim, private, Capt. Peter Nagel's Co., in Col. Joseph Hiester's Battalion.

John Kerner, sergeant, Capt. Nagel's Co.; re-enlisted in Capt. Moser's Co.; wounded October, 1777, and lost two fingers; transferred to Capt. Finney's Co.; discharged 1781; died in Union County, 1829, aged 84 years.

John King, lieutenant in Capt. George Douglass' Co. in "Flying Camp."

Adam Koch, private in Armand's Legion.

William Munebach, private in Artillery Artificers.

William Machemer, private in Capt. Joseph Hiester's Co.

George Marks, Reading, private in Von Ottendorf's Corps, January 24, 1777; then corporal in Selin's Co., same corps; died January 16, 1782, whilst attached to Hazen's Regt., on return from the South.

William Marks, Reading; drummer in Selin's Co.

Conrad Poll, private in Capt. William Scull's Co. Killed in action in New Jersey.

Edward Scull, of Reading. He was an adjutant in Haller's Flying Battalion; promoted captain January 3, 1777; resigned May 16, 1778, and was appointed secretary of the Board of War. June 20, 1777, he was brigade major of the 3rd and 4th Battalions.

Lieutenant Whitman, of Reading, wounded at the Battle of Germantown; regarded as fatal, but he recovered and lived many years afterward.

Jacob Michael Wilhelm, private in 1st Partisan Legion. He died in Virginia on July 8, 1834.

Ennion Williams, of Bethel township, major of Miles' 1st Penna. Regt., March 13, 1776. Resigned February 4, 1777, on account of promotion over him.

Jacob Vanderslice (son of Henry Vanderslice, of Reading) was born Feb. 7, 1757. He was a Lieut. in the 9th Penna. Regt., as appears by the following reference:

"Lieut Jacob Vanderslice, of the 9th Penna. Regt., laid before the Council instructions for his entering on the recruiting service given him by the Lieut.-Col. of the Regt., and thereupon recruiting instructions were issued to him in the County of Berks, with orders to the Lieutenant of the County for money, Sept. 14, 1778."

In the account of Col. Jacob Morgan, Lieutenant of the County, the following entry appears:

Lieut. Jacob Vanderslice, paid him for recruiting service Sept. 26, 1778, £225, and on Nov. 6, 1778, £220; total, £445.

Jacob Yoder, of Reading. He was a soldier in the Revolution during 1777 and 1778, but it is not known in which company he served. He migrated to the West in 1780, and in 1782 was the first man to descend the Mississippi River to New Orleans in a flat boat with a cargo. He died in Kentucky in 1832, aged 74 years.

Thomas Hartley was born near Reading in 1748. When 18 years old he went to York, Penna., and subsequently became a distinguished attorney of York. He was active in the Revolution, serving as a colonel during 1777 and 1778, and prominently identified with the State Assembly and the National Congress. He died at York in 1800. His distinguished career justifies this honorable mention.

ARMY SURGEONS FROM THE COUNTY.

A number of the surgeons in the Revolution were from Berks County. Two became especially promi-

First Reformed Church, 1761—1832. One of three churches used as hospitals.

nent and rendered distinguished services in connection with the hospitals. The names of those that I could ascertain were the following:

Dr. Bodo Otto.   Dr. Daniel Welcher.   Dr. Andrew Forrest.
Dr. Jonathan Potts.   Dr. John Umstead.   Dr. Nicholas Snell.
Dr. John A. Otto.

Hospitals at Reading.—Col. Isaac Melcher was in charge of the barracks at different places. While on a visit at Reading in October, 1777, he addressed a letter to Executive Council on the 8th inst. in which he stated that "we are now taking public places of worship here for hospitals, and private houses, which is very distressing to the county, particularly at this period, when many of our worthy fellow-citizens are wandering from place to place for shelter." He added that there were sick and wounded in the place, and he had engaged a quantity of wood at Reading to supply 200 or 300 sick the ensuing Winter.

REPORTS OF MEN SUPPLIED FROM THE COUNTY.

In my extended researches for the men that were supplied by Berks County during the Revolution, I found the following reports in the *Colonial Records* and *Pennsylvania Archives*. They must be considered in connection with the companies and men hereinbefore mentioned in order to get at the probable number engaged in actual service.

The total number of men from Pennsylvania in actual pay on July 1, 1776, was reported as follows:

In the Army, 1432; in the Navy, 743. On August 1, 1776, it was: Army, 1365; in the Navy, 768.

The company of Capt. Henry Christ was the only company from Berks County in service at that time. At the first report it had 62 men; at the second, 64 men.

I could not ascertain the names of any men from Berks County who were in the naval service, nor that any were in the military service below Philadelphia.

Reports.

Oct. 16, 1776.—The Council proposed to raise four battalions of militia for the immediate defence of the State, 500 men to be supplied by Berks County, and the same number by York, Cumberland and Lancaster Counties. [These may have been made up by Col. Haller's Regiment.]

Dec. 11, 1776.—Capt. Stephen Crumrine was paid £15 to be distributed among the families of the poor Associators who were in his company.

April 24, 1777.—Congress asked Pennsylvania to call out 3000 militia, one-half to rendezvous at Chester, on the Delaware, and the other half at Bristol; and, in pursuance of this request, an order was sent to Col. Morgan on the 25th to furnish 500 men from Berks County and march them immediately to Bristol, with as many arms and accoutrements as could be procured in the county. If the first class should not amount to that number, the second class was also to march. Each man was to be supplied with a blanket. He was directed to exert himself to the utmost to comply with this order, because it was thought the British were then preparing to make an immediate attack upon Pennsylvania. He received this order on the 26th, while he and his sub-lieutenants were in session receiving the militia returns of the inhabitants of the county. In a letter to Council on April 27th he added:

"It would be impracticable to forward the business sooner, as the county is so very extensive, half the inhabitants would not have timely notice. As for my own part, your Excellency [President of Council] may rest well assured I shall leave no stone unturned that tends in the least to promote the good and welfare of my Country, and the General Cause of the Independent States which I have really so much at heart."

June 13, 1777.—Council informed Col. Morgan that they were "for some time impatiently expecting to hear that the 1st class of militia had joined the Camp at Bristol, and that the 2nd was ready to march on the shortest notice." On the 27th, he reported that two companies of the 1st class were ready to march on the next day.

The subsequent orders were modified. Troops were eventually forwarded shortly afterward, consisting of two battalions, commanded by Col. Daniel Hunter and Col. Daniel Udree.

September 6th.—The Lieutenants were asked to have all the militia ready on account of a supposed intention of the British to invade the State and get possession of Philadelphia; and Berks County was ordered to forward a class to Derby.

September 12th.—The 3rd and 4th classes of militia were called out, and on the 18th, Col. Morgan reported that he hoped to have them ready to march soon, but that they were badly off for want of arms.

In October there were altogether only about 1600 militia of the State in service, and it was expected that they would fall far short of that number in a few days.

Oct. 17, 1777.—Gen'l Washington reported that the term of service of great numbers of the Pennsylvania militia had then expired, and said that, inasmuch as the British were in Philadelphia, "at least one-half of the men capable to bear arms should be called into the field." He expressed surprise "that Pennsylvania, the most opulent and populous of all the States has but 1200 militia in the field at a time when the enemy are endeavoring to fix their Winter quarters in her Capitol," and added that on an average, the State battalions were never above one-third full, and many even far below that.

In the Battle of Germantown about 1500 militia of Pennsylvania were engaged. From the biographical sketch of Col. Joseph Hiester, which was prepared in 1832, I am led to say that some of the Berks County Militia were included in this number, but how many I am not able to state, though I made diligent search in the *Colonial Records, Pennsylvania Archives*, and other publications for data bearing on this particular occurrence.

In January, 1778, General Washington recommended that Capt. Edward Scull recruit 150 men in Berks County for the Battalion of the State in the Continental army.

January 5, 1778.—Council sent a circular to the Lieutenant of the county, calling out the 6th and 7th classes of militia, as completely accoutred and equipped as possible, and directing the men to be forwarded immediately, because the time of service of those in the field was about to expire. By this circular it appears that Council required "returns of the militia" which went into service. No returns, however, have yet been discovered, showing what companies and men were forwarded from Berks County to fill certain orders.

Feb. 10, 1778.—Capt. Edward Scull and Lieut. William Henderson, of the 4th Penna. Regt., were ordered on the recruiting service.

March 24, 1778.—Ordered that 200 militia of Berks County be detailed for duty at Reading, to guard magazines of military stores, provisions, etc., pursuant to a resolution of Congress on March 19, 1778. This order was filled on April 15, 1778.

April 24, 1778.—A guard of one sergeant and nine privates was placed at Boone's mill, eight miles below Reading (near Stonersville), where Morgan (Q. M.) had placed that week 500 knapsacks to be painted, and some person had set fire to them and so destroyed them.

May 22, 1778.—The Vice-President of Council directed the guard at Reading to be discontinued, excepting a small guard for the stores, which should not exceed 50; and on the 27th, Col. Morgan reported that he had reduced the guard at Reading to 50, rank and file.

September 16, 1778.—Capt. James Wilson, of Reading, was recommended for recruiting service by his commanding officer.

October 19, 1778.—The Executive Council received intelligence from New York that the British were about to make an important movement, and it was determined that Maj.-Gen'l Armstrong should go to Philadelphia and take command of the militia in case of an invasion. The quota of southeastern Pennsylvania was fixed at 15 battalions—the quota of Berks County at 2. I could not find any returns of men forwarded at that time.

A company of 52 volunteers, raised in Berks County, was sent by Col. Morgan to Philadelphia on June 27, 1780, under the command of Maj. Edward Scull, with a muster roll. The remaining men of the order were to be sent on the following Monday. I could not ascertain what the number was.

The 5th Regt. of Infantry in the Penna. Line was ordered on January 23, 1781, to be recruited at Reading; and on the 30th an order for £500 was drawn to Henry Christ for enlisting men into this regiment.

Sept. 22, 1781.—"Passed through [Lancaster] this afternoon 153 recruits from York, but raised at Reading, for Philadelphia." [Marshall's Diary, p. 283].

June 14, 1783.—A petition from Capt. Peter Smith was presented to the Executive Council, "in behalf of the Militia of Greenwich and Maxatawny townships, in the County of Berks, praying that they may be paid for a tour of duty performed in 1781."

October 2, 1784.—A detachment of 50 men out of Berks County Militia was ordered to be sent to Wyoming to quiet the disturbances there and support the civil authority.

April 6, 1790.—Capt. Jacob Ladich was paid £294, 5sh, 10d, balance due of £332, 9sh, 4d, for the pay and bounty of his company of Berks County Militia while employed in the service of the United States under the command of Col. Samuel Ely from Oct. 1, 1781, until Oct. 17, 1781, including their extra pay.

Nov. 24, 1790.—Lieut. Daniel Stroud was paid £95, 18sh, for the residue of pay due to his company of Berks County Militia while employed in guarding prisoners of war in August and September, 1781.

Dec. 9, 1790.—The Comptroller-General approved of the following claims:

Capt. ——— Spatts, balance of £130, 17sh., 2d. to pay his company of Berks Co. Militia for militia service in 1781.

Capt. George Riehm, balance of £217, 15sh., 6d. to pay his company for services in 1781.

Dec. 17, 1790.—He also approved the following accounts presented:

Lieut. ——— Miller, £33, 9sh., 4d. to pay six men of his company in the 6th Battalion of Berks Co. Militia while guarding Convention prisoners of war at Reading in 1781.

Lieut. Jacob Rehrer, £260, 16sh., 6d. to pay his company of the 2nd Battalion of Berks Co. Militia for similar service in 1781.

Dr. Nicholas Snell, £27 for 18 days' pay as a Surgeon of Col. Samuel Ely's Battalion of Berks County Militia from Oct. 1, 1781, to Oct. 18, 1781, while on a tour of duty to Newtown, in Bucks County, under Gen'l Lacy.

On Dec. 15, 1790, Jacob Severts was paid £2, 19sh., 6d. for serving as Q. M.-Sergeant on same tour of duty, 17 days, in this battalion.

Payments for County Militia.

The following payments were found to have been made during this period to, for and on account of the militia in Berks County:

March 28, 1776.—A payment of £12 was made to Capt. Dirck Pennybacker of Berks County. At that time he resided in Amity township, where he carried on a grist mill and farm, together containing 200 acres. He was still assessed in the township in 1781.

Oct. 12, 1776.—Maj. Ennion Williams was paid £9, 17sh, 6d, for guard duty at the State House, powder house, etc., from July to November, 1775, to pay 66 privates and 13 officers. And on the same day Col. Daniel Brodhead was allowed $30 per month during captivity of Col. Miles, while he commanded the Pennsylvania troops, this being for the support of his table. Both were from Berks County.

Dec. 31, 1776.—Adam Witman, Commissioner of Berks Co., was paid $2000 for Committee of Safety.

Jan. 15, 1777.—Capt. —— Fisher was paid £1, 12sh, for subsistence of his company in 3rd Battalion of County Militia.

Jan. 22, 1777.—John Hufty was paid £1 for firing and lodging three companies of the County Militia.

Jan. 23, 1777.—Capt. John Old was paid $125 for a month's wages of a Colonel and Major.

Aug. 25, 1777.—Col. Daniel Hunter was re-appointed Paymaster of the County Militia. He was filling this office then; but finding it inconvenient to continue, Henry Spyker was appointed in his stead on Aug. 26, 1777.

Sept. 10, 1777.—An order was drawn to Col. Jacob Morgan for £500.

March 28, 1778.—Order drawn on treasurer in favor of Henry Spyker, Paymaster of Berks Co. Militia, for £5000; April, 17, 1778, £6000; and May 20, 1778, £5000.

Nov. 30, 1780.—Order on treasurer drawn to Henry Spyker, Paymaster of Berks County, for £163,000 to pay militia of said County, if so much in the treasury, arising from militia fines in the said County. This must be an error in the *Colonial Records*.

Dec. 13, 1780.—Resolved that Jacob Morgan pay off militia who marched on late tour of duty.

CHAPTER VII.

PRISONERS OF WAR AT READING.

Reading was a prominent place for locating prisoners of war that were taken at different times in the course of prosecuting the Revolution. They comprised different nationalities, but principally English, Hessians and Germans, and the following particulars are detailed, respecting the several classes.

ENGLISH PRISONERS.

Owing to the arrival of certain English prisoners at Reading in February, 1776, without any notice or preparation, the following letter was forwarded to the Pennsylvania delegates in the Continental Congress:

READING, February 4, 1776.

Gentlemen: A number of English soldiers, who were lately taken in Canada, have arrived here, with their wives and children. The Committee were immediately assembled, and, although they were much surprised at so large a party being ordered here without any previous notice and without any person attending them to supply them with necessaries, yet, understanding it was the pleasure of Congress the said soldiers should be quartered here, they immediately appointed Mr. Henry Haller, a member of the Committee, to provide houses, fire-wood and provisions for the party who must have otherwise suffered much at this severe season. As we are totally unacquainted with the pleasure of the honorable Congress as to the particular quantities of provisions to be allowed these prisoners, we have despatched an express to you, gentlemen, desiring you will, by his return, be pleased to procure and send to us the directions of Congress to govern us in the matter.

As Mr. Haller has been an active member of this Committee, and is a very suitable person, we beg leave to recommend him to be continued as Commissary for the soldiers stationed here.

We are, gentlemen, your most obedient, humble servants.

By order of the Committee of Correspondence.

MARK BIRD, *Chairman.*

On April 17, 1776, the *officers*, who were prisoners of war at Reading, were ordered to be removed to Lebanon; and on July 10th, Congress ordered that the *privates* who were prisoners there should be removed to Lancaster.

In September, 1776, the conduct and late hours of the prisoners excited the citizens to such an extent that a meeting of the Committee of Berks County was called on September 3rd and resolutions were adopted praying the Council of Safety to require the prisoners to disarm themselves and repair to their respective lodgings at a seasonable hour—8 P. M.—every evening. Capt. John Witman, Thomas Warren and Michael Graus were appointed to take possession of fire-arms, etc.; and on the 4th, Daniel Rose, Philip Kremer and Krauff Hiener were appointed to assist them. On the 5th, they reported that Gen'l Prescott had refused to deliver up his pistols until he had first broken and rendered them useless, and that he had declared they acted like robbers. He admitted his conduct, and the committee resolved "that he be committed to the Common Gaol till the opinion of the Council of Safety be known." James Read, chairman, reported this action to the Council, and made request that "a guard be kept as security from any attempts which may be made by the prisoners in our present defenceless situation." The Council heard the matter on the 10th, and ordered guard to be kept as long as the prisoners remained, at the Council's expense.

Joseph McIlvain was paid £66 on December 11, 1776, for removing prisoners from Bristol to Reading.

Read's Letter to Council.—On December 26, 1776, seven persons as prisoners reached Reading, having been taken there from Northampton County, as suspects inimical to the Revolution. Their arrival induced James Read, Esq., to address a letter to the Council of Safety on the next day, which was as follows :

"Reading being the nearest place, we, who have already more prisoners, French and Scotch, than we have men at arms, (old and young together) in this place, shall have all the Tories that Northampton can find, whereby the ruin of this town is justly apprehended. Lancaster has Barracks, and neither that town, nor York, has any prisoners in it. But if the people of Northampton have their choice of three places, they will always send to the nearest of them. Thus Reading must be endangered, and at best burthened. Our prison is small, that of Lancaster large, and that town is three times as large as this. Pray, sir, let these things be immediately considered. We are distressed. The militia from Northumberland disturb us by their importunity for salt; which, surely, we are not to provide, when there is such a scanty portion in every family.

"We have heard that a Hospital is to be made in this place. Strange this! when we have not one house in town unoccupied. Many families have come hither from Philadelphia. I need say no more on this head. I am obliged to write in great haste. I cannot, however, conclude, without pressing you, sir [the President, Thomas Wharton, jr.] to try to relieve us of these tories and other prisoners, and saying that hereafter it will be impossible to get a waggon, or any service done without ready pay. The people who have hitherto done public services are very importunate and grow angry that they are not paid."

Pursuant to the request of Gen'l Washington, the Council of Safety on March 1, 1777, directed Col. Haller to remove the French prisoners at Reading to Easton, in order that an exchange might take place, and when he reached Easton he was to dispatch a messenger to Gen'l Washington to let him know it, so as to receive such further directions respecting their route as he might think proper to give.

Quaker Prisoners from Philadelphia.—Certain prisoners, (twenty prominent Quakers) were stationed in the "Mason's Lodge" at Philadelphia. On September 10, 1777, they were ordered to be escorted to Reading; and on the 12th, the Bucks County Militia were ordered to act as a guard in conducting the British prisoners to Reading and such others as may be necessary to be added. They stayed for a time at the public house kept by Eve Withington, the widow of Capt. Withington. She presented a petition to the Executive Council on January 9, 1789, praying payment of her account. The balance due her was paid June 23, 1789. They were escorted by two of the light-horse of Philadelphia in this circuitous route to avoid the British, and doubtless proceeded by way of Lancaster, Carlisle, Hagerstown and the Shenandoah Valley to their destination at Staunton, in Augusta County, Virginia. On January 1, 1778, an order for £159 was drawn to pay the expense of removing certain Quaker prisoners to Reading.

In May, 1779, a disturbance between the British prisoners and the inhabitants of Reading was reported to the Council of War by President Reed and their removal to New Jersey was suggested.

County Jail at Reading, 5th and Washington streets, 1770 to 1848.

June 1, 1779.—A letter was addressed by Col. Henry Haller to the Executive Council, enclosing sundry papers respecting the prisoners at Reading, and the disturbances between them and the inhabitants of the town. These papers were ordered to be sent to the Board of War with the request that the said prisoners be sent to some other place.

By a letter from the Secretary of the Board of War to the Executive Council on July 19, 1780, it would appear that there were then only about 100 prisoners of war at Reading. At that time, Col. Henry Haller was the "Commissary of Prisoners" at Reading, and he complained of the great scarcity of provisions. This must refer only to those in the town, not near by.

Geist's Company on Guard Duty.

The following detachment of Capt. Conrad Geist's Company, of the 6th Battalion of County Militia was detailed to guard the prisoners while in the Reading Jail from which they had attempted to break out, and also while they were being conducted from Reading to Lancaster. This was in 1776:

Captain.
Conrad Geist.

Ensign.		*Sergeants.*
Jacob Stehly.		George Gertner.
		William Shener.

Privates.

Matthias Babb.	Peter Feather.	George Houser.
Peter Custard.	Conrad Fesig.	George Jaeger.
Christian Deringer.	Peter Fesig.	Philip Klinger.
Christopher Diem.	Christopher Fisher.	William Knorr.
George Donnelly.	John Fister.	Matthias Leib.
Paul Ege.	George Fry.	Abraham Levan.
George Eisenbeis.	Jesse Grinding.	Daniel McCoy.
Isaac Ermold.	John Hiener.	Dewalt Miller.

John Miller.	Zacharias Rexroad.	James Simpson.
Frederick Nagel.	Christian Setley.	John Snyder.
Philip Nagel.	Henry Setley.	Henry Wolf.
Jacob Petre.	Christian Shreffler.	

HESSIAN PRISONERS.

In 1775, the King of Great Britain obtained by treaty from the German Princes 17,000 men for the purpose of sending them to America to assist in subduing the American Colonies. These men were sent early in 1776. Many of them, (Hessians) were taken prisoners at the Battle of Trenton on December 26, 1776, and conveyed to Lancaster.

The Continental troops then took the following prisoners, arms, etc. : 750 Hessians, 1 lieutenant-colonel, 2 majors, 4 captains, 15 subalterns, 3 standards, 6 brass field pieces and near 1000 stand of arms. Two days afterward, Gen'l Washington commanded them to be forwarded to Lancaster.

The following letter was addressed to Daniel Clymer, Esq., at Lancaster, in 1777, by Joseph Nourn, from Philadelphia, in reference to the removal of prisoners from that place to Reading :

"The Board have directed me to write to William Atlee, Deputy Commissary of Prisoners, to whom you'll please to render all the assistance in your power in the removal of the Prisoners of War from Lancaster towards Reading and Lebanon. Congress having just been informed by Express that the Enemy are landing in Maryland above Baltimore, & its being past a doubt the rescuing their Prisoners & the destruction of our Stores are the objects they have in view. On this important occasion, anything in your power, the Board are well satisfied will be done. You'll please to have an eye to the Prisoners at York, & if Mr. Atlee can do the Business by himself at Lancaster, it is the desire of the Board you proceed thither, & the Committee are hereby earnestly requested to furnish such a number of Militia as shall put it out of the power of the Prisoners to effect an escape. We are unacquainted with the number of Prisoners at York; you will, therefore, act as your own good sense may dictate."

Some of these prisoners were afterward stationed at Reading. The first location in the town was in the southern section. The exact place was along the Schuylkill a short distance below the ferry, where the "Lancaster Bridge" is now situated. After remaining in that locality several years, they were removed to the southern declivity of Penn's Mount. This removal was caused by the frequent disturbances which arose between the prisoners and the citizens of the town.

On June 27, 1781, President Reed wrote to Valentine Eckert, "that it was the desire that the prisoners should be encamped in huts at some small distance from Reading, where wood and water were convenient; that Colonel Morgan had mentioned a piece of ground which had belonged to the proprietaries, which would be convenient and proper." Three persons were appointed to select a location—Valentine Eckert, Lieutenant of Berks County; Maj. Bayley and Col. Wood, of Lancaster. On the 17th of July, Col. Wood wrote to President Reed, "that he could not decide where to locate the prisoners; that certain persons, who thought they did not have a legal title to the Commons, had paid the taxes and claimed the land." He, therefore, referred the matter to him for a decision.

The "Commons" was not selected; but the committee went half a mile to the eastward and selected a place on the hill-side, where they caused huts to be erected, and in which they stationed the prisoners.

This place has since been known as "Hessian Camp." The greater part of these huts were standing in 1841. The exact location was on an enclosed portion of land that lay between the Rose Valley Creek (at a point where the Mineral Spring Dam now is) and the "Hill Road" as now laid out. Then the trees were few in number and there was no road along the upper end of the camp.

Some of the Hessian prisoners at Reading, during the course of their imprisonment, were hired out to service, notably to George Ege at Charming Forge and to John Patton at Berkshire Furnace.

At the close of the Revolution, the Hessian prisoners were returned by the British or satisfactorily accounted for, according to contract. It has been persistently stated as a tradition that many of these Hessians remained and settled in the county roundabout Reading; but in my opinion this is erroneous. They could not have remained here except as deserters.

Hessian Camp Surprised.—The following interesting incident transpired at the Hessian camp on Christmas day, 1781. The Hessian prisoners and their guard were suddenly alarmed by certain soldiers in the disguise of Indians, which caused them to fly from the encampment. A court-martial was afterwards held, but no one was punished.

"Van Campen, whilst at McClure's Fort, which was on the Susquehanna River, above Sunbury, upon the service of conducting scouts around the line of the settlements, was ordered with his company to Lancaster, late in the fall of 1781. He descended the river in boats as far as Middletown (a place ten miles below Harris's Ferry), where the order was countermanded by another, directing him to march to Reading, Berks County, where he was joined by a part of the 3rd and 5th Pennsylvania Regiments, and a company of the Congress Regiment. Their principal duty, while here, was to take care of a large body of Hessians that had been taken prisoners with General Burgoyne. These had been under the guard of a company of militiamen, whose time had not yet expired. The march which Van Campen's soldiers had performed was, on account of lateness of the season and bad roads, extremely fatiguing, and, as the time for which the militia were engaged continued them in service a little longer, he allowed them the space which intervened as a season of rest. This proved grateful to the soldiers, and it no doubt served to invigorate their spirits, for in the approaching Christmas holidays, they were found to be sufficiently recruited to engage in the exercises of sport. Some of those belonging to Van Campen's company determined to have a frolic with the militiamen before they should be discharged from their posts. These were stationed at a little distance out of the village, near the direct road from Reading to Philadelphia, on the side of a hill, around which the way turned, and which hid the view to the road before reaching the place. When Christmas came, twelve or fifteen young soldiers set out, with music in their heads, for the militiamen's camp. Just before they came to where the road turned around the hill, and while they were yet out of sight, they arrayed themselves in Indian dress and crept along up the ascending ground until they came in sight of the militiamen's camp. There they fired their guns, which contained an unusual charge of powder, and followed the discharge of these by loud and continued yells. They presented themselves to the view of the soldiers, and began to jump from tree to tree so as to produce an enlarged idea of their numbers. Their unexpected appearance produced the intended effect. The soldiers were startled by the sudden roar of the rifles, which echoed through the deep forest like the terrible thundering of cannon. The loud yells, too, from the supposed Indians, were enough to have startled them in a time of peace, much more when the savage was looked for at any moment to commit his deeds of violence. The soldiers conceived an instantaneous alarm; fear was scattered throughout their ranks, and, with a sudden bound, they started from their encampment. The sentinels fled without firing a single gun and the whole company deserted their posts, leaving the poor Hessians (whom they were placed to guard) without a man to prevent their being retaken. But these, too, apprehensive that they might be mistaken for rebels, were infected with the universal panic and showed their heels to the enemy. The camp was entirely deserted in a few moments after the first alarm had been given. No sooner had the militiamen deserted their camp than they began to spread the alarm, saying, 'that all Niagara was let loose; that a party of several hundred Indians had attacked their camp, and that they had just escaped with their lives.' The intelligence was soon brought to the troops at Reading, who were immediately placed in the order of defence, and who began forthwith to march, with Van Campen at their head, towards the enemy. They had not gone far, however, before they were met by some of their own soldiers, who assured them that they had started out upon a false alarm, at the same time giving them a history of the secret of the attack and of the brave defence which had been made by the militiamen. They returned to their quarters, very much amused and with the laugh upon the poor soldiers who had made such a display of their bravery.

"But this little event (which had been conceived only in sport, like many others of the same origin) was the occasion of serious difficulty. To one party it afforded the highest amusement, but, to those who had committed their valor to their heels, it was a subject of constant annoyance. They could not endure the chagrin that was brought upon them by having been put to flight by a few boys who had been disguised as Indians, and who had so successfully played off their wits upon them of a Christmas holiday. The militia officers, whose bravery was somewhat implicated in the affair, declared that they would be satisfied with no reconciliation short of the punishment of those who had been concerned in creating the alarm.

"A court-martial was held, in which Lieutenant Van Campen sat with the militia officers, to decide the point at issue. These affirmed it to be but right—that those who had occasioned the mischief should be whipped; while Van Campen, whose soldiers were implicated, unwilling that his men (who belonged to some of the most respectable families of that part of Pennsylvania) should suffer such a disgrace, would allow of this only upon condition that the sentinels, who had fled from their posts without firing, should be punished as the martial-law required—with death. These terms were not agreeable to the minds of the officers, and Van Campen, who declared that he would sooner see his men shot than whipped, continued to sit in court-martial for the space of three weeks. A compromise was finally made between the two, it being proposed that the sergeant, who had been one of the leaders in the affair, should be broken of his rank. This was allowed, and harmony was again restored between the two parties. The sergeant was broken of his rank at night and restored the next morning; so that his punishment, after all, was more nominal than real. Immediately after, Van Campen and his men entered upon the care of the Hessian soldiers and remained in this service until the next spring, when they were relieved by the militia, who again took them under charge."

The foregoing extract was taken from the "Life and Adventures of Moses Van Campen" by his grandson, John N. Hubbard, (published in 1841) pps. 239 to 243. Near the beginning of this extract he states that the Hessians at Reading had been taken prisoners with Burgoyne. This is not correct. No prisoners were taken in that important battle, October 17, 1777. The British Army surrendered to General Gates at Saratoga with the agreement that they "should march out with all the honors of war, and have free passage to England, upon condition that they should not serve again during the war."

Hessian Officer Drowned.—During the time that the Hessian prisoners were at Reading, a Hessian officer of rank was fishing from a canoe one day in the Schuylkill, and fell overboard. A servant on the shore saw the accident, but, instead of alarming the occupants in a house near by, he ran and informed the commanding officer. When the officer arrived, he found the Hessian at the bottom of the river, drowned, and his efforts to resuscitate life were fruitless.

Sickness and Burial of Hessians.—During the Winter of 1776-77 there was much sickness amongst the prisoners. Many of them died. The burials were made in "Potter's Field," which comprised two lots of ground, numbers 398 and 399 on the west side of North Sixth Street, south of Walnut, in Reading. The deaths were so numerous at times that it became necessary to bury two, and even three, in one grave. I heard this statement made frequently by some of the older residents, but I always questioned its reliability, for I could not believe that dead prisoners would be carried from the Camp and buried within two squares of the principal thoroughfare and near the centre of the town. It is probable that the men buried there were sick soldiers who died in the churches that were used as hospitals, the churches having been near by on Washington street to the east and west of 6th street.

GERMAN PRISONERS.

On June 16, 1781, a large number of Convention prisoners of war, 1050, all Germans, excepting 63 Brittons, arrived at Reading under guard of the York County Militia. Col. Valentine Eckert called out two classes of companies from the 6th Battalion of Berks County Militia to guard the encampment. They were under the command of Major Bayley. During the week following, additional prisoners were brought, so that the whole number was near 1100. They were encamped on the east bank of the Schuylkill, near the ferry on the road to Lancaster, having been ordered to be put into huts where wood and water were convenient. Col. Eckert and Col. James Wood suggested "that the Continental stables and a large store house might be converted into barracks to advantage by raising them about two feet and underpinning with stone, by which it would make them two stories, and, with some small additions, would shelter the whole of the troops. However, this would be attended with inconvenience, as their fire wood must be waggoned, but not any considerable distance. My [Wood's] intention is if the troops are to be hutted, and the Quarter Master can procure tools and a person acquainted with building to superintend the work, to have them built by the troops and in such a manner as to be of use upon any other or future occasion."

The stable was 20 by 175 feet, and the store house 20 by 60 feet.

Krause's Company on Guard Duty.

The following detachment of Capt. Charles Krause's Company of the 1st Battalion Berks County Militia was detailed on August 13, 1781, to guard the Convention prisoners of war near Reading, from August 16 to October 16, 1781. The captain was paid the balance due, £277, on April 28, 1790:

Captain.
Charles Krause.

Sergeants.		*Corporals.*
Ernst Gries.		Christian Schmeck.
Philip Dresher.		Isaac Harmany.
John Burchard.		John Harmany.

Privates.

Philip Kline.	Mathias Bower.	Michael Christman.
George Mumma.	Jacob Sigfried.	Henry Grub.
Jno. Fenstermacher.	George Klapp.	Fred'k Mengel.
Abraham Gross.	Baltzer Lutz.	John Saul.

Adam Labar.	Adam Knettle.	Peter Shomo.
Casper Merkel.	John Heines.	Lorentz Christ.
Christian Wilhelm.	Peter Rundorf.	John Norbeck.
Conrad Sitler.	Titan McCarty.	Mathias Flack.
Christian Becker.	Philip Christ.	John Klockner.
Theobald Keffer.	Philip Dull.	

Additional Men as Guard.

After peace was declared, a petition was presented to the Executive Council, subscribed by forty-three names, which prayed for an allowance to pay for military services rendered. The petitioners set forth that they had been ordered out to guard the Convention Troops upon constant service from 1781 until peace happened; that these troops were prisoners of war confined in the vicinity of Reading; that the militia of that district had performed constant guard duty during the stay of the prisoners, to the great hinderance of their several occupations, with a firm reliance that their country would make such satisfaction as the Militia laws should entitle them; and that they had made numerous applications for pay, but their efforts were in vain.

The subscribing names were as follows:

John Folweiler.	Philip Ruppert.	Henry Spengler.
George Eisenbeis.	Jacob Stahle.	Peter Stichter.
George Gerdner.	Conrad Geist.	Abraham Phillippi.
Nicholas Scherrer.	Henry Miller.	George Seitz.
Stephen Fitterer.	Daniel Hiester.	Alexander Klinger.
George Young.	John Phillippi.	John Shenfelder.
Michael Reifsnyder.	Henry Hahn, Jr.	Benjamin Parks, Jr.
Jacob Merch.	George Snell.	John Seitter.
William Mears.	John Felix.	Jacob Klingman.
Philip Weiss.	George Brendlinger.	Jacob Kesel.
Jacob Petery.	Bernard Kepner.	Ernst Gries.

David Herman.	Andrew Eisenbeis.	George Shoemaker.
George Roland.	Adam Spohn.	John Lewis.
Godfried Leman.	Jonas Baum.	
Gottlieb Christian.	Valentine Boyer.	

I could not find that any action was taken on this petition. Conrad Geist, one of the petitioners, had commanded a company as captain which served as guard of prisoners in 1776.

The above names may not represent all the men who served at that time, for some may have died or moved away between the declaration of peace and the signing of the petition.

From the contents of the petition, we must conclude that the militia of the county, especially from the vicinity of Reading, (which constituted the 1st Battalion under the command of Col. Nicholas Lotz), were in constant service of this kind, and judging from other evidence of men in that service, they were detailed for short terms.

Continental Troops as Guard.

Maj.-Gen'l Lincoln, Minister of the War Department, informed the Executive Council on January 2, 1782, that Gen'l Hazen's Regiment was appointed to guard the prisoners in the counties of Lancaster, Berks and York, whereupon the Council directed the Lieutenants of the said counties to discharge the militia then on duty so soon as the Continental troops should take charge of the prisoners.

Militia as Guard for Military Prisoners.

On February 23, 1782, the Lieutenant of the county was ordered to call out the first class of militia to guard the military prisoners at Reading ; but only 40 men were wanted at a time for this purpose. The order was as follows :

"*Ordered*, That the Lieutenant of the county of Berks be directed to call out a class of the militia of the said county, for the purpose of guarding the military prisoners of that county ; that as forty men are only wanted at one time for the said purpose, the lieutenant be directed to call out no more than that number, and that the battalion be called up in their numerical order, beginning at the first, for the said one class, so far as may be necessary to furnish the said number ; and when the time of the first forty shall expire, he then call on the next battalion or battalions for the like number, so as to have the succeeding numbers ready to take charge of the said prisoners when the time of the first shall expire, and so on until the said one class shall have served their tour of duty, or until further orders from this Council."

Nagel's Company on Guard Duty.

The following detachment of Capt. Peter Nagel's Company, in the 6th Battalion of Berks County Militia, was on duty guarding prisoners of war who were conducted from Reading to Philadelphia. I could not ascertain the time when the service was rendered. It was probably on September 19, 1782, when they were ordered to "mount guard."

Captain.
Peter Nagel.

Sergeant.
Casper Heiner.

Privates.

Christian Deringer.	Joseph Kendall.	George Phillipi.
Nicholas Dick.	Samuel Keiser.	George Schultz.
Peter Feather.	Hartman Leitheiser.	George Seitz.
John Heiner.	George Merkel.	Abraham Witman.
Benj. Hoover.	Philip Nagel.	Jacob Yoder.

CHAPTER VIII.

ESTIMATE OF MEN IN SERVICE.

The following statement shows the probable number of men from Berks County who were in actual service at some time during the Revolution. The figures at the end of each company indicate the number of men that appears in the rosters as published, except in several instances where it has been corrected by positive returns. The companies, when organized and forwarded, were to have the regular number, and it is probable that they generally had this number, excepting when special orders were given to supply guards for the prisoners at Reading or men for defending the frontiers of Berks and Northumberland counties. How the number came to be reduced in nearly all the companies I am not able to explain. The reduced figures may represent the strength of the companies when mustered out of service.

In reference to the battalions given, I have taken the number, either at the number ordered by the Executive Council which was to be supplied by the county, or estimated it at what was commonly known to comprise a battalion.

All the orders for guarding prisoners I have fixed at 40 men, unless otherwise published. Previous to 1782, the number at one time acting as guard exceeded 40 men, but I cannot state how many. From the order of February 23, 1782, it is apparent that the changes were frequent, and that five men were taken from each company in a battalion, and when the term of service expired, another class was taken in the same manner from the next battalion, and so on in numerical order until each of the six battalions supplied its quota. The estimate presented is evidently less than the number of men who were in actual service.

In several instances, the estimates of battalions and companies may be excessive. But, because there is no way by which to ascertain the figures accurately, we can not on that account ignore the evidence of men altogether, whether simply ordered or forwarded. When orders were made for troops to fill the quota of the county, and returns found, we can assert that they were filled; but if no returns were found, it can not be said that the orders were not filled. I found evidence of payments made long after 1783 for military services rendered before that time, notwithstanding I did not find any orders or returns for such services.

For the year 1779, I did not find any returns. It is hardly probable that, for a whole year, there were no orders at all for troops from Berks County. From this, however, we are not to conclude that there were no men in actual service from the county during 1779, for some were in service by previous enlistment and re-enlistment for terms that extended into and beyond that year.

For the year 1775.

June—Company of Capt. George Nagel.................... 95

For the year 1776.

January—Company of Capt. Jonathan Jones	83
" " " " John Spohn	78
" " " " Peter Decker	86
February—Detachment of Capt. Peter Nagel's Co. for guarding prisoners	17
March—Company of Capt. Henry Christ	87
July—Company of Capt. Benj. Weiser	53
Other men in German Regiment	13
July—Battalion of Lt.-Col. Nicholas Lotz, quota required	666
August—Battalion of Col. John Patton (four companies)	191
" Company of Capt. Will—estimated	72
" " " " Daniel DeTurk	72
" Battalion of Col. Mark Bird	300
September—Battalion of Col. Balser Geehr—estimated	500
" Detachment of Capt. Conrad Geist's Co. guarding prisoners	39
October—Quota ordered from county	500

Believed to have been supplied from 1st and 6th Battalions commanded by Col. Henry Haller and Col. Daniel Hunter.

For the year 1777.

January—Order for 2nd Battalion—estimated	500

Partly filled by companies of Will, Diehl and Scheffer.

February—Company of Capt. Jacob Moser	67
" " " " Jacob Bower—(part)	24
Sundry enlistments in Continental Line	37
August—Two battalions commanded by Cols. Daniel Hunter and Daniel Udree	656
September—Two companies guarding stores at Reading—estimated 50 each	100
November—Battalion of Col. Henry Spyker	400

For the year 1778.

January—Recruited by Capt. Edward Scull	150
April—Guard ordered at Reading	200
" " " " Boone's Mill	10

June—Von Heer's Dragoons............................ 16
August—Forwarded to Sunbury.................................180
  "   "   " Easton 123
October—Quota from county—two battalions............... ——

For the year 1779.

No troops were discovered as having been forwarded from the county during the year 1779.

For the Year 1780.

June—Forwarded to Philadelphia, under Capt. Edward
      Scull.. 52
July—Quota from County, (mostly filled by six companies of
      6th Battalion, and selections from 3rd...............600
August—Two companies from 1st Battalion for frontiers—esti-
      mated........... 120
——Men in pursuit of Indians.............................112

For the Year 1781.

May—One class, 4th Battalion............................. 64
June—Two classes, 6th Battalion...........................128
August—Detachment of Krause's Company................... 36
August—Detachment of Stroud's Company.................. 40
September—Recruits from Reading...........................153
October—Ely's Battalion at Newtown........................300
October—Livingood's Company of Riflemen.............. 83
October—Three companies to Newtown.......................180
——Militia from Greenwich and Maxatawny townships.......120
——Guarding prisoners—men supplied from 2nd and 6th Bat-
      talions 169

For the Year 1782.

February—Robinson's Company to Northumberland county.... 60
February—Guard for prisoners at Reading................... 40
August—Frontiers of Berks County.......................... 27
August—Frontiers of Berks and Northumberland Counties..... 50
September—Frontiers of Northumberland County.............125
September—Guard for prisoners at Reading.................. 17

Recapitulation.

For the year 1775..........95	For the year 1780..........884
" " " 1776........2757	" " " 1781........1273
" " " 1777........1784	" " " 1782..........319
" " " 1778..........679	
" " " 1779..........—	Estimated Total 7791

Of these 7791 men, the foregoing narrative shows the names of 1542; and included in the latter number are the names of sixty-five captains and sixteen colonels. The number of men for the years 1776 and 1777 appears incredible, but the reader will take into consideration that the men for each year were not all in service at one time. Taking the reports of men in service that I have given in detail, and understanding that I have not been able to discover all the men that were enlisted, it can be said that the estimated total, as arranged, is not above, but rather below, the real number supplied by the county during the Revolution. The system of supplying men was simple, and it was carried on in such a manner as to render assistance to the government with as little injury as possible to the several districts from which the men were called. The number demanded at one time was not extraordinary, compared with the total number subject to military duty, and the term of service was limited to such a period that the business interests of the people should not suffer serious losses. In this way, it was possible to have at least several hundred men from a county in service all the time. Averaging the quota of Berks County at only 300, and changing the men every ninety days, four times a year, for seven years, from 1776 to 1782, the total would exceed the number given. This is not a correct way to get at the probable number; still it can be made apparent thereby that my estimate is not excessive.

Names of Captains.

Jacob Baldy.	George Kemp.	Edward Scull.
George Battorf.	Charles Krause.	Peter Scull.
George Beaver.	John Ludwig.	Henry Shepler.
Jacob Bower.	Jacob Ladich.	Conrad Sherman.
Michael Bretz.	Sebastian Lentz.	Casper Smeck.
Henry Christ.	John Lesher.	Peter Smith.
Stephen Crumrine.	Jacob Livingood.	John Soder.
Peter Decker.	Jacob Maurer.	John Spoon.
Daniel DeTurck.	George May.	Leonard Stone.
Samuel Dewees.	John Mears.	Henry Strauch.
John Diehl.	George Miller.	Bartholomew Von Heer.
George Douglass.	Jacob Moser.	
Conrad Eckert.	George Nagel.	Michael Voyge.
Michael Furrer.	Peter Nagel.	Peter Wanner.
George Focht.	John Old.	Benjamin Weiser.
Conrad Geist.	Dirck Pennybacker.	Conrad Weiser.
Charles Gobin.	Jacob Rickstein.	Henry Weaver.
Jacob Graul.	George Riehm.	Matthias Wick.
Thomas Herbert.	Ferdinand Ritter.	George Will.
Joseph Hiester.	John Robinson.	Peter Withington.
Jacob Hill.	Jacob Rothermel.	James Wilson.
Jonathan Jones.	Nicholas Scheffer.	Michael Wolf.

Names of Colonels.

Mark Bird.	Joseph Hiester.	George Nagel.
Daniel Brodhead.	Daniel Hunter.	John Patton.
Valentine Eckert.	Michael Lindemuth.	Henry Spyker.
Samuel Ely.	Nicholas Lotz.	Daniel Udree.
Balser Gechr.	Jacob Morgan.	
Henry Haller.	Jacob Morgan, Jr.	

CHAPTER IX.

ARMY SUPPLIES FROM THE COUNTY.

During the Revolution, many army supplies were either manufactured or produced in the County of Berks, more especially in the years 1775, 1776 and 1777; and these were collected from the several townships and deposited at Reading, for the purpose of enabling the Commissioners of Forage to fill the proportional allotments of the district with reasonable dispatch. They consisted of grain, flour, hay, powder, clothing, accoutrements, horses and wagons.

The superior geographical situation of Reading led Congress to select the place as a general depot for storing supplies of all kinds. It was far enough from Philadelphia so that Gen'l Howe could not entertain any thoughts of capturing the stores with safety to his army, and yet it was near enough to enable the storekeeper to promptly fill orders made upon him.

Store House at Reading.—In a letter of Col. Morgan to the Executive Council, dated September 18, 1777, besides acknowledging receipt of an order for calling out the 3rd and 4th Classes of Militia, he stated as follows:

"There is at present a great quantity of powder and other stores belonging to the States in this town [Reading] and there are two companies now out of said classes mounting guard over said stores. The people of the town are vastly uneasy at having so much powder here, and, unless it be very well guarded, that uneasiness will increase to a great degree, as fire happening to the house where the powder is lodged would tear the town to pieces and destroy the whole body of inhabitants. Many persons of the town, above 53 years of age, would make part of a guard if taken into pay, which would render it easy to send so many more of the militia as would otherwise be requisite for such guard. The Continental Press and Medicinal store also require some guard."

By a letter of the same day from Christ and Shoemaker [Justices] to the Council it would appear that they had called two companies of militia to guard the said stores—"not forgetting the Continental Treasurer." The stores included a "vast number of ammunition in the town, or near it." The companies had been in actual service for over three weeks.

Supplies Manufactured.

The following items were found relating to the supplies that were manufactured in Berks County, and forwarded in pursuance of orders given by the Executive Council:

John Mears, of Berks County, carried on the manufacture of saltpetre. On Feb. 9, 1776, James Biddle was directed to supply him with £100 for that purpose, taking good security for the money and providing for the delivery of saltpetre to that amount in twelve months. Mears lived at Reading and subsequently became a captain in the 4th Regiment of the Continental Line of Pennsylvania.

Feb. 22, 1776.—An order for £90 was drawn to pay John Reithmyer, John Deisler and Peter Brecht for 150 cartridge boxes, etc., which they manufactured in Berks County and supplied to the Committee. And on May 8th, an order for £108, 15sh., was drawn to them to pay for 150 more.

Isaac Levan, Jr., was one of the persons appointed by the Committee of Berks County to purchase arms for the use of the province, and on April 9, 1776, an order for £19, 12sh., was drawn in favor of Dr. Jonathan Potts for repairing 9 muskets which belonged to the province. These muskets were ordered to be delivered to Capt. Thomas Herbert, of Berks County, who was then in the service of the province. He lived at Reading.

May 18, 1776.—Mark Bird addressed a letter to the Committee of Safety, of Philadelphia, in which he made mention of muskets, &c., as follows:

"If the Committee of Safety will send me the price of 100 muskets and accoutrements, with orders on the Commissioners to deliver to me such as they have ready, or my paying what they cost, I am of opinion in two weeks after the receipt of their orders and cash, I shall be able to deliver in Philadelphia the number mentioned. If each county will do the same, all the troops now in pay of the Continent and this Province may be armed in three weeks from this date—I mean the Continental troops in the barracks at Philadelphia. * * * * I am convinced you may collect in the different counties a thousand muskets, but few accoutrements. If you send the cash to the different counties to some person you can confide in, the arms will be ready immediately, but till you send the cash to pay the smiths they will deny giving up the muskets. They like to see the cash without having the trouble of going so far as Philadelphia for it."

This offer was accepted by the Executive Council and an order to him for £400 was drawn. And in August, 1776, the Committee of Safety also drew an order in favor of Samuel High, (a county commissioner,) for £600, on account of arms making in the county.

Gun manufacturing was carried on along the Wyomissing Creek in Cumru township, beyond Mohnsville, about seven miles south-west from Reading. There were many gunsmiths in the county, prominent among them being Balser Geehr.

July 2, 1776.—An order for £300 was drawn in favor of George Ege for 100 tons of cannon balls.

July 8, 1776.—Council passed the following resolution:

"That the Iron Masters employed in casting cannon or shot for the public service in the counties of Chester, Lancaster and Berks, be permitted to employ any of the soldiers, prisoners of war at Lancaster and Reading, as laborers in the said business, giving an account to the Committees of Lancaster and Reading of the time of such soldiers as they shall so employ."

This permission was given in view of the public exigency which required additional artillery and war materials to repel the invasion of the country by the army of Gen'l Howe, who had recently appeared at New York with the British fleet.

July 22, 1776.—An order was drawn in favor of Michael Bright, (a county commissioner,) for £600 to pay for firelocks made in Berks County for the Province.

May 16, 1777.—Col. Morgan reported that orders had been issued for collecting the allotted number of blankets in the county for the Continental service, and also 300 for the county militia. He made inquiry about arms and found that about 150 with accoutrements could be procured at Reading, which might be made fit for service in a fortnight; as to drums, colors and fifes none had yet been collected. He then made an estimate that $3200 would be necessary to purchase blankets and carry the militia law in execution, and asked that this amount be remitted to him immediately.

May 22, 1777.—An order was drawn to Col. Jacob Morgan for £600 for blankets and paying substitutes in the county. On June 10th, another order was drawn to him for £500, and at same time an order for 150 stand of arms and 1500 flints; and on the 12th, an order was drawn to him for 150 knapsacks and cartridge boxes, and 250 canteens, for the county militia.

Feb. 19, 1778.—A report was made to the Executive Council that Col. Mark Bird had sent by water to Philadelphia 1000 barrels of flour during some time previous.

Nov. 14, 1780.—George Ege, then lessee of Berkshire Furnace, supplied the National Government with shot and shell, amounting to £2894. An account was opened in his books against the "United States."

Shot: 843, 24-pd.; 2137, 18-pd.; 289, 12-pd.
Shell: 867, 10-in.; 714, 8-in.

SUPPLIES COLLECTED.

And the following items were found, relating to supplies collected in the county:

Sept. 26, 1775.—The Council of Safety directed an order to be drawn in favor of the Commissioners of Berks County for £400 towards paying for the arms and accoutrements supplied.

Dec. 1775.—The Council of Safety ordered all the arms belonging to the province, found in Berks County, to be collected for the people and forwarded to Philadelphia as fast as collected.

Aug. 22, 1776.—Order from Council of Safety to Mark Bird for £107, 2sh., 6d., for arms taken from Non-Associators for the use of his battalion.

Dec. 6, 1776.—Col. Balser Geehr was paid £11, 7sh., 4d. for repairing arms and £85, 8sh. for arms taken from Non-Associators; and at the same time Col. Sebastian Levan was also paid £88, 2sh., 6d. for arms taken from Non-Associators.

Dec. 11, 1776.—James Old was paid £2000 and John Patton £350 on account of cannon shot which they cast for the State. Old lived in Chester County, but Patton in Berks County.

Dec. 19, 1776.—Three accounts were ordered to be paid for arms taken from Non-Associators in Berks County, amounting to £131 and charged to the 6th Battalion of Militia commanded by Col. Daniel Hunter.

In 1777, the proportion of grain for horse feed from Berks County was 4000 bushels.

June 14, 1777.—Morgan was directed to supply the State with 30 wagons as quota from the county.

Sept. 8, 1777.—Council ordered 100 wagons to be sent to Philadelphia from Berks County to assist in removing stores of different kinds, and the property belonging to the families of poor militiamen, in anticipation of Gen'l Howe's invasion of Philadelphia.

In Nov., 1777, in pursuance of orders received, 350 wagons were sent from Berks County to Philadelphia; also, a wagon master-general and wagon masters. When they reached Philadelphia, the enemy had left, and the wagons got nothing. Twenty were taken into service. The men returned and demanded pay. Henry Christ, Jacob Shoemaker and John Ludwig requested the Executive Council to forward money for this purpose. The sum required was between £2500 and £3000.

Council, in writing to Gen'l Potter on Nov. 7, 1777, from Lancaster, as to a supply of muskets from the several counties, stated: "Berks, we dare say, will not be behind. Col. Morgan has been successful heretofore. Bucks and the two other older counties, [meaning Philadelphia and Chester] are less under notice here."

Jan. 15, 1778.—Congress ordered 8000 barrels of flour to be deposited at or near Reading.

Jan. 30, 1778.—The county was ordered to furnish 50 wagons for immediate service of the army as her quota of 280 wagons.

In 1778, the supplies at Reading were large and valuable; and then Congress requested the State to station 200 militia at this point to defend the magazines of military stores, and keep communications secure from sudden incursion of the enemy. The Executive Council made such an order.

Feb. 10, 1778.—Col. Lutterloh reported to Gen'l Washington that he found a considerable quantity of clothing collected at Reading, waiting for an order to be sent forward.

Feb. 18, 1778.—Berks County was ordered to furnish a quota of 32 wagons.

Feb. 20, 1778.—Ordered that the sum of £24,000 be sent by Col. Jacob Morgan to Valentine Eckert and John Lesher for purchasing supplies; also an order to the treasurer for £150 for recruiting, etc.

Feb. 20, 1778.—Col. Joseph Cowperthwaite, of Lancaster, was appointed storekeeper at Reading. He had been colonel of the 5th Battalion of Pennsylvania troops for a time.

May 18, 1778.—The quota of tax levied from Berks County for the year 1778, for the purposes of war, was £16,544.

By the correspondence of James Young, the Wagon-Master-General of Pennsylvania, it appears that he was stationed at Reading from February to May in 1778. In March, he reported the wagons of the county as constantly employed in carrying flour and forage to the Schuylkill, and thence the articles were transported by water, because then the roads were almost impassable with loaded wagons. Col. Lutterloh, the Quarter-Master-General of Washington's Army, was stationed at Reading with Mr. Young during March, and was ill for a time.

Sep. 27, 1778.—A quota of 110 wagons was ordered from Berks County to carry provisions from Philadelphia to New Windsor without delay.

June 11, 1779.—A warrant was issued to the Wagon Master of Berks County to supply 60 wagons; and on October 16, following, 30 wagons.

In June 1779, Col. Jacob Morgan, Jr., addressed a letter to the Executive Council in which he stated that he had sent into service 36 good Continental teams and 54 spare horses; also a brigade of 12 teams properly equipped. And prompted by a hopeful, enthusiastic spirit, he concluded the letter by adding: "There shall not be an idle horse in the county that is fit for the service. I made myself so bare that I put all the public riding horses into teams and one of my own. I am determined that neither man nor horse that is in the public service shall eat idle bread in this county. I think we should now exert ourselves, as I am in hopes this will be the last campaign."

July 13, 1779.—Col. Jacob Morgan, Jr., was required to purchase and forward immediately to Philadelphia 500 barrels of flour for the use of the officers of the Continental Line.

In April, 1780, the Executive Council was directed by Gen'l Washington to furnish the State out of the supplies at Reading, with the following articles: 200 barrels of flour; 560 gallons of rum; 180 tons of hay; and 14,000 bushels of corn.

Col. Nicholas Lotz, as commissioner of forage, reported on June 5, 1780, that he had purchased 40 tons of flour, 172 bushels of oats and 19 bags; and on June 19th, he reported the purchase of 10 head of cattle and 40 sheep, which he was obliged to take under the law. Cattle and sheep he reported to be scarce, because many butchers and drovers had come from Philadelphia and other places and bought them up. On June 21st, an order for £1000 was drawn in his favor for expenses in purchasing cattle for the use of the army; and on the same day a demand was made for 40 wagons from Berks County.

The quota of articles, etc., from Berks County to the State in July, 1780, was—600 barrels of flour per month; 600 bushels of forage per month; 20 wagons and 200 horses; and 300 militia: and there having been a great want of teams in the army then, a requisition was made on the county to furnish 20 wagons.

It was reported to Council on Aug. 12, 1780, that Col. John Patton, by agreement with Capt. Joy, agreed to supply the Board of War with 90 tons of shell and shot; for which purpose he put his Berkshire Furnace in blast. He was then at work; but how long he would continue he could not tell because his workmen were not exempted from military duty. Then they were ordered out, and unless they were released he could not keep his works going. He had some Hessian prisoners employed. These were demanded from him; and if they were not returned, his bond was to be put into suit.

June 22, 1787.—The Executive Council ordered Nicholas Sweyer to be paid £48, 10sh. for transporting military stores from Oley Furnace in Berks County to Philadelphia in 1781, pursuant to a resolution of the Assembly, September 20, 1781.

Sept. 16, 1789.—Conrad Riehl was paid £9, 10sh. for 16 days' service in collecting and conducting a brigade of wagons to Reading for public service in November, 1781, by order of the Wagon Master-General.

By the foregoing orders and returns of supplies collected, it appears that the county furnished 512 wagons and 48 teams. Each wagon had a team of six horses, and was in charge of two men. Accordingly, there were also at least 1100 men from the county in this important branch of service in the Revolution.

SUPPLIES TAKEN IN OLEY IN 1778.

John Lesher, a prominent iron master of Oley, addressed a letter to the Executive Council on January 9, 1778, in reference to supplies for the army that were forcibly taken from him, and, in order to present the general situation that then existed throughout the county as to inconvenience and loss sustained by the people, it is introduced in this connection:

"I conceive it to be my duty to acquaint you that I am no more master of any individual thing I possess, for, besides the damages I have heretofore sustained by a number of troops and Continental wagons in taking from me 8 tons of hay, destroyed apples sufficient for 10 hhds. of cider, eating up my pasture, burning my fences, etc., and 2 beeves I was obliged to buy at 1sh. per pound to answer their immediate want of provisions, and at several other times since I have supplied detachments from the army with provisions. There has lately been taken from me 14 head of cattle and 4 swine, the cattle at a very low estimate to my infinite damage, as they were all the beef I had for my workmen for carrying on my iron works. I had rather delivered the beef and reserved the hides, tallow, etc., but no argument would prevail, all must be delivered to a number of armed men at the point of the bayonet. As my family, which I am necessitated to maintain, consists of near 30 persons, not reckoning colliers, wood cutters and other day laborers, my provisions and forage being taken from me, my forge must stand idle, my furnace (which I am about carrying on) must of consequence be dropt, which will be a loss to the public as well as myself, as there is so great a call for iron at present for public use, and some forges and furnaces must of necessity fail for want of wood and ore.

"The case in this neighborhood is truly alarming, when the strongest exertions of economy and frugality ought to be practiced by all ranks of men, thereby the better to enable us to repel the designs of a daring Enemy who are now in our Land. It strikes me with horror to see a number of our own Officers and Soldiers wantonly waste and destroy the good people's properties; by such conduct they destroy the cause they seek to maintain. Instead of judicious men appointed in every township, or as the case may require, to proportion the demands equal according to the circumstances of every farmer and the general benefit of the whole, these men, under the shadow of the bayonet and the appellation Tory, act as they please, our wheat, rye, oats and hay taken away at discretion and shamefully wasted and our cattle destroyed. I know some farmers who have not a bushel of oats left for seed, nor beef sufficient for their own consumption, while some others lose nothing—as a man who has 100 head of Cattle lost not one. Such proceedings I think to be very partial. Many farmers are so much discouraged by such conduct that I have heard several say they would neither plow nor sow if this takes place. The consequence may be easily foreseen, unless some speedy and effectual method be taken to put a stop to such irregular proceedings, and encouragement and protection extended to the good people of this Commonwealth. I shudder at the consequence. I humbly submit the whole to your serious consideration."

MASTS FOR THE U. S. NAVY.

During August, 1780, Captain Dennis Leary was engaged on the land of James Wilson, Esq., along the river Schuylkill, some thirty miles north of Reading, superintending the cutting of masts for the Navy of the United States, where workmen were employed in that business, but he and the men were hindered by depredations of the savages. He informed Council "that masts suitable not only for our ships but for those of our illustrious Ally may be cut in that quarter; that, in fact, a number of very fine masts are cut, ready to be hauled to the river, and that many more may be procured if protection should be afforded to the workmen." A company of 50 or 60 men was asked for this purpose.

RECEIPT BOOK OF COL. LOTZ.

In 1893, I saw the receipt book of Col. Nicholas Lotz in which receipts were taken for moneys paid from August 12, 1780, to December 5, 1781. The total amount was $202,033. Some of the items were reckoned in pounds, shillings and pence, but the most of them were in dollars. In this we have undoubted evidence that the county performed her whole duty in the struggle. A great part of the amount was paid in currency, which was never redeemed, whereby he and others suffered great losses.

PROMINENT INDUSTRIES.

Twelve prominent iron industries were carried on successfully in the county during the Revolution. They were situated in the four sections of the county, along strong streams of water, as follows:

Furnaces.

Oley, in Oley, on Manatawny Creek.
Mt. Pleasant, in Colebrookdale, on West Branch of Perkiomen.
Hopewell, in Union, on French Creek.
Berkshire, in Heidelberg, on tributary of Tulpehocken Creek.
Reading Furnace is frequently taken as of Berks County, but it was situated in Chester County not far from the Berks County line.

Forges.

Pine, Spring and Oley in Douglass, District, and Oley, on Manatawny Creek.
Mt. Pleasant, in Colebrookdale, on West Branch.
Bird's, in Robeson, on Hay Creek.
Gibraltar, in Robeson, on Allegheny Creek.
Moselem, in Richmond, on Ontelaunee Creek.
Charming, in Tulpehocken, on Tulpehocken Creek.

Iron Masters.—The iron masters, who were the proprietors of the foregoing industries, were Mark Bird, John Patton, John Lesher, David Potts, John Old, Daniel Udree, George Ege and Christian Lower. The assessed value of the property of these men in the different sections of the county amounted to a very large sum in the aggregate, showing that they were in a situation to contribute a strong influence towards the successful prosecution of the war for the Revolution. They supplied the Continental Government with cannon balls, cast iron and wrought iron in various shapes, and they co-operated heartily in the great social movement for representative government. Their assistance was of the greatest consequence and cannot be overestimated. We can take great pride in the fact that the county then possessed such enterprising, public-spirited and patriotic men.

Other Industries.—There were other industries that are equally worthy of mention, such as numerous grist mills, saw mills, gun factories, wheelwright shops and blacksmith shops. These were also situated along the strong streams in different sections of the county and rendered great assistance to Congress and the Council. Nicholas Lotz, Sebastian Levan and Daniel Brodhead were three extensive millers, and Valentine Eckert and Christian Lower were two influential blacksmiths, who identified themselves prominently in the public affairs that related to the Revolution. Knapsacks and gun barrels were made in different parts of the county. And numerous energetic, hopeful and persistent farmers constituted the very foundation of the public welfare.

PRICES DURING THE REVOLUTION.

Prices in October, 1776.

Linen, per yd............12sh.	Wood, per cord.............£2
Shoes, per pr.............15 "	Meat, per lb..............10d.
Salt, per bu..............25 "	The prices of articles generally were two and three times what they were before 1775.
Pork, per quarter........13 "	
Butter, per lb............ 2 "	

In 1777.

Prices in October, 1777, as fixed by the Commissary General :

Wheat, per bu........8sh., 6d.	Pork, per 100 lb......$7 and $8
Rye " ....8sh., 6d.	Whiskey, per gall ....8sh., 6d.
Indian Corn, per bu...6sh., 6d.	Hay, per ton. 1st crop, £7, 10sh.
Beef, per 100 lb............$10	" " 2nd " £6

Other Prices.

Salt, per bu........£10 and £15	Potatoes, per bu ....16sh.
Cord Wood, per cord.....65sh.	Chickens, apiece..........10sh.

When the Committee was appointed on November 8, 1777, to collect clothing, arms, etc., the articles taken were to be appraised as follows :

New single blanket...£3.
    In proportion for inferior kinds.
Strong, large, well-made shoes, per pr......................25sh.
Good yarn stockings, per pr........   ....22sh., 6d.
Good well-manufactured cloth, ¾ yd. wide, per yd ....30sh.
Good linsey woolsey, 1 yd. wide, per yd....................15sh.
Good linen for soldiers' shirts, 1 yd. wide, per yd...... ....15sh.
Good tow linen, per yd..8sh.

The Committeemen were allowed 20sh. per day for every day employed in performing their duty.

In 1780.

Col. Nicholas Lotz, as Commissioner of Purchases for Berks County, addressed a letter to the Executive Council, dated at Reading, June 5, 1780, in which the prices of certain articles at that time appear. They were as follows:

Corn, per bu	5sh., 6d.	Flour, per cwt	30sh.
Oats, "	3sh., 9d.	Hay, per ton	80sh.
Buckwheat, per bu	4sh.		

He assured the people that the merchants would take the new money at the same rate as specie; and that the money would be received in taxes at *one for forty of the present currency.* He offered for hauling 2sh. per ton per mile; 5sh. for each bag, and 3sh. for each cask; which were the lowest prices payable in gold or silver.

PAY OF MEN IN SERVICE.

The estimated strength of a regiment in the Continental service in 1776, and the pay of the officers and men, according to a resolution of Congress in October, 1776, were as follows:

	Pay.	Rations.		Pay.	Rations.
Colonel	$75	6	Adjutant	40	3
Lt.-Col	60	5	Q. Master	27½	2
Major	50	4	Surgeon	33	3
Captain	40	3	Surgeon Mate	18	2
1st Lieut	27	2	Sergt. Major	9	1
2nd Lieut	27	2	Drum Major	9	1
Ensign	20	2	Fife Major	9	
Regt. Q. M	40	3	Q. M. Sergt	9	
Chaplain	33⅓	2			

Each company was required to have, in addition to the officers enumerated, 4 sergeants, 4 corporals, 1 drummer, 1 fifer and 76 privates.

The allowance for each private was $1 per week, and for each commissioned officer on recruiting service $2⅔. Lieutenants of county, $12 per diem; Sub-Lieutenants, $10.

Each company consisted of 90 men, including officers, and each regiment of eight companies, altogether numbering 733 men.

CONTINENTAL PAPER MONEY.

During the progress of the Revolution, the Government of the United States was compelled to resort to the emission of "bills of credit" with which to purchase army supplies, etc., and to satisfy the demands of carrying on the war. Gold and silver were not then known to exist in the country in any quantity equal to the demands of the war, nor could they be procured. Direct taxation, though practicable, was deemed impolitic. The only plausible expedient in the power of Congress was the emission of bills of credit, which were to represent specie under a public engagement of redemption through taxation, or of exchange for gold or silver. This practice had been familiar from the first settlement of the colonies; and, under proper restrictions, it had been found highly advantageous. Congress, therefore, resolved, in June, 1775, to emit such bills to the amount of two millions of dollars; in July, ordered a million more, and in November, three millions more; and for their redemption, Congress pledged the Confederated Colonies. Subsequently other emissions were made; and such was the animation of the times, that these several emissions, amounting to twenty millions, circulated for some time without any depreciation, and commanded the resources of the country for public service equally with gold or silver. For a considerable time the Government derived much benefit from this paper creation of their own, though it was without any established funds for its support or redemption. Whilst the ministry of England were puzzling themselves for new taxes and funds on which to raise supplies, Congress raised theirs by resolutions, directing paper of no intrinsic value to be struck off in the form of promissory notes. But there was a point both in time and quantity beyond which this process ceased to operate; that time was about eighteen months from the date of first emission and that quantity twenty millions. The rulers thought it still premature to urge taxation, and they, therefore, resorted to the expedient of further emissions. The ease with which the means of procuring supplies were furnished by simply striking off bills of credit and the readiness with which the people received them, prompted Congress to multiply them beyond the limits of prudence, and a depreciation of their value was the unavoidable consequence.

At first, this depreciation was scarcely perceptible, but it increased daily, till finally the currency became worthless. It began at different periods in different States; but in general about the middle of the year 1777, and then increased progressively for several years. In the latter part of 1777 it was two dollars in currency for one in specie; in 1778, five for one; in 1779, twenty-seven for one; in 1780, fifty for one. After 1780, the circulation was limited to certain localities; but where the currency passed, it depreciated to one hundred and fifty dollars for one. In Pennsylvania, the Executive Council resolved, as late as February 1, 1781, that Continental money should be received for public dues at the exchange of seventy-five dollars in currency for one in specie. But an Act provided that after June 1st, following, only specie or equivalent bills of credit should be received for taxes or other public dues; and this rendered the currency worthless in the State. This extraordinary depreciation brought great loss to many of the people who had aided the Government in the grand struggle for freedom. In this respect the soldiers suffered most. The people of Reading, and especially of the county, met with considerable losses thereby. Some of them had large quantities which were transmitted for some time until lost or destroyed. It was not redeemed.

In the issue of this paper money, certain prominent men were selected from the different sections of the several colonies for the purpose of signing the issues. James Read, of Reading, was selected to sign the Continental notes; and on April 7, 1781, John Patton, of Heidelberg, was selected to sign the issue of the Pennsylvania currency for £500,000.

Col. Henry Haller, of Reading, was selected by the Executive Council, on June 14, 1779, to solicit subscriptions in Berks County for the loan of twenty million dollars by Congress.

CHAPTER X.

PROCLAMATIONS FOR THE FAVOR OF GOD.

During the Revolution, proclamations were recommended by Congress, requesting the people to pray for the favor of God, and to co-operate for success in the cause of free government. These public expressions indicate the high degree of religious faith which existed during that period. They are worthy of great praise and admiration. The composition, arrangement of ideas and selection of words are superb. Studying them carefully, I am led to say that the existence of this spirit amongst the people, especially as influenced and encouraged by men in political power, was a factor whose importance cannot be fully measured at this time. Without it, I question whether the movement of the disconnected colonies, scattered so far from one another, with little preparation for such a hazardous undertaking against a well-organized and powerful nation, could have been successful; but with it, the people generally were inspired with hope, confidence, perseverance, determination and courage, elements that were highly necessary in warfare, and these led them onward through the most adverse circumstances to victory.

First Recommendation for Prayer.—The first recommendation for this purpose was made by Congress on December 11, 1776, in the words following :

"*Whereas*, The just war into which the United States of America have been forced by Great Britain is likely to be still continued by the same violence and injustice which have hitherto animated the enemies of American freedom.

"*And Whereas*, It becomes all public bodies, as well as private persons, to reverence the Providence of God and look up to Him as the Supreme Disposer of all events, and the Arbiter of the Fate of Nations; therefore the Congress hereby *Resolve*—

"That it be recommended to all the States, as soon as possible, to appoint a day of solemn fasting and humiliation, to implore of Almighty God the forgiveness of the many sins prevailing among all ranks, and to beg the countenance and assistance of His Providence in the prosecution of this just and necessary War. The Congress do also, in the most earnest manner, recommend to all the members of the United States, and particularly to the Officers, Civil and Military, under them, the exercise of repentance and reformation; and further do require of the said officers of the Military Department the strict observation of the Articles of War in general, and particularly that of the said Article which forbids profane swearing and all other immoralities, of which all such officers are desired to take notice. It is left to each State to issue Proclamations, fixing the day that appears the most proper for their several bounds."

In pursuance of this Recommendation, the Supreme Executive Council of Pennsylvania appointed Thursday, the 3rd day of April, 1777, for the said purpose, and issued a Proclamation accordingly on March 7, 1777. An order was made that it be published in all the newspapers, English and German, and that 500 copies be printed, (300 in English and 200 in German) and forwarded by the earliest opportunity to the distant parts of the State.

Appeal for Support in Warfare.—When intelligence was received that the British were moving towards Philadelphia in September, 1777, the Executive Council issued the following earnest appeal to the people and caused it to be published:

A Proclamation.

"The time is at length come in which the fate of ourselves, our wives, children and property must be speedily determined. Gen'l Howe, at the head of a British Army, the only hope and last resource of our enemies, has invaded this State, dismissing his ships and disencumbering himself of his heavy artillery and baggage, he appears to have risked all upon the event of a movement which must either deliver up to plunder and devastation this Capitol of Pennsylvania and of America, or forever blast the cruel designs of our implacable foes.

"Blessed be God, Providence seems to have left it to ourselves to determine whether we shall triumph in victory and rest in freedom and peace, or, by tamely submitting or weakly resisting, deliver ourselves up a prey to an enemy, than whom none more cruel and perfidious was ever suffered to vex and destroy any people.

"View then, on the one hand, the freedom and independence, the glory and happiness of our rising States, which are set before us as the reward of our courage. Seriously consider on the other hand the wanton ravages, the rapes and butcheries which have been perpetrated by these men in the State of New Jersey, and on the frontiers of New York. Above all, consider the mournful prospect of seeing Americans like the wretched inhabitants of India stripped of their freedom, robbed of their property, degraded beneath the brutes and left to starve amid plenty, at the will of their lordly masters, and let us determine once for all that we will *Die or Be Free.*

"The foe are manifestly aiming either by force to conquer, or by stratagem and stolen marches to elude the vigilance of our brave commander, and declining a battle with our countrymen they have attempted to steal upon us by surprise. They have been hitherto defeated, but numbers are absolutely necessary to watch them on every quarter at once. The neighboring States are hurrying forward their militia, and we hope by rising as one man, and besetting the foe at a distance from his fleet, we shall speedily enclose him like a lion in his toils.

"The Council therefore most humbly beseech and entreat all persons whatsoever to exert themselves without delay to seize this present opportunity of crushing the foe now in the bowels of our Country, by marching forth instantly under their respective officers to the assistance of our great General, that he may be enabled to environ and demolish the only British Army that remains formidable in America or in the World. Animated with the hope that Heaven—as before it has done in all times of difficulty and danger—will again crown our righteous efforts with success, we look forward to the prospect of seeing our insulting foe cut off from all means of escape, and, by the goodness of the Almighty, the Lord of Hosts, and God of Battles, wholly delivered into our hands."

On the same day, the 5th and 6th classes of Philadelphia were ordered out; the next day, every able-bodied man of Bucks County was ordered to turn out with his arms, &c., and "those who had no arms were to take with them axes, spades and every other kind of intrenching tools;" and on the 12th of September, the 3rd and 4th classes of Berks and Northampton, the 3rd of York, the 4th of Chester and the 2nd of Northumberland.

Proclamations for fasting, praise and thanksgiving were issued in the Spring and Fall of each succeeding year from 1777 to 1783 by Council, in pursuance of special recommendations of Congress; also for victory over Cornwallis in 1781, and for peace in 1783.

I have not found any written or printed evidence that these proclamations were generally observed; but an intimate association with many people in all the districts of Berks County in their homes and churches for thirty years, a study of their manners, customs and religious convictions as transmitted almost unchanged from generation to generation for over a hundred years, and extensive researches into the social and moral history of their ancestors have made me sufficiently acquainted to express the opinion that such appeals during the dark days of the Revolution were thoroughly appreciated by them.

CHAPTER XI.

COUNTY INCUMBENTS OF POSITIONS.

The following men from Berks County occupied the positions named, for the time stated, during the Revolution:

National.

Delegate in Continental Congress.—Edward Biddle, 1774-5; 1775-6; 1778-9.

Secretary of Board of War.—Edward Scull, May 16, 1778.

Surgeons.—Dr. Jonathan Potts, Dr. Bodo Otto.

Surveying Department.—William Scull, Jan., 1778 to Sept., 1779.

Deputy Quarter-Master General.—Jacob Morgan, Jr., Apr., 1778 to 1783.

State.

Delegates to Provincial Conference.—June 18, 1776.—Jacob Morgan, Henry Haller, Mark Bird, Bodo Otto, Benjamin Spyker, Daniel Hunter, Valentine Eckert, Nicholas Lotz, Joseph Hiester, Charles Shoemaker.

Delegates to Constitutional Convention.—July 15, 1776.—Jacob Morgan, Gabriel Hiester, John Lesher, Benjamin Spyker, Daniel Hunter, Valentine Eckert, Charles Shoemaker, Thomas Jones, Jr.

Members of Assembly.—Edward Biddle, 1774, '75, '78; Henry Christ, 1774, '75; Henry Haller, 1776; John Lesher, 1776; James Read, 1777; Benjamin Spyker, 1777; Sebastian Levan, 1777, '78, '79; Daniel Hunter, 1777, '78, '81; Balser Geehr, 1777, '80, '81; Jonathan Potts, 1778; Mark Bird, 1778, '80; Gabriel Hiester, 1778, '79, '81; Valentine Eckert, 1779; Christian Lower, 1779, '82, '83; George Ege, 1779, '80, '82; Jonathan Jones, 1779; John Patton, 1780, '82; Thomas Mifflin, 1780; Joseph Hiester, 1780, '81; Benjamin Weiser, 1781; John Bishop, 1781; Daniel Clymer, 1782, '83; Abraham Lincoln, 1782, '83; Nicholas Lotz, 1782, '83; John Ludwig, 1782; John Rice, 1783.

Edward Biddle was Speaker of the Assembly for the year 1774-5.

The representation of the county was as follows: Two for the years 1774 and 1775, and six for the remaining years.

The foregoing Representatives were elected the several years named for the term of one year.

Executive Councillors.—Richard Tea, (Iron master of Hereford township) was a Councillor for a time. He was elected in 1776, and served until April, 1777, when he resigned.

Jacob Morgan, Jr., was qualified on Sept. 3, 1777. He resigned April 4, 1778, upon accepting the appointment of D. Q. M. General. On May 25, 1778, an order was drawn to him for £301, 5sh., for attending Council 180 days, including mileage.

James Read succeeded him, and was qualified on June 30, 1778. On Dec. 1, 1778, he received one vote for President of the Executive Council. He resigned June 4, 1781, and on the 5th, was elected Register of the Court of Admiralty of Pennsylvania.

Sebastian Levan, of Maxatawny, was also a Councillor, and officiated from Oct. 31, 1781, to Oct. 15, 1784.

Wagon Master General.—Henry Haller, June, 1779, to Aug. 14, 1780. Jacob Morgan, Jr., Aug. 14, 1780, to 1783.

Superintendent of Commissioners of Purchases.—Jacob Morgan, Jr., Aug. 14, 1780, to 1783.

Register of Court of Admiralty.—James Read, June 5, 1781.

Prothonotary of Supreme Court.—Edward Burd, Esq., appointed Aug. 12, 1778. He continued until Jan. 26, 1786, when he was re-appointed.

County.

Committee on Correspondence.—July 2, 1774.—Edward Biddle, James Read, Daniel Brodhead, Henry Christ, Christopher Schultz, Thomas Dundas, Jonathan Potts.

Committee on Observation.—December 5, 1774.—Edward Biddle, Christopher Schultz, Jonathan Potts, William Reeser, Balser Geehr, Michael Bright, John Patton, Mark Bird, John Jones, John Old, Sebastian Levan, George Nagel, Christopher Witman, Jacob Shoemaker, James Lewis.

Colonels of Associated Battalions.—1775.—Edward Biddle, Mark Bird, Daniel Brodhead, Balser Geehr, Christian Lower.

Standing Committee.—1775.—Edward Biddle, Mark Bird, Jonathan Potts, Daniel Brodhead, Balser Geehr, Collinson Read, Sec., Valentine Eckert, Nicholas Lotz, Chairman, Sebastian Levan, Richard Tea.

Lieutenants of County.—Jacob Morgan, June 9, 1777, to 1780; Valentine Eckert, Jan. 8, 1781, to 1783.

Sub-Lieutenants.—Henry Shoemaker, Christian Lower, Jr., Valentine Eckert, Daniel Udree, Jacob Sweyer, John Mears.

Paymasters of County Militia.—Daniel Hunter, 1776 to Aug. 25, 1777; Henry Spyker, Aug. 26, 1777, to 1783.

Superintendent of Purchases.—John Patton, 1778.

Commissioners of Forage.—Valentine Eckert, 1778; John Lesher, 1778; Nicholas Lotz, 1780 to 1783.

In Oct., 1779, Col. Michael Lindemuth was appointed Commissioner to purchase flour for the French fleet.

Collectors of Excise.—John Biddle, 1774; Daniel Levan, 1779–80; John Witman, 1780–81; Conrad Foos, 1782, 1783.

Waggon Master.—Henry Haller, 1778 to 1783.

Quarter-Master.—Jacob Morgan, Jr., 1778.

Storekeeper at Reading.—Joseph Cowperthwaite, 1778.

Local Committees.—Owing to the aid given by divers inhabitants to the enemy, the Council in Sept., 1777, appointed committees to dispose of the property of such offenders and make return of their proceedings under oath. The following committee was appointed for Berks County: Thomas Parry, David Morgan, Peter Nagel, Henry Haller, Daniel Udree, Henry Spyker and Joseph Hiester.

This committee appointed two persons in each district to make provision for distressed families whose husbands and fathers were in service. The appointees for Reading were Henry Hahn and Peter Feather.

On Nov. 8, the Council also appointed committees to collect arms, clothing, etc., from the inhabitants who did not take the oath of allegiance, or who aided the enemy, and to deliver them to the clothier-general. The committee in Berks County was—Henry Christ, Henry Haller, Thomas Parry, Daniel Udree, Philip Miller, Nathan Lewis, John Lower, Godfrey Riehm, Jacob Seltzer and Nicholas Scheffer.

Committee on Attainder and Vesting Forfeited Estates.—1778—Henry Haller, Thomas Parry, David Morgan.

Auditing Committee.—Francis Richardson, Reynold Keene, Collinson Read, James Biddle and Henry Haller were appointed January 23, 1777, commissioners for the county, to audit and settle the accounts for arms and accoutrements purchased, the property of persons lost in actual service, and of those who were killed, died in service, or were made prisoners.

Judges.—Peter Spyker, 1775-83; George Douglass, 1775-83; Balser Geehr, 1775-83; John Patton, 1775-77; Jacob Morgan, 1775-77; Mark Bird, 1775-76; Jonathan Potts, 1776-77; Daniel Levan, 1777; Sebastian Zimmerman, 1778-83; William Reeser, 1778-83.

Peter Spyker was appointed President Judge of all the Courts on November 18, 1780.

Justices of the Peace.—1777—Henry Christ, Reading; Jacob Shoemaker, Windsor; James Read, Reading; Daniel Hiester, Heidelberg; Peter Spyker, Tulpehocken; Jacob Weaver, John Old, Amity; John Ludwig, Exeter; Benj. Shott; Christopher Schultz, Hereford; Samuel Ely, Richmond; Jacob Wagoner, Bern; Daniel Rothermel, Maidencreek; Charles Shoemaker, Windsor; Egedius Meyer; Jacob Morgan, Caernarvon; Thomas Parry, Union. 1778—Benjamin Weiser, Heidelberg; Michael Lindemuth, Bern; Gabriel Hiester, Bern. 1780—John Guldin, Oley.

County Commissioners.—Samuel Hoch, 1775-76; Michael Bright, 1775-77; Abraham Lincoln, 1775-78; Christian Lower, 1777-79; John Kerlin, 1778-80; Adam Witman, 1779-81; Thomas Jones, 1780-82; Thomas Parry, 1781-83; Daniel Messersmith, 1782-83; Michael Furrer, 1783.

Sheriffs.—George Nagel, 1775; Henry Vanderslice, 1776-77; Daniel Levan, 1778-79; Henry Haffa, 1780-81; Philip Kraemer, 1782-83.

Treasurers.—Christopher Witman, 1775-79; Daniel Levan, 1780-83.

Assessors.—The assessors appointed by the County Commissioners for the years named, were:

1776.—Vernor Stamm, Michael Furrer, Paul Geiger, John Spohn, John Kerlin, John Egner.

1777.—John Hartman, Michael Furrer, John Robinson, John Egner, George Kelchner, Joseph Sands.

CHAPTER XII.

AFFAIRS AT READING.

PUBLIC PAPERS REMOVED FROM PHILADELPHIA.

When the Executive Council anticipated the invasion of the British Army into Pennsylvania, they regarded the public papers and documents unsafe at Philadelphia, and therefore directed them to be removed to Reading. On December 4, 1776, they issued an order to James Biddle for £15 to pay the expense of removal. I could not find any action of the Council directing their return. They were doubtless taken back to Philadelphia about 1778, after remaining here for over a year until the tide of warfare turned in favor of the Confederation.

SOCIAL CONDITION IN 1777.

Alexander Graydon lived at Reading for a time during the Revolution. In his "Memoirs" he mentions the situation of social affairs during the Winter of 1777–78. The following interesting extracts are presented:

"The steady advance of the English upon Philadelphia during the Summer of 1777 had thrown the city into a great panic. Many persons went to Reading as a place of safety—the fugitive families having been estimated at a score or more. The ensuing Winter (1777-78) at Reading was gay and agreeable, notwithstanding that the enemy was in possession of the metropolis. The society was sufficiently large and select, and a sense of common suffering in being driven from their homes had the effect of more closely uniting its members. Besides the families established in this place, it was seldom without a number of visitors, gentlemen of the army and others. The dissipation of cards, sleighing parties, balls, etc., were numerous. Gen'l Mifflin, at this era, was at home—a chief out of war, complaining, though not ill, considerably malcontent, and apparently not in high favor at headquarters. According to him, the ear of the commander-in-chief was exclusively possessed by Greene, who was represented to be neither the most wise, the most brave, nor the most patriotic of counsellors. In short, the campaign in this quarter was stigmatized as a series of blunders, and the incapacity of those who had conducted it was unsparingly reprobated. The better fortune of the Northern Army was ascribed to the superior talents of its leader; and it began to be whispered that Gates was the man who should, of right, have the station so incompetently sustained by Washington. There was, to all appearance, a cabal forming for his deposition, in which it is not improbable that Gates, Mifflin and Conway were already engaged, and in which the congenial spirit of Lee on his exchange immediately took a share. The well known apostrophe of Conway to America, importing 'that Heaven had passed a decree in her favor or her ruin must long before have ensued from the imbecility of her military counsels,' was at this time familiar at Reading. And I [Graydon] heard him myself—when he was afterwards on a visit to that place—express himself to this effect; 'That no man was more of a gentleman than Gen'l Washington, or appeared to more advantage at his table or in the usual intercourse of life; but, as to his talents for the command of any army (with a French shrug), they were miserable.' Observations of this kind, continually repeated, could not fail to make an impression within the sphere of their circulation; and it may be said that the popularity of the commander in-chief was a good deal impaired at Reading.

"Among the persons who, this Winter, spent much time in Reading, was one Luttiloe, a foreigner, who was afterward arrested in London on suspicion of hostile designs; also William Duer, who either was or lately had been a member of Congress. * * * There was a Major Stine, a Captain Sobbe and a Captain Wetherhold, of the Hessians, whom I sometimes fell in with. One old gentleman, a colonel, was a great professional reader, whom, on his application, I accommodated with such books of the kind as

I had. Another of them, a very portly personage, apparently replete with national phlegm, was nevertheless enthusiastically devoted to music, in which he was so much absorbed as seldom to go abroad. From that obsolete instrument, the harp, he extracted the sounds that so much delighted him. But of all the prisoners, one Graff, a Brunswick officer taken by Gen'l Gates's army, was admitted to the greatest privileges. Under the patronage of Dr. Potts, who had been principal surgeon in the northern department, he had been introduced to our dancing parties, and being always afterwards invited, he never failed to attend. He was a young man of mild and pleasing manners, with urbanity enough to witness the little triumphs of party, without being incited to ill humor by them. Over hearing a dance called for, one evening, which we named "Burgoyne's Surrender," he observed to his partner that it was a very pretty dance, notwithstanding the name, and that Gen'l Burgoyne himself would be happy to dance it in such good company. There was also a Mr. Stutzoe, of the Brunswick dragoons, than whose, I have seldom seen a figure more martial, or a manner more indicative of that manly openness which is supposed to belong to the character of a soldier."

CONWAY-CABAL.

The "Conway-Cabal" was a secret movement by which it was intended to remove Washington and put Gates in his place. Conway spent the Winter of 1777–78 at York, intriguing with Mifflin, Lee and certain members of Congress to bring about the removal of Washington. The correspondence between Gates, Mifflin and Conway, reflecting upon Washington, became known through the indiscretion of Wilkinson, who had seen one of the letters and repeated its purport to Stirling. The unfavorable impression produced by this discovery was not removed when Gates, with some bluster, first demanded of Washington to know who had tampered with his letters, and then denied that Conway had written the letter whose words had been quoted. Mifflin had written to Gates, informing him that an extract from Conway's letter had been procured and sent to headquarters. This perplexed Gates and caused him to suspect that his portfolio had been stealthily opened and his letters copied, and in a state of mental trepidation he wrote to Washington on the 8th of December, in which, among other things, he said: "I conjure your Excellency to give me all the assistance you can in tracing the author of the infidelity which put extracts from General Conway's letter to me in your hands." Washington replied with characteristic dignity and candor on the 4th of January following,—saying, among other things:

"I am to inform you then, that Colonel Wilkinson, on his way to Congress in the month of October last, fell in with Lord Stirling at Reading and— not in confidence that I ever understood— informed his aid-de-camp, Major McWilliams, that General Conway had written this to you: 'Heaven has been determined to save your country, or a weak general and bad counsellors would have ruined it.' Lord Stirling—from motives of friendship— transmitted the account with this remark: 'The enclosed was communicated by Colonel Wilkinson to Major McWilliams.' Such wicked duplicity of conduct I shall always think it my duty to detect."

Attempts to influence State legislatures proved equally unsuccessful, and when the purpose of the "Cabal" became known to the country and to the army, it met with universal condemnation.

It has been said that this "Cabal" was conceived at Reading, one tradition locating the place of meeting in a low one-story log building on the south side of Penn street, 60 feet above Eighth, (which was torn down in 1884), and another tradition in a two-story stone building on the south side of Penn street, 120 feet above Tenth, called for many years the "Fountain Inn." But these traditions are not correct. Conway was not at Reading but at York at that time. He visited Reading afterward. Wilkinson was on his way from Saratoga through Reading to York, where Congress was then assembled, with dispatches from Gen'l Gates concerning the surrender of Burgoyne's Army on the 17th of October. Accordingly, the people of Reading came to know of the surrender before Congress.

DUEL AT READING.

Col. Richard Butler's regiment was quartered at Reading during 1780-81. Most of its officers were very worthy men. It was commanded by Lieut. Col. Metzger, in the absence of the Colonel, who was not at Reading most of the Winter. Metzger was one of the very few foreign officers who were valuable to the colonists. There was a Capt. Bowen in the Regiment. He was recognized as an excellent officer; but he had a warm temper which occasioned some disturbance at Reading about that time. On one occasion he took offense when none was intended, and on that account fought a duel with the major of the regiment. The duellists each fired a shot, and Bowen had a button shot from his coat. Their seconds then settled the matter between them. An investigation of the cause of the difficulty was then made. It appeared the major was walking with some girls on the night before, and they burst out laughing just after Bowen had passed them. Their laughter was caused by the major telling them of his and Bowen's being at a dance on the evening before, when the blind fiddler broke one of the strings of his fiddle and the landlady took a candle and held it for him while he was fitting a new string. This story even set the seconds to laughing and they all returned in good humor. Upon another occasion, soon afterward, while Bowen and Charles Biddle (who was then residing at Reading) were playing backgammon, at a certain place, Capt. Bower—an officer in the same regiment, came into the room and, addressing himself to Bowen, said: "I hope you are very well, Major." Bowen immediately started up and replied to him: "Don't major me, sir! None of your majors! You know I am not a major, sir! What do you mean, sir?" Bower declared that he had not intended to give any offense. Bowen then took Biddle into an adjoining room and inquired if he should not challenge Bower. Biddle replied to him that "a man who would not fight on some occasions was not fit to live, nor was a man fit to live who was always quarreling." They returned, and Biddle made the captains shake hands, and so avoided a second duel. Bowen held the appointment of Town-Major for a time.

PRE-REVOLUTIONARY BUILDINGS AT READING.

At Reading three buildings have been permitted to stand, though erected before the Revolution. The foundations and walls are the same, but the external appearance is changed. They are:

Farmers' Inn: Fifth and Washington streets; erected as a two-story cut-stone building in 1760 by Michael Bright, and enlarged afterward.

Federal Inn: Penn Square, two-story stone building; erected in 1763 and subsequently altered several times; used as a bank since 1814.

County Jail: Fifth and Washington streets, two-story stone building, with high wall extensions; erected in 1770 by County Commissioners. It was used as such until 1848, when it was sold and converted into a store.

Other prominent buildings during the Revolution, whose likenesses have been preserved, are the following:

Weiser Store Building: East Penn Square, two-story stone building; erected in 1750 by Conrad Weiser; destroyed by fire in 1871.

First Reformed Church: Washington and Reed streets, large stone structure; erected in 1761; torn down in 1832.

County Court House: Penn Square, two-story cut-stone building; erected in 1762; torn down in 1841.

Friends' Meeting House: Washington above Fourth street, one-story log building; erected in 1765 and torn down in 1868.

Trinity Lutheran School Building: Sixth and Washington streets, one-story stone building; erected in 1765; torn down in 1893.

During that time, there were three churches at Reading: *Trinity Lutheran,* Washington below Sixth; *First Reformed;* and *Friends'.* These were the churches that were used for hospital purposes.

CHAPTER XIII.

CONCLUSION.

INDEPENDENCE AND PEACE.

The surrender of Lord Cornwallis at Yorktown on October 19, 1781, was virtually the end of the war between Great Britain and America. The news of the surrender reached London on the 25th of November, following. Several months afterward, the warfare in the American Colonies was discussed and its continuance discouraged in the House of Commons, a resolution having been passed, declaring that they who advised the continuation of the war were enemies of their country. These discussions were continued with earnestness till they culminated in a preliminary treaty of peace on November 30, 1782. In the first article of this treaty, "the independence of the thirteen United States of America" was recognized. The treaty was not made final then, owing to the three allied powers—Great Britain, France and Spain—having been pledged to one another not to conclude a treaty except by common consent; and the consent of France and Spain was to be obtained. This occasioned further delay and obliged the United States to await the adjustment of the differences between them. The final treaty of peace was concluded at Paris on September 3, 1783, and thereby the United States were acknowledged to be "free, sovereign and independent."

During these two years of negotiation and delay there were no general military operations. But great anxiety was felt over the prospects for a permanent peace. Through the inactivity of the army, the officers and soldiers became restless; also discontented, because they were not rewarded for their patriotic services. An attempt was made by anonymous and seditious publications to inflame their minds and to induce them to unite in redressing their grievances whilst they had arms in their hands. But Washington succeeded in quieting them. His wisdom and eloquence elicited from the officers the unanimous adoption of a resolution by which they declared "that no circumstances of distress or danger should induce a conduct that might tend to sully the reputation and glory they had acquired; that the army continued to have unshaken confidence in the justice of Congress and their country; and that they viewed with abhorrence and rejected with disdain the infamous proposition in the late anonymous address to the officers of the army."

RETURN OF THE SOLDIERS.

In order to avoid the inconveniences of dismissing a great number of soldiers in a body, furloughs were freely granted. In this way a great part of the unpaid army was disbanded and dispersed over the States without tumult or disorder. As they had been easily and speedily formed out of farmers, mechanics and laborers in 1775, so with equal facility did they throw off their military character and resume their former occupations. They had taken up arms earnestly for political freedom, but when these were no longer necessary, they laid them down peaceably to become again good, industrious citizens as they had been for eight years devoted and patriotic soldiers. The manner and time of the return of Berks County troops from the seat of war have not as yet been ascertained.

REVOLUTIONARY SURVIVORS.

In 1823, there were forty-six survivors of the Revolution, still living at Reading. During the gubernatorial campaign of that year, thirty-nine of these survivors held a public meeting on the 19th of August, for the purpose of endorsing Andrew Gregg, the Federal Candidate for Governor. Their names were:

Peter Nagel.	Andrew Fichthorn.	Alexander Eisenbise.
John Strohecker.	Peter Stichter.	Balser Ottenheimer.
Nicholas Dick.	James Haiden.	George Slear.
George Snell.	John Giley.	John Bingeman.
Henry Miller.	John Sell.	John Fox.
Henry Stiles.	Frederick Heller.	Henry Hahn.
Michael Reifsnyder.	John Snyder.	Christopher Diem.
Michael Spatz.	Michael Madeira.	George Yerger.
John Snell.	Jacob Dick.	John Row.
George Price.	Daniel Rose.	Ludwig Katzenmyer.
David Fox.	Gottlieb Christine.	Christian Hoffman.
Christian Miller.	William Mannerback.	Samuel Homan.
Jacob Petree.	Philip Nagel.	Henry Diehl.

Capt. Peter Nagel acted as chairman of the meeting, and Michael Madeira as secretary. Daniel Rose, John Strohecker and Balthaser Ottenheimer reported appropriate resolutions, which were unanimously adopted. The following expressive and enthusiastic language was used in the introductory part of the resolutions:

"Our hoary locks and trembling limbs forbid the expectation that many of us will assemble again in this life on a similar occasion. We wish to retire from the world and its cares, but when the Constitution of our country is assailed, whose rights are invaded for which we have seen so much blood and treasure expended, when the men of the Revolution are denounced as *Tories*, because they refuse to join the standard of the enemy of that constitution and those rights, shall we, who, regardless of the name of *Rebel*, and in defiance of British bayonets, once stepped forward in defence of our country, now shrink from our duty to that country at the cry of Federalist or Tory, blue light or Hartford conventionist? No, forbid it the memory of our deceased fellow-patriots. No, by the spirit of '76, which is yet glowing in our bosoms, we come an united band of soldiers for life in our country's cause, to rally round our constitution, offering our example to the rising generation, and solemnly declaring that if the public liberties must fall, *we are ready to be buried in the ruins.* [*Berks and Schuylkill Journal, Aug 23, 1823.*]

The candidate on the Democratic ticket was the Rev. John Andrew Shulze, a native of Berks County, but then a resident of Lebanon County. The survivors of the Revolution exerted a strong political influence at Reading, but Shulze was elected by 25,706 majority, and the constitution was not assailed. Its principles were so successfully upheld by him, and its provisions carried out, that he was re-elected three years afterward with little opposition.

In 1840, the Census reported nine surviving Revolutionary soldiers in Reading, who were then drawing pensions from the State Government, the figures indicating their age at that time:

Michael Spatz, 78.   William James, 79.   Henry Stiles, 84.
Peter Stichter, 78.   Sebastian Allgaier, 83.   Joseph Snablee, 84.
Aaron Wright, 78.   John P. Nagel, 83.   Christian Miller, 85.

In 1846 two still survived—Michael Spatz and William James.

BOOK II.

BIOGRAPHICAL SKETCHES.

EDWARD BIDDLE.

Edward Biddle was born in 1732. He was the fourth son of William Biddle, a native of New Jersey, whose grandfather was one of the original proprietors of that State, having left England with his father in 1681. His mother was Mary Scull, the daughter of Nicholas Scull, who was Surveyor-General of Pennsylvania from 1748 to 1761. James, Nicholas and Charles Biddle were three of his brothers.

On February 3, 1758, he was commissioned an ensign in the Provincial Army of Pennsylvania and was present at the taking of Fort Niagara in the French and Indian War. In 1759 he was promoted to lieutenant, and in 1760 he was commissioned as a captain, after which he resigned from the army and received 5000 acres of land for his services. He then selected the law as his profession, and after the usual course of study at Philadelphia, most likely in the office of his elder brother, James, he located at Reading, and soon established himself as a lawyer.

In 1767, he was elected to represent Berks County in the Provincial Assembly, and he was annually re-elected until 1775, and again in 1778. In 1774 and 1775, he officiated as Speaker, but he was obliged to resign this responsible position on March 15, 1775, on account of illness. He had previously been placed upon the most important committees, and had taken an active part in all the current business.

When the citizens of Reading held a public meeting on July 2, 1774, to take initiatory steps in behalf of the Revolution, they selected Edward Biddle to preside over their deliberations, and the expressive resolutions then adopted by them were doubtless drafted by him. His patriotic utterances on that occasion won their admiration, and they unanimously gave him a vote of thanks in appreciation of his efforts in the cause of the rights and liberties of America.

On the same day, while he was presiding at this meeting, the Assembly of Pennsylvania was in session and elected eight delegates as representatives to the "First Continental Congress," and among them was Edward Biddle, of Reading. When this Congress assembled at Philadelphia on September 5, 1774, the subject which principally occupied its attention was referred to a committee of two delegates from each Colony, and Biddle was selected as one of them. They were directed "to state the rights of the colonies in general, the instances in which those rights were violated, and the means most proper to be pursued for obtaining a restitution of them." The able declaration, which the committee reported, was earnestly supported by Biddle, though opposed by his colleague.

The report of the Pennsylvania delegates to the Assembly was approved by it, and this action gave Pennsylvania the credit of being the first constitutional House of Representatives that ratified the Acts of Congress.

Biddle was again selected as one of the delegates to the new Congress, which was to be held on May 10, 1775. On his way from Reading to Philadelphia, by boat, to attend the second convention, he accidentally fell overboard into the Schuylkill, and circumstances compelling him to sleep in his wet clothing, he took a cold, which resulted in a violent attack of illness. Besides leaving him a confirmed invalid for the rest of his life, he was deprived of the sight of one of his eyes. He was one of the twenty-two members of Congress who did not sign the "Declaration of Independence." His illness may account for his non-attendance and non-subscription of that great document for our political freedom. He was elected three times as a delegate to Congress. The first two terms extended from September 5, 1774, to December 12, 1776, and the last from 1778 to 1779. I could not find any information of his public actions, from 1776 to 1779, excepting his attendance of the meetings of the Committee of Safety at Philadelphia in the beginning of January, 1776.

The public records in the county offices, especially in the Prothonotary's office, disclose a large and lucrative practice as an attorney-at-law, and this extended from 1760 to the time of his decease in 1779. It seems to have been as much, if not more than that of all the other attorneys taken together.

He died on September 5, 1779, at Baltimore, Md., whither he had gone for medical treatment. He was married to Elizabeth Ross, a daughter of Rev. George Ross, of New Castle, Delaware, by whom he had two daughters, Catharine (married to George Lux, Esq., of Baltimore), and Abigail (married to Capt. Peter Scull.) His connection with this distinguished family gave him great social and political prominence. After his decease, notices appeared in various publications highly complimentary of his character.

MARK BIRD.

Mark Bird was the son of William Bird, one of the most prominent iron men of Berks County from 1740 to 1762, whose works were situated near the mouth of Hay Creek, in Union township. He was born at that place in January, 1739, and learned to carry on the iron business. After his father's death, he took charge of the estate, and, by partition proceedings in the Orphans' Court, came to own the properties consisting of 3000 acres of land, three forges, a grist mill and saw mill. About that time he laid out a town there and named it Birdsboro. By the time the Revolution broke out, he had enlarged his possessions very much and had come to be one of the richest and most prominent and enterprising men in this section of the State. The Recorder's office shows that he also owned at different times various properties at Reading.

In the popular demonstrations at Reading for the Revolution, he took an active part. At the public meeting on Dec. 5, 1774, he was selected as one of the Committee on Observation recommended by Congress, and on January 2, 1775, he was chosen one of the Delegates to the Provincial Conference, and also placed on the Committee of Correspondence. He was also prominently identified with the military movements, and at the meeting at Lancaster on July 4, 1776, for the election of two Brigadier-Generals, he received seven votes. During the years 1775 and 1776, he officiated as one of the Judges of the County Courts.

In 1775 and 1776, Mark Bird was the Lieutenant-Colonel of the 2nd Battalion of the County Militia, which was formed out of companies in the vicinity of Birdsboro; and in August, 1776, as a colonel, he fitted out 300 men of his battalion with uniforms, tents and provisions at his own expense. I could not ascertain that he led them into any engagement. They were in service at or near South Amboy in the Fall of 1776, and may have constituted a part of the "Flying Camp."

In 1785, his landed possessions in Berks County included 8000 acres, upon which were the extensive iron works at Birdsboro, and also the Hopewell Furnace on Six Penny Creek, which he had erected about 1765. And it is said that he owned large property interests in New Jersey and Maryland. The wide distribution of his investments led him to remark boastfully upon one occasion that he could not be overcome by fire, wind or water. By a strange coincidence, he actually became embarrassed by losses through fire, wind and water in the several localities where his possessions were situated, and in 1786, he was compelled to make an assignment of his estate for the benefit of creditors. About 1788, he removed to North Carolina, where he died some years afterward, the exact place and time I have not been able to ascertain.

He was married in 1763, to Mary Ross, a daughter of Rev. George Ross, by whom he had children, but the number and names could not be ascertained. He was a brother-in-law of Edward Biddle; also of George Ross, of Lancaster, a signer of the Declaration of Independence.

JACOB BOWER.

Jacob Bower was born in 1757 and entered the Revolution as first lieutenant in the company of Capt. Benjamin Weiser, which was raised in Heidelberg township, in the vicinity of Womelsdorf. At that time he was still a young man under age. Subsequently, he was promoted to captain, and as such served until peace was declared in 1783. At the close of the war, he settled at Reading and became a prominent county official. He first filled the office of sheriff for one term, from 1788 to 1790; then county commissioner, from 1790 to 1793; recorder, register and clerk of the Orphans' Court, from 1792 to 1798; and county auditor for the years 1799 and 1800. Some time after 1800, he removed to Womelsdorf and became an invalid, where he died Aug. 3, 1818.

The following obituary notice appeared in the *Berks and Schuylkill Journal, Aug. 8, 1818*, at the time of his decease :

" Died at Womelsdorf, in this county, on Monday last, after a tedious and severe illness, aged 61 years, Gen'l Jacob Bower. The deceased was a faithful and active officer during the whole of the Revolutionary war. He sacrificed at the shrine of Liberty a large patrimony, but, like many other veterans of the Revolution, was doomed to feel the stings of adversity in his old age."

He was a son of Conrad Bower, innkeeper, of Reading, who died in 1765, and whose widow became the second wife of Michael Bright.

MICHAEL BRIGHT.

Michael Bright was born November 24, 1732, in Heidelberg township, Lancaster (now Lebanon) County, near Sheridan. His father, Michael Brecht, emigrated from Schriessheim, in the Palatinate, to Pennsylvania, in 1726, when 20 years old. He learned the trade of saddler and located at Reading about 1755. He carried on this occupation successfully until 1762, when he became an innkeeper and owner of the Farmers' Inn, on the north-west corner of Fifth and Washington streets, which is still standing, though enlarged and owned by his grandson,

Francis Bright. In 1774, he was elected as a county commissioner and served three years. This position at that time was one of large responsibility. In December of that year, he was appointed one of the "Committee of Observation" of the county, whose duties were to collect funds for the relief of Boston, to watch the disaffected citizens and require them to give up their arms, and in general to provide for the common defense. This committee was also known as the "Standing Committee." He was a man of considerable character and acquired a large amount of property. He died at Reading in August, 1814. He was married twice, first to Sarah Stoner, by whom he had two sons, Michael and Jacob; and next to Catharine Bower (widow of Conrad Bower), by whom he had three sons, David, Peter and John, and a daughter Sarah, married to Leonard Rupert.

DANIEL BRODHEAD.

Daniel Brodhead was born at Albany, N. Y., in 1725. In 1738, his father migrated to Pennsylvania, and settled in Monroe County, now East Stroudsburg, where he grew up in a frontier life. Their house was attacked by Indians in 1755. In 1771, he removed to Heidelberg township, Berks County, where he purchased and carried on a grist mill. Soon afterward, he was appointed deputy-surveyor under John Lukens, Surveyor-General. In July, 1775, he was appointed a delegate from Berks County to the Provincial Convention at Philadelphia. In March, 1776, he was appointed lieutenant-colonel of Miles' rifle regiment; and in October following, he was transferred to the 3rd Pennsylvania Battalion, known as Shee's. On March 12, 1777, he was promoted to colonel of the 8th Pennsylvania Continental Line, to rank from September 29, 1776. Upon the capture of Colonel Miles, at the battle of Long Island, in August, 1776, the command of the remainder of the battalion devolved upon him; and he was, in fact, after the battle, in command of the whole Pennsylvania contingent, being then the senior officer remaining in the army. Shortly afterward, he went home on sick-leave, and when he rejoined the army it was as colonel of the 8th Regiment.

He was stationed at Fort Pitt, in the western part of Pennsylvania, in 1779 and 1780. His correspondence from April, 1779, to October, 1780, while there, is published in the Appendix to the *Pennsylvania Archives*, and covers 173 pages. In January, 1781, he was transferred to the 1st Pennsylvania Line, and he was still colonel of the regiment in September, 1783. He made some important treaties with the Indians, and for this he expected to be ordered to move into the Indian country, but he was disappointed, the command having been given to Colonel Clark, a Virginia officer. The war having then been virtually ended, he was not assigned to any command. It is believed that he received the appointment of brigadier-general before the close of the war.

In 1789, he represented Berks County in the General Assembly and participated in the important discussion relating to the alteration and amendment of the Constitution of 1776. He voted in the affirmative. Subsequently, in the same year, when the Assembly reconvened, he voted for the calling of a convention to amend the Constitution. In 1789, he received the appointment of Surveyor-General of Pennsylvania, which he held for eleven years. About that time he removed to Milford, Pike County, Pa., where he died November 15, 1809.

In 1778, he married the widow of Samuel Mifflin, of Philadelphia, who was the brother of Gen'l Thomas Mifflin, afterward Governor of Pennsylvania. They then lived at Reading, and at her death in 1788, they were residents of the same place.

EDWARD BURD.

Edward Burd was a practicing attorney at Reading, having been admitted to practice in the courts of Berks County in 1772. He moved to Reading from Lancaster. When the company of Capt. George Nagel marched to Cambridge, in Massachusetts, during July and August, in 1775, Burd was one of a number of devoted and patriotic sons who went along at their own expense; and when the "Flying Camp" was raised, he was chosen major of Haller's Regiment. In the Battle of Long

Island, in August, 1776, he was taken prisoner, and while imprisoned addressed a letter to Hon. Jasper Yeates, at Lancaster. On August 12, 1778, he was appointed prothonotary of the Supreme Court, and he continued to officiate in this position by reappointment until January 2, 1800.

HENRY CHRIST.

Henry Christ was a man of prominence at Reading in 1760, and officiated as sheriff of Berks County for the years 1761 and 1762. He showed a proper enthusiasm in the first movement at Reading for the Revolution in 1774, and was appointed by Edward Biddle as one of the Committee on Correspondence. In 1776 he raised and commanded a company of rifle-men in the campaign of Long Island, though not actually engaged in the battle. In 1777 he was placed on the Committee to collect arms, &c.

Upon his return, he was appointed a justice of the peace of Reading, and in 1784 he was reappointed for another term of seven years. While holding this office he also served as recorder, register and clerk of the Orphans' Court of the county from 1777 to 1789, excepting the last-named office for the year 1789; and he was also clerk of the Quarter Sessions for 1779.

He died at Reading in August, 1789, and left a large estate. He had four sons—Henry, Jacob, John and Daniel—and six daughters—Barbara (married to John Gallentine), Maria (married to George Spangler), Catharine (married to Capt. Jacob Graul), Margaret (married to Jacob Zimmerman), Susanna (married to Frederick Gossler) and Magdalena (married to Michael Lutz).

PETER DECKER.

Peter Decker was a retired gentlemen at Reading in 1768, and at the beginning of the Revolution raised a company which was to have been a part of the regiment from Berks County in the "Flying Camp," commanded by Lt.-Col. Nicholas Lotz, but the county quota was made up without his company and it became connected with the regiment commanded by Col. Robert Magaw, of the 5th Pennsylvania Battalion. He participated in the Long Island Campaign. In 1779, he was a resident of Cumru township, where he carried on a tavern until he died in 1784.

GEORGE DOUGLASS.

George Douglass, son of Andrew Douglass, and Jane Ross, (a daughter of the Earl of Ross,) was born at Pequea, in Lancaster County, Pa., on February 25, 1726. He removed to Berks County when a young man. He was located in Brecknock township in 1757, and by 1760 came to own a large grist mill and plantation of 247 acres which he carried on for some time. About 1761 he settled in Amity township, and there he remained until his decease. He served as a Justice of the Peace of the township named for several years before 1770, and he officiated as one of the Judges of the county courts from 1772 to 1784.

In the organization of Lotz's Battalion for the "Flying Camp," a company was included that was commanded by one Douglass whose first name is not given in the returns. It is believed that George Doug-

lass was this captain, for there was no other George Douglass in the county in 1776, excepting his son George, and he was only nine years old. The men in his company resided in Amity township and vicinity.

His wife was Mary Piersol. He died March 10, 1799, and left six children—Richard, Andrew, George, Elizabeth (married to John Jenkins), Rebecca (married to Mordecai Piersol), and Bridget (married to James May.) Andrew, the second son, was married to Rachel Morgan, a daughter of Col. Jacob Morgan, Jr.

THOMAS DUNDAS.

Thomas Dundas was a prominent merchant at Reading for many years. He was the third son of the Earl of Dundas. When the feelings of the inhabitants were being excited in behalf of the Revolution, he was found among the number that favored the cause of freedom. He took an active part at the first public meeting which was held at Reading, on July 2, 1774, and was appointed on the committee to carry on correspondence with the similar committees from the other counties of the Province. During the year 1776, he officiated as Prothonotary of the county. He died at Reading on April 25, 1805, and left a son William, and a daughter Jane, who was married to Marks John Biddle, a lawyer at Reading.

The *Weekly Advertiser*, a newspaper published at Reading, made the following mention of his decease in the issue of April 27th:

"Thomas Dundas was a very respectable inhabitant of this borough, where he had resided nearly forty years. As a man of business, and as a gentleman of sound understanding and liberal manners, his death may be regarded as a public loss; but by a numerous circle of private friends, his memory will be long and affectionately cherished for his urbanity and social virtues."

He was a particular friend of Dr. Jonathan Potts—the doctor having appreciated his kindness so highly that upon his death in 1781, he bequeathed to him 100 guineas in money, and his Revolutionary sword and pistols.

VALENTINE ECKERT.

Valentine Eckert was born at Longasalza, in the Kingdom of Hanover, in 1733. He came to America with his parents in 1741, who settled in the Tulpehocken Valley at a point east of where Womelsdorf is now situate. He was naturalized in September, 1761. In June, 1776, he was one of the ten members of the Provincial Conference who represented Berks County in that important body; and in July following, he was selected as a delegate from the county to the Provincial Convention which was assembled for the purpose of framing a new government founded on the authority of the people. In 1776 and 1779 he represented the county in the Provincial Assembly. He was a resident of Cumru township and a blacksmith by occupation. He offered his services to the Government in the Revolutionary War, which were accepted, and he commanded a company of cavalry Associators for a time. He and his company participated in the Battle of Germantown, in October, 1777, where he was wounded. He was appointed Sub-Lieutenant of the county on March 21, 1777, and served in this office until his promotion to Lieutenant of the County in January, 1781. He continued to act as Lieutenant until the close of the war. While serving as Sub-Lieutenant, he also acted as a commissioner for the purchase of army supplies.

In 1784, he was appointed judge of the Court of Common Pleas of the county and occupied this office for a term of seven years, when, by the Constitution of 1790, a president judge of all the courts was appointed to take the place of the several judges. In the Pennsylvania Militia, he was brigade inspector for the county from April 11, 1793, for a period of 20 years. About the year 1816, he moved to the State of Virginia, and died at Winchester in December, 1821, in the 88th year of his age.

CONRAD ECKERT.

Conrad Eckert was born at Longasalza, in the Kingdom of Hanover, on February 6, 1741. During that year his father, John Eckert, emigrated from the place named to Pennsylvania, and settled in Heidelberg township, Lancaster (now Berks) County. He was brought up at farming, and when a young man became a blacksmith, which he pursued for some time. When the Revolution began, he was one of the active Associators of the county. As such he commanded a company which was raised in Heidelberg township, and became a part of the 1st Battalion, commanded by Col. Henry Haller. This battalion marched to service in New Jersey in December, 1776, but the companies left and returned home without permission, because they had not been paid according to the terms of their enlistment. Captain Eckert is the "Captain Echard" mentioned by Gen'l Israel Putnam as one of the captains who informed him that "their companies had run away to a man, excepting a lieutenant, sergeant and drummer." His company afterwards formed a part of Spyker's Battalion, and participated in the campaign at and about Germantown and White Marsh during the Fall of 1777. In this service, he was wounded in the battle at the former place, and his health in consequence became so impaired that he never fully recovered. Subsequently, in 1778 and 1780, his company was connected with the 4th Battalion of County Militia.

Upon his return from military service, he carried on farming on the Eckert homestead, near Womelsdorf, until his death, August 25, 1791. He was married to Elizabeth Hain, a daughter of —— Hain, in Heidelberg township, by whom he had seven sons, John, Peter, George, David, Daniel, Solomon and Conrad, and two daughters, Catharine (married to Henry Copenhaven), and Barbara (married to Daniel Reeser). His remains were buried in the graveyard connected with Hain's Church.

Col. Valentine Eckert was an elder brother.

GEORGE EGE.

George Ege was born March 9, 1748, and settled in Berks County about the year 1774, when he became the sole owner of the Charming Forge, a prominent industry then situated on the Tulpehocken Creek, in Tulpehocken (now Marion) township. During the Revolution he was an ardent patriot and supplied the Government with large quantities of cannon balls. He represented the county in the General Assembly for the years 1779, 1780 and 1782. Upon the adoption of the State Constitution of 1790, he was appointed an Associate Judge in 1791, and he served continuously until 1818, a period of twenty-eight years, when he resigned to devote his attention entirely to the management of his extensive business in the manufacture of iron.

In 1804, he was the largest manufacturer and land owner in the county. Then he owned and carried on the Charming Forge with 4000 acres, Berkshire Furnace with 6000 acres, Schuylkill Forge, near Port Clinton, with 6000 acres, and four large farms in Tulpehocken and Heidelberg townships, together containing 1000 acres. In 1824, the assessed value of all his property was near $400,000.

He died at his home on the Charming Forge property, December 14, 1829, aged nearly 82 years. He had been actively engaged in business from 1774 to 1825, a period exceeding half a century, and for some years after he had reached the age of three score and ten. His remains were interred in the cemetery connected with Zion's Church at Womelsdorf. His daughter Rebecca was married to Joseph Old, a prominent iron master who carried on the Reading Furnace in Chester County, and a son Michael was married to Maria Margaretta Shulze, who was a daughter of Rev. Emanuel Shulze.

Judge Ege was distinguished for great kindness of heart and humane impulses. Among his possessions were many slaves, numbering about forty, and he was always known to treat them with much consideration. Occasionally renegade slaves from the South found a comfortable home with him and also employment at one or other of his iron industries. A trusty slave, by the name of Tom Nelson, is particularly remembered for his integrity and devotion to the interests of his master, the Judge, having frequently been intrusted with large sums of money which he carried from Charming Forge to the bank at Reading. Judge Ege was then a director in the "Bank of Deposit," the first bank at Reading. When Washington stopped at Womelsdorf in 1794 on his way to Carlisle, during the excitement growing out of the "Whiskey Insurrection," Tom was especially desirous of driving his master to Womelsdorf, not only to enable the Judge to pay his compliments to the great Revolutionary hero and first President of the United States, but to afford himself the opportunity of seeing him. Judge Ege was personally known to Washington on account of his patriotic spirit during the Revolution, and of his prominence as a large manufacturer of iron, cannon balls, &c.

BALSER GEEHR.

Balser Geehr was born of German parentage at Germantown, near Philadelphia, on January 22, 1740, and removed to Amity township, in Berks County, when a young man. By the year 1767, he was living in Oley township, employed as a gunsmith. While in Oley, he was married to Catharine Hunter (Iaeger), a daughter of Anthony Iaeger, and a sister of Col. Daniel Hunter. In 1771, he purchased a large plantation of nearly 500 acres in Bern township, several miles to the south of the Blue Mountain, and moved upon it in 1772.

When the Revolution began, he was a man of large influence in the northern section of the county, and upon the selection of a Standing Committee in 1774, for a proper guidance of popular sentiment in its behalf, he was naturally chosen to represent that section on this important committee. In the formation of the Associators of Pennsylvania, Balser Geehr was one of the five delegates from Berks County who attended a meeting at Philadelphia in August, 1775. These delegates were known as the "Colonels of the Associated Battalions." He took an active part in the county militia. In 1775 and 1776 he was lieutenant-colonel of the 4th Battalion, which was composed of companies in the northern section of the county. In September, 1776, his battalion participated in the campaign about New York, but I cannot state what particular service was rendered.

He officiated continuously as a judge of the county courts from 1775 to 1784, and represented the county in the General Assembly for the years 1782, 1786, and from 1792 to 1799. These positions show the popular esteem in which he was held.

It is stated that he attended a levee given by President Washington in Independence Hall, in company with friends from Reading. In that day, cards were not commonly used but the names were announced. Upon arriving at the hall door, he gave his name upon request, and then it was called out to an usher at the first landing of the stairway, who in turn called it out again to another at the doorway of the assembly room, where it was again announced in a distinct manner. Not having been acquainted with the custom, this public use of his name excited him so that he exclaimed in a loud tone of voice—" Yes, yes, I'm coming ; give me time," to the great amusement of other invited guests about him.

He carried on farming extensively on the Bern plantation until 1796, and then removed to a farm of 231 acres in Maxatawny township, several miles north of Kutztown, which he had purchased shortly before. He died June 19, 1801, and his remains were interred in a private burying ground near the centre of the plantation last mentioned.

By his decease without a last will, and the decease of his two sons John and Jacob also, and his two granddaughters (the children of Jacob), dying intestate without issue, the Maxatawny farm became involved in very tedious and costly ejectment litigation, covering a period of fifteen years. One of the cases involving the trial is reported in *Outerbridge Reports* (Penna. State) vol. 9, p. 577, (1884); and another in *Crumrine Reports*, (Penna. State) vol. 28, p. 311 (1891). The trials excited much general interest amongst the legal profession, and the cases reported are regarded as leading cases on the subject of title to land by descent.

ALEXANDER GRAYDON.

Alexander Graydon was born at Bristol, in Bucks County, Penn'a, on April 10, 1752. He went to Philadelphia while young and was educated principally at the Quaker school. He then studied law, but did not come to be admitted to the Bar at that place. He was a volunteer in the Revolution, and commanded a company in the Long Island campaign. In the capture of Fort Washington, he was taken prisoner. Upon his release, he afterward went to Reading and was admitted to the Bar on May 14, 1779. He carried on practice for a time, then removed to Harrisburg, where he died, May 2, 1818. His remains were buried in the Old Pine Street Presbyterian Church burial ground at Philadelphia. While at Harrisburg, his memoirs were published in 1811. William Graydon, a practicing lawyer at that place, and the author of Graydon's Forms, was a brother.

HENRY HALLER.

Henry Haller was a tailor at Reading in 1765, and in 1775 was engaged as an innkeeper, by which time he had become a man of considerable social and political influence. In the formation of a regiment in Berks County, as its quota of the 4500 men for the Flying Camp, he was chosen Colonel, but he did not accompany the regiment in its march to Long Island, and did not participate in that battle. Shortly afterward, however, he commanded another battalion which went into service in New Jersey.

In the public actions for encouraging the Revolution, he took a prominent part, and next to Edward Biddle, George Nagel, Jacob Morgan and Bodo Otto, was as prominent as any other man at Reading. He was a delegate to the Provincial Conference in 1776, and also a member of the Committee of Safety, the Committee on Attainder, and the Committee to Collect Arms, etc. He served as a member of the Assembly from 1776 to 1781. During the years 1778, 1779 and 1780, he was wagon-master of Berks County, and during 1779 and 1780, wagon-master-general of the Continental Army. The first public office that he filled was coroner of the county in 1767.

After the Revolution, he moved up the Schuylkill Valley beyond the Blue Mountains, in Brunswick township, then still part of Berks County, and there he died in September, 1793, possessed of a very large estate. He had eight sons, Frederick, Jacob, Henry, John, William, Isaac, Benjamin and Lewis ; and two daughters, Elizabeth (married to William Mears), and Sarah (married to Samuel Webb).

GABRIEL HIESTER.

Gabriel Hiester, a son of Daniel Hiester and Catharine Shueler (natives of Witzenstein, Westphalia), was born in Bern township June 17, 1749. He was brought up as a farmer and given such an education as the neighborhood afforded at the school connected with the Bern Church. In 1776, he was selected as one of the representatives from Berks County to the Provincial Convention for the formation of a Constitution. In 1778 he received the appointment of justice of the Common Pleas Court of the county, which he held for four years. He was afterward elected to the Assembly, and represented the county for eight years, 1782, 1787–89, 1791 and 1802–04. He was in the Assembly when the question of framing a new Constitution was discussed, but he voted against the propriety of calling a convention for this purpose. He was Senator from the district which comprised Berks and Dauphin Counties for ten years, 1795–96 and 1805–12. This continued selection by his fellow-citicitizens indicates their confidence in him as a man of ability and integrity.

He died on his farm, in Bern township, September 1, 1824. He was a brother of Col. Daniel Hiester, of Montgomery County; of Col. John Hiester, of Chester County, and a cousin of Col. Joseph Hiester, of Berks County. His wife was Elizabeth Bausman, who survived him eight years, dying in the 81st year of her age. He had four sons, Gabriel, Jonathan, William and Jacob, and two daughters, Mary (married to Frederick A. Shulze), and Elizabeth.

The family name was commonly written Hiester, but he wrote it, as given, Heister.

JOSEPH HIESTER.

Joseph Hiester was born in Bern township, Berks County, on November 18, 1752. His father, John Hiester, emigrated to Pennsylvania in 1732, in the 25th year of his age, from the village of Elsoff, in the province of Westphalia, Germany, and some years afterward settled in Bern township, where he married Mary Barbara Epler, a daughter of one of the first settlers in that section of the county.

The son was brought up on the farm until he was a young man. In the intervals of farm labor, he attended the school at Bern Church, and there he acquired the rudiments of an English and also a German education. The homestead was situated about a mile north of the church.

He went to Reading before he was of age, and entered the general store of Adam Witman. He remained in the store until 1776, and then, manifesting an active sympathy for the Revolution, he was selected as a delegate to the Provincial Conference. Upon returning home, he raised a company of men which became a part of the "Flying Camp" in the regiment of Lt.-Col. Nicholas Lotz, and with it participated in the Battle of Long Island, where he was taken prisoner. Upon his exchange he returned to Reading, and after recovering from the effects of his imprisonment, he rejoined the army. He participated in the battle of Germantown in 1777, and in 1780 commanded a regiment which was in service in New Jersey for thirty days.

About the close of the Revolution, he entered into partnership with his father-in-law, and some years afterward became the sole proprietor of the store. He conducted business operations very successfully for a number of years. Public affairs also received much of his attention. In 1787, he was elected a member of the General Assembly and re-elected twice. In 1789, he was chosen a delegate to the Constitutional Convention, and in 1790, the first State Senator from Berks County. In 1797, he was elected to represent this district in Congress and afterward re-elected five times. After an intermission of eight years, which he devoted entirely to business at Reading, he was again sent to Congress in 1815, and re-elected twice.

While holding this office, he became the nominee of the Federalist party for Governor in 1817, and though not then elected, his popularity was shown in the vote which he received. He was the first candidate on the Federal ticket who received a majority of the votes in Berks County against the Democratic candidate, and also in the southeastern section of the State. The party naturally selected him in 1820 a second time as the most available candidate, and he was elected. The election returns reveal the fact that the devotion of the people of Berks County caused his election. His numerous friends signalized this triumph by a grand festival at Reading on November 1, 1820. His administration was characterized by great activity in promoting the growth of the Commonwealth, especially through internal improvements. He suggested that such improvements could be made advantageously, and domestic manufactures encouraged with success, and that there existed an imperative duty to support a liberal system of education. At the end of his term he lived in retirement at Reading. He died June 10, 1832. His remains were interred in the burying ground of the Reformed Church, and some years afterward removed to the Charles Evans Cemetery. He had a son, John S. Hiester, and four daughters.

DANIEL HUNTER.

The parents of Daniel Hunter were emigrants from Germany, amongst the early settlers of Oley township. The name was Iaeger in German. He was born in this township on April 8, 1742, and carried on farming all his life. At the breaking out of the Revolution, he manifested an earnest interest in public affairs. His prominence and patriotic spirit led to his selection as a representative from the county to the Provincial Conference in June, 1776, and to the Convention in July following. The Supreme Executive Council appointed him a paymaster of the militia in 1776, and he served in this position until August, 1777. In militia affairs he was particularly prominent. In the Winter and Fall of 1777, he commanded a regiment of militia, formed of companies from Oley and vicinity, which was engaged in the Revolutionary service, first in the campaign about Trenton, and then in the campaign about the Brandywine. He represented the county in the General Assembly for the year 1782. While serving this office, he was taken ill, and from this illness he died at home, February 3, 1783, in the 41st year of his age.

His wife was Maria Lease. He left three surviving children—Daniel, Frederick and Catharine (who was married to Jacob Kemp). His sister Catharine was the wife of Balser Geehr.

THOMAS JONES, JR.

Thomas Jones, Jr., was a son of Thomas Jones, an early Welsh settler in Cumru township, who took up a large tract of land in 1735. He was born in 1742 in this township, and was brought up to farming. At the beginning of the Revolution, he assisted in organizing the Associators of Berks County, and was in active service for a time as a major in one of the battalions. He was a member of the first Constitutional Convention from Berks County, and he also served as a county commissioner for two terms, from 1779 to 1782, and from 1783 to 1786. He died in 1800, aged 58 years. His residence was in Heidelberg township. He left one son, Samuel, and four daughters—Martha, Susanna, Sarah and Mary.

JOHN LESHER.

John Lesher was a native of Germany. He was born January 5, 1711, the only son and heir-at-law of Nicholas Lesher. He emigrated to Pennsylvania in 1734, and was naturalized in 1743. He first settled in the upper section of Bucks County, but subsequently removed to Oley township, Berks County. Along the Manatawny Creek, near the Oley Churches, he, with two other men (John Yoder and John Ross), erected a forge in 1744. This was known as the "Oley Forge." From that time, for a period of fifty years, he was prominently identified with the iron industry of Berks County. He represented the county in the Constitutional Convention of 1776, and served in the General Assembly from 1776 until 1782. While in the Convention, he was one of the important committee who prepared and reported the "Declaration of Rights." During the Revolution, he acted as one of the Commissioners for purchasing army supplies. He addressed an interesting letter to the Supreme

Executive Council in 1778, relating to the taking of supplies from him. [See p. 181.]

He died in Oley township April 5, 1794, aged 83 years. He left a wife, two sons, John and Jacob; and five daughters—Barbara (married to Jacob Morgan), Hannah (married to George Focht), Maria (married to John Potts, Jr.), Catharine (married to John Tysher), and Elizabeth.

DANIEL LEVAN.

Daniel Levan was the son of Daniel Levan, of Maxatawny township, in Berks County, who died in June, 1777. He was born in that township, and, after having been brought up on a farm, removed to Reading. He studied law with Edward Biddle, Esq., on whose motion he was admitted to practice in the several courts of Berks County on November 11, 1768.

He officiated as the sheriff of the county during the years 1778 and 1779, and as the county treasurer from 1780 to 1783. His residence was situated on the south-east corner of 5th and Cherry streets, and there he died in March, 1792, leaving to survive him four sons, Isaac, Daniel, Jacob and Samuel.

SEBASTIAN LEVAN.

Sebastian Levan was born in Maxatawny township, Berks County. He was a son of Jacob Levan, one of the first judges of the County from 1752 to 1762. He was raised on his father's farm and learned the trade of miller, which he afterward carried on for himself. At the breaking out of the Revolution, he represented his district on the Standing Committee. Subsequently, he served in the the State Assembly during 1779 and 1780, and as a Councillor on the Supreme Executive Council from 1782 to 1784. He was also active in the County Militia, being colonel of a battalion. He died in August, 1794.

ABRAHAM LINCOLN.

Abraham Lincoln was a son of Mordecai and Mary Lincoln. He was born a posthumous son in 1736, in Exeter township, Berks County, (then part of Philadelphia County). His father—who died in May of that year, a few months before his birth—was the paternal ancestor of Abraham Lincoln, President of the United States. He was brought up on a farm and received a fair education. Prior to the Revolution, he served as a county commissioner from 1772 to 1775, and continued in office by re-election until 1778. On March 21, 1777, he was appointed one of the sub-lieutenants of the county, but it is not known how long he served in this position.

He represented the county in the General Assembly from 1782 to 1786, and was a delegate to the Pennsylvania Convention to ratify the Federal Constitution in 1787. He did not sign the ratification. He was also a member of the Constitutional Convention of 1789–90.

He died at his residence in Exeter township, January 31, 1806, in the 70th year of his age. In 1761, he married Anne Boone, a daughter of James Boone and Mary Foulke. She was a full cousin of Col.

Early Home of Lincolns

Daniel Boone, the Pioneer of Kentucky. The Boones were Quakers and the Lincolns Congregationalists. Hence it appears by the minutes of the Exeter Meeting, October 27, 1761, that she "condoned" her marriage to one who was not a member of the Society. He left four sons, Mordecai, James, Thomas and John, and five daughters, Mary (married to Joseph Boone), Martha, Ann (married to William Glassgow), Anna, and Phebe (married to David Jones).

The above cut represents the building where the children of Mordecai Lincoln, Sr., were born. It is situated about a mile below Exeter Station, several hundred feet north from the railroad, near a small stream. An extension was built to the west end.

JACOB LIVINGOOD.

Jacob Livingood, a captain of a company of riflemen during the Revolution in 1781, was born in Tulpehocken township, Berks County, on January 26, 1752, on the property commonly known as the " Livingood Mill," which is situated on a branch of the Little Swatara, within a mile of its outlet into that stream. His father and grandfather, both of the same name, had lived there for a number of years, the latter having migrated from New York in 1729 with a small colony of Germans, under the leadership of Conrad Weiser. He was brought up to farming and milling.

In the Fall of 1781, he raised a company of riflemen at and near Womelsdorf for the Continental Army, which was in service for ninety days. Upon his discharge and return home, he resumed his avocation as a miller. For some years afterward, he was engaged in the grain business, disposing of the grain collected at Philadelphia. He was also at Reading for a time. Subsequently, he returned to Tulpehocken and lived by himself in a small log building, which was erected by members of the family expressly for him, on the Mill premises, where he frequently entertained the surviving members of his company. It is stated that the meetings of his Continental associates were occasions of great hilarity, and he always welcomed them in his military uniform. So proud was he of this dress that he died with it on; and out of respect for his known wishes, he was thus laid to rest in the burying ground of the Lutheran Church, a mile west of Stouchsburg. The day of his decease is not known.

NICHOLAS LOTZ.

Nicholas Lotz was born February 20, 1740, in the Palatinate, and emigrated to Pennsylvania when a young man. He first settled in the western section of the county. Some time previous to the Revolution, he located at Reading and became the owner of two mills at the mouth of the Wyomissing Creek, which he conducted very successfully. When the struggle for independence began, he was prominently identified with the patriotic movement at Reading. In January, 1775, he was selected as chairman of the Standing Committee. He served as a delegate to the Provincial Conference in June, 1776, and upon his return home took an active part in the enlistment of men. He was commissioned a lieutenant-colonel and participated in the campaign of the " Flying Camp " at New York, where he was engaged in the battle of Long Island and taken prisoner. He was admitted to parole within certain bounds on April 16, 1777, and exchanged on September 10, 1779. He showed great interest in Militia affairs, being at the head of the battalion in the central section of the county from 1775 for many years.

In 1780 he was appointed Commissioner of Forage, and, as such, purchased supplies for the army until the close of the war. The Executive Council addressed him as a Colonel and so recognized him.

Nicholas Lotz

Col. Lotz represented Berks County in the General Assembly from 1784 to 1786, and again from 1790 to 1794; and he filled the office of Associate-Judge of the county from 1795 to 1806. Gov. Thomas Mifflin gave him the appointment, there having been great intimacy between them.

When Gen'l Washington, while President, was at Reading, on his way to Carlisle, in 1794, Col. Lotz was at the head of a party of prominent men who signalized the occasion by giving a military parade on Penn Square in honor of the distinguished visitor. The review was made from the second story of the "Federal Inn" (now the Farmer's Bank building). In personal appearance, he was a tall, finely-proportioned man, being over six feet in height and weighing about 300 pounds; and upon that occasion he attracted marked attention, not only by reason of his commanding presence, but also of his military, political and social prominence.

Federal Inn, Penn Square, Reading.

He died November 28, 1807, and left to survive him eight children: seven sons, Philip, Nicholas,

Jacob, John, Henry, Michael and William, and a daughter, Rosa (married to John Yeager). His remains were buried in the graveyard of the Reformed Church, and from thence removed to the Charles Evans Cemetery.

CHRISTIAN LOWER.

Christian Lower was of German descent. In that language the name was spelled Lauer, but in writing it himself he spelled it Lower.

The name of his father, Christian Lauer, appears in the list of families that migrated from Schoharie in New York to Tulpehocken in 1723, and his grandfather, Michael Lauer, followed in 1728.

He was born in Tulpehocken township and brought up to the trade of a blacksmith. He took an active part in the Revolution and was prominent in the political affairs of the county for many years. In August, 1775, he was selected as one of the Colonels of the Associated Battalions and attended the Convention at Philadelphia. He officiated as a County Commissioner during the years 1777, 1778 and 1779, served as a Sub-Lieutenant in supplying the quota of troops from 1780 to the close of the war, and represented the county in the General Assembly for the years 1779, 1782 to 1785, 1793, 1794 and 1796.

Before the Revolution, his father was the owner of the Moselem Forge. He was a man of social prominence and died possessed of a large estate in September, 1786, leaving to survive him two sons, Christian and John, and three daughters, Elizabeth (married to George Holston), Magdalena (married to Michael Ley), and Catharine (married to Benjamin Spyker).

The son Christian, the subject of this sketch, died in January, 1807, and left a widow and seven children: three of age, Elizabeth (married to John Battorf), Catharine (married to Jacob Kohr), and Magdelena (married to John Dieffenbach); and four under age, John, George, Margaret and Mary. The remains of both father and son were interred in the burying ground of Tulpehocken Church.

JOHN LUDWIG.

John Ludwig was a son of Dan'l Ludwig, the elder, of Heidelberg township, where he was born, and raised at farming. At the opening of the Revolution, he was a man of prominence in the central section of the county. He raised a company of men, which formed part of the "Flying Camp" in Lotz's Battalion, and it appears that he and his company were subsequently engaged in the battles of Trenton and Princeton. He also commanded a company which comprised part of Hiester's Battalion in 1780, that was with Reed's Army in New Jersey.

He was commissioned a justice of the peace in 1777, and recommissioned in 1784. He was a delegate to the Pennsylvania Convention to ratify the Federal Constitution in 1787, but, with his colleagues, did not sign the ratification. He served in the General Assembly in 1782–83, and again in 1788–90; and he also served as a member of the Pennsylvania House of Representatives from 1790 to 1793. In 1795, Gov. Mifflin appointed him a justice of the peace, and he was still in commission at the time of his death in July, 1802.

JACOB MORGAN.

Jacob Morgan was the most prominent Revolutionary character of Berks County from 1777 to 1780, and as such brought great credit to the county and great honor to himself.

He was born in the district or shire of Cærnarvon, in the northern part of Wales, in 1716, and emigrated with his father, Thomas Morgan, to Pennsylvania some time previous to 1730. About that time a colony of Welsh people, including Thomas Morgan and his family, migrated up the Schuylkill Valley from Philadelphia to the mouth of the French Creek, and thence along and beyond the headwaters of that creek until they reached the headwaters of the Conestoga Creek, in Cærnarvon township. There they settled and took up large tracts of land. That section of territory was then a part of Lancaster County, but since 1752 a part of Berks County. The tract taken up by his father was in the vicinity of Morgantown. It included the town plan which he subsequently came to lay out in 1770, and which he named after the family, a custom quite common in that day throughout the county.

When the French and Indian War came to affect Pennsylvania in 1755, Jacob Morgan was 39 years old, and until that time had been engaged at farming. In December of that year, he was commissioned as a captain under the Provincial Government, and he continued actively engaged in this military service until

Jacob Morgan

1760, when he returned home and resumed farming. For his services, he became entitled to 3000 acres of land by proclamation of the King of Great Britain in 1763, but it would seem that he did not take up the land, for in his last will he devised his right to the grant to four of his children.

When the Revolution began, he was nearly 60 years of age. In June, 1776, he was selected to represent the county as a delegate to the Provincial Conference, and in July following as a delegate to the Constitutional Convention; and in 1777, upon the creation of the office of Lieutenant of the several counties for the purpose of aiding the Executive

Council in effectively prosecuting the war, he was selected by the Council to fill this very important position. This evidences his distinguished character, for at that time Berks County possessed a number of prominent and influential men. In the prompt and faithful performance of his duties, he was very successful, the Executive Council in their letters to him frequently complimenting his energy in having the county to promptly fill the numerous orders for troops. He resigned in December, 1780. While filling this office, he was always recognized as a colonel, and was addressed as such by the Executive Council.

He officiated as a judge of the county for the years 1768, 1769, 1772, and from 1774 to 1777; and as a justice of the peace for the southern district of Berks County, which included Caernarvon township, from 1777 to 1791, by appointment for two consecutive terms of seven years each.

A story, illustrating his courage and self-possession at an advanced age, is told of him after his retirement to Morgantown. About the year 1784, one evening, while seated in his sleeping room on the first floor, three masked men entered and demanded his money or his life. He refused in a positive manner, and one of them struck him on the head with a club, which caused him to fall and roll under the bed. In falling, the table (at which he sat) was upset and the light extinguished. Just then an indentured girl, "Patty Barefoot," who was in the room, hid from fear behind the bed, took his sword (which lay on a projecting ledge of the partition several feet from the floor) and handed it to him, when he arose suddenly, struck out violently in the darkness to the right and left upon the heads and across the backs of the intruders, and thus drove them away.

He died at Morgantown on November 11, 1792, at the age of 76 years, and was buried in the graveyard of the St. Thomas Episcopal Church at that place. He left a last will, by which it appears that he died possessed of a large estate, including over 700 acres of farming and wood land in Berks County, and the right to over 7000 acres of land by virtue of grants from the Government.

He had two sons, Jacob and Benjamin; and three daughters, Sarah (married to —— Jenkins), Mary (married to Nicholas Hudson), and Rebecca (married to John Price, an attorney at Reading). Rachel, a daughter of John Price, was married to Samuel Wetherill in 1788.

JACOB MORGAN, JR.

Jacob Morgan, a son of Jacob Morgan, and commonly known as Jacob Morgan, Jr., was born in Cærnarvon township, Berks County, in 1742. At the age of 16 years, he was appointed an ensign, and served in the French and Indian War at Fort Augusta, then on the extreme northern frontiers of Berks County. He also accompanied the second expedition against Fort Duquesne; and in 1760, he was a lieutenant in the 2nd Battalion of Associators, acting as an adjutant under the command of Col. Hugh Mercer.

At an early age he went to Philadelphia, and, after clerking for a while, became a successful merchant.

When the Revolution began, he was a man of prominence. On December 4, 1776, the Executive Coun-

cil of Pennsylvania appointed him Colonel of the 1st Battalion of Associators of the City of Philadelphia and Northern Liberties. He and his battalion were engaged in the Battle of Princeton, and there on the field, he received the sword of his friend, Gen'l Mercer, while attending him in his dying moments; and shortly afterward they also participated in the Battle of Monmouth.

The Executive Council selected him for the position of Lieutenant of the City of Philadelphia, but he declined this appointment, doubtless, because he contemplated changing his residence to Reading, for I find that, in September, 1777, he became the representative from Berks County in the Board of Executive Council. This election would indicate that he had moved there some time in April or May. He continued to serve as a Councillor until April 14, 1778, when he was selected to be the Quartermaster-General of the county, and then, thinking that by accepting this appointment he could render more service to his country, he resigned. In 1780, he was also appointed Superintendent of the Commissioners of purchases for the army, and of the Wagon-Masters of the State; and he served these three highly responsible positions in a most faithful and satisfactory manner until the close of the Revolution.

Certain deeds, conveying real estate in Berks County to and from him in 1779, describe his residence as of Reading. The letters to him from the Executive Council, which are published in the *Colonial Records*, were addressed to him at Reading, and those from him to the Council were dated at Reading, the dates of both extending from 1777 to 1782.

Shortly after the war, he returned to Philadelphia. A deed from him for land in Berks County, dated in

1791, describes him as a merchant at that place. He was then, and continued until the time of his decease, engaged in business with his son-in-law, Andrew Douglass, under the firm name of Douglass & Morgan. It is said that this firm was one of the first to manufacture refined sugar at Philadelphia.

He died on September 18, 1802, in the 61st year of his age, and his remains were interred in the burying-ground of Christ Church, at the corner of Fifth and Arch streets, in which were buried the remains of many distinguished men.

Col. Morgan was married to Barbara Jenkins, of Reading, by whom he had six children: Rachel (married to Andrew Douglass), Elizabeth (married to William Sergeant), George, John, Jacob and Hannah—the last three dying, while young, of yellow fever at Philadelphia in 1793.

DAVID MORGAN.

David Morgan was a brother of Col. Jacob Morgan. He was born on the Morgan homestead and raised on the farm. He participated in the Revolution by acting on several local committees, being one of the Committee to seize the property of Tories in the county, and one of the Committee to vest the title to forfeited estates. Upon the decease of his brother, the Colonel, he was appointed to the office of justice of the peace of the district, and he continued to fill this position until his decease. He always resided at Morgantown, and died there in July, 1812. Four children survived him, Elizabeth (married to Michael Bower), James, David and John.

GEORGE NAGEL.

Joachim Nagel was born at Eisenberg, a town situated three miles from Coblentz, in the southern district of the Rhenish Province, on February 21, 1706. He married a young woman of that vicinity, and had by her four sons, George, Frederick, Peter and John; and two daughters, Margaret (married to —— Geyer), and Catharine (married to Elias Youngman). How many of the children were born there, I was not able to ascertain. By way of anticipating his emigration, he sent his eldest son, George, to Pennsylvania in 1748 for the purpose of examining the country. The report was evidently favorable, for he and his wife, and the children still with him, emigrated in 1751, landing at Philadelphia in the Fall of that year. Thence he went to Berks County, where he settled on a tract of land situated in Douglass township, at the confluence of the Manatawny creek and its lower tributary, the Ironstone, and erected a grist mill, which he carried on until his death, July 26, 1795, in the 90th year of his age.

George Nagel was born at Eisenberg, about the year 1728. He located at Reading about 1755, and engaged at blacksmithing. He was enlisted in the French and Indian War as an ensign, and for a time was stationed at Fort Augusta. He continued in service until the close of the war in 1763, when he returned to Reading and resumed his trade. When the Revolution began, he was imbued with a high patriotic spirit, and raised the first company of men in Berks County, which participated in the Massachusetts campaign at and about Cambridge. He continued in active service until 1783, rising to the rank of colonel. [See page 77.]

Upon his return to Reading, he engaged in the mercantile business, which he carried on until his death in March, 1789. The inventory in the settlement of his estate shows many unpaid book accounts. His remains were buried in the Reformed graveyard. He was married to Rebecca, a daughter of Mordecai Lincoln, of Exeter township, by whom he had two children, a son, Jacob, and a daughter, who was married to Thomas McCartle, of Westminster, Maryland.

PETER NAGEL.

Peter Nagel was one of the four sons of Joachim Nagel. He was born October 31, 1750, at Eisenberg, and emigrated with his father to Douglass township, in Berks County, Pennsylvania, in September, 1751. When a young man, he moved to Reading

Peter Nagel

and learned the trade of hatter, serving an apprenticeship of seven years under Samuel Jackson, the first hat manufacturer at Reading. He carried on this occupation for some years as a journeyman, and then as a successful manufacturer until 1804.

He was prominently identified with the County Militia during the Revolution, his name appearing as a captain in the Returns from 1777 to 1783. The company under his command guarded prisoners of war at Reading upon different occasions. He was appointed a justice of the peace in 1793 by Gov. Thomas Mifflin (who was a warm personal friend), and he continued to serve this position by reappointment until his decease, a period covering over forty years. In 1803, when the County of Berks was divided into districts for justices of the peace, Reading was made the first district, and Peter Nagel was selected as one of the four appointees. He also officiated as coroner of the county from 1781 to 1787, and as treasurer of Reading from 1815 to 1828. His son, Peter Nagel, officiated as county treasurer from 1835 to 1843; his grandson, Henry Nagel, from 1843 to 1845, and his great-grandson, Dr. Hiester M. Nagel, from 1873 to 1875.

When Washington was at Reading in 1794, Peter Nagel participated in the review of the military parade in honor of the distinguished visitor. Upon that occasion he held a reception at his residence (which was situated on North Fifth street, east side, on the second lot south of Washington, now constituting the lower half of the Post Office property), to enable the citizens to meet the great hero of the Revolution. Another incident is that he and his eldest daughter, Elizabeth, attended one of Washington's receptions at Philadelphia.

Capt. Nagel was a portly man, nearly six feet tall, of fine personal appearance and commanding presence. He died November 30, 1834, and his remains were interred in the Reformed burying-ground, whence they were removed to Charles Evans Cemetery. He was married twice, first to Barbara Ann Imler, with whom he had eight children : one who died in infancy ; Elizabeth (married to William Old, who was a grandson of Baron Henry William Stiegel), Sarah (married to Jacob R. Boyer), Mary (married to George Buehler), Rebecca (married to Nicholas Coleman,) Catharine (married to Isaac Kimmel), Peter Nagel and George Nagel ; and then to the widow of Isaac High (who was the daughter of William Hottenstein, and the mother of Gen'l William High, a prominent man of the Militia of Berks County), with whom he had three children : Harriet (married to Daniel Mears), Susan (married to Jacob Boyer), and John High Nagel.

BODO OTTO.

Next to Washington, Gates, Mifflin, Wayne and other leading generals, Dr. Bodo Otto, of Reading, occupied a prominence and rendered useful services equal to any other man who was engaged in the great cause of the Revolution, not on the field of battle, leading his fellows into danger and death, but amongst the hospitals as a senior surgeon, caring for and administering to the sick, wounded and dying soldiers. And yet his name is not mentioned in history ! He was born of distinguished parentage in 1709, in the Kingdom of Hanover, Germany, and was especially educated as a surgeon under the authority of the Government in the University of Gœttingen. In 1755,

he emigrated with his family from Amsterdam, and landed at Philadelphia, where he practiced his profession very successfully until 1773, when he removed to Reading.

When the Revolution began, Dr. Otto took a prominent part in the public demonstrations; and in the selection of delegates from Berks County to the Provincial Conference in 1776, the people naturally looked to him as a thoroughly qualified man. This was the only representative position that he was enabled to take, for when the struggle began in earnest, and hospitals had to be established, he was appointed a senior surgeon of the hospitals in the Colonies. This was certainly bearing his share of responsibility in the cause, and all his time was evidently taken up in the proper performance of his duty. During the gloomy and discouraging Winter of 1777–78, while the army lay encamped at Valley Forge, he was in charge of the camp hospital, and was assisted by his two sons, Bodo and John Augustus. Toward the close, the following meritorious certificate was issued to him by the Director of Military Hospitals:

"This is to certify that Dr. Bodo Otto served in the capacity of a senior surgeon in the Hospitals of the United States in the year 1776, and when the new arrangement, in April, 1777, took place, he was continued in that station until the subsequent arrangement of September, 1780, when he was appointed hospital physician and surgeon, in which capacity he officiated until a reduction of a number of the officers of said department, in January, 1782, was made. During the whole of the time he acted in the above stations he discharged his duty with great faithfulness, care and attention. The humanity, for which he was distinguished, towards the brave American soldiery, claims the thanks of every lover of his country, and the success attending his practice will be a sufficient recommendation of his abilities in his profession. Given under my hand, the 26th day of January, 1782.

"JOHN COCHRAN,
"*Director of the Military Hospitals.*"

In the beginning of 1782, after serving as senior surgeon for nearly six years, he resumed his practice at Reading, though then 73 years of age, and carried it on until his death in 1787. His remains were interred in the Trinity Lutheran Church lot at the western end of the building. He was married three times, and among the children surviving were Bodo Otto, Jr., and John Augustus Otto, who were brought up in the same profession and became distinguished as medical practitioners. He resided on the north side of Penn Square, midway between Fifth and Sixth streets.

JOHN A. OTTO.

John Augustus Otto, a son of Dr. Bodo Otto, was born in Hanover, Germany, on July 30, 1751, and emigrated with his father to Philadelphia in 1755. While living at the latter place, he was given a thorough education and specially prepared to practice medicine and surgery. When his father removed to Reading in 1773, he accompanied the family. During the Revolution, he assisted his father in surgical operations and in attending the military hospitals. After the Revolution, he established a large practice at Reading and was recognized as an eminent physician. He served as a justice of the peace of Reading from 1785 to 1789, and in 1790 he filled the office of prothonotary.

He was married to Catharine Hitner, of Montgomery County, and died December 14, 1834. His children were Dr. John B. Otto, Daniel H. Otto, Margaret (married to Benjamin Witman), Mary (married to Hon. Gabriel Hiester), Sarah (married to Jonathan Hiester, Esq., an attorney at Reading), Elizabeth (married to Henry Richards), and Maria (married to Joseph Wood).

JOHN PATTON.

In the transfer of real estate in Berks County, John Patton is described as residing at Reading in 1764, and in 1782. In the campaign beginning with the Battle of Long Island, he commanded a regiment, but the only mention of it was found in connection with the march of the company of Capt. John Lesher from Womelsdorf by way of Kutztown and the East Penn Valley, to Perth Amboy in 1776. The regimental officers were from Tulpehocken and Heidelberg townships.

In 1774, John Patton was assessed in Heidelberg township. By the amount of the assessment, he was evidently a rich property owner. He was married to the widow of William Bird, and was interested in the manufacture of iron. By the *Colonial Records*, it appears that he supplied the Continental Army with cannon balls.

He officiated as a Judge of the county courts from 1770 to 1777, excepting 1776, when he was absent in the Long Island campaign; and he represented the county in the General Assembly for the years 1780 and 1782.

I think he came from Philadelphia and was an elderly man at the time, judging from his marriage to the widow of William Bird, but where he went to after 1782, I have not been able to ascertain.

A Col. John Patton is mentioned in the *Pennsylvania Archives*, but from the sketch given there it would seem that he was a different man from the John Patton who lived in Berks County.

JONATHAN POTTS.

Jonathan Potts was born in the lower part of Berks County, April 11, 1745. After obtaining a good education at Ephrata and Philadelphia, he went to Edinburgh, 1766. He was accompanied by Benjamin Rush. They carried letters of introduction from Benjamin Franklin. Potts returned in 1767, and graduated at the Medical Institute of Philadelphia, at its first commencement in 1768. He delivered the valedictory oration, and was highly complimented. He began the practice of medicine at Reading and became a noted practitioner. He wrote an article on "Utility of Vaccination" in 1771, which was published in *Pennsylvanien Staatsbote*. He mentioned the time small-pox visited Reading, and that 106 children died—one in three who had the disease.

He exhibited great patriotism during the Revolution, and represented Berks County at Philadelphia on several important occasions during 1775 and 1776. In the beginning, he was Secretary of the Committee on Correspondence, and after the movement in behalf of the Revolution was thoroughly started, he became prominently identified with the surgical department of the army. In June, 1776, he was appointed Surgeon for the Continental Army in Canada and at Lake George. In December, 1776, he was stationed at Philadelphia, and in April, 1777, at Albany. While there, he was Director-General of the hospitals of the Northern Department. Through his zeal in public service, he was prostrated by illness. He died at Reading in October, 1781, and left to survive him a widow and five children : three sons, Benjamin, Francis and Edward ; and two daughters, Mary and Deborah. He was a brother of Samuel Potts, Esq., of Pottsgrove, Montgomery County.

COLLINSON READ.

Collinson Read was one of the early leading attorneys of the Bar at Reading. He was admitted to practice on August 13, 1772. "He distinguished himself as a profound lawyer, and his publications will be remembered in Pennsylvania with high regard, as well by the merchant and private gentleman, as by the members of the Bar. He was of extensive erudition in the Greek, Latin, French and German languages. In this accomplished gentleman, there was a peculiar kindness of heart that disarmed all enmity in his opponents, and his exertions of friendship, whether in or out of the profession, were ever judicious and such as made him beloved by all his acquaintances. He died of pleurisy on March 2, 1815, aged 62 years, after an illness of only two days."—(*Weekly Advertiser, March 4, 1815.*)

He officiated as register of wills of the county in 1775 and 1776. The Standing Committee selected him as their secretary in 1775, and he served this position until the close of the Revolution.

JAMES READ.

James Read was born at Philadelphia. He came to Reading upon the erection of Berks County in 1752; and, by appointment from the Provincial Government,  filled the county offices of prothonotary, recorder, register, clerk of Orphans' Court and clerk of the Quarter Sessions continuously from 1752 to 1776. He was one of the first attorneys admitted to the Bar at Reading, and also practiced his profession while filling the offices named. The official records are in his own handwriting and indicate that he was a man of careful habits. He officiated as one of the justices of the county courts under the Provincial Government, and served as a member of the Supreme Executive Council for one term, from 1778 to 1781. He resigned the office June 4, 1781, " on account of considerations of duty to his family," and his resignation was accepted the next day. It would seem that he was after a higher office, for, on June 5th, he was one of six applicants for the position of Register of the Court of Admiralty and succeeded in making the appointment. Subsequently, in 1787, he was again elected as a Councillor from Berks County, and continued until 1790. Under the Constitution of 1776, he was elected in 1783 as a Censor to represent Berks County in the Council of Censors, who were " to inquire whether the Constitution was preserved inviolate in every part." On April 22, 1785, he was appointed flour inspector of Philadelphia, and reappointed on April 22, 1789. The numerous positions filled by him indicate that he was a man of recognized ability. He owned a number of properties at Reading at different times. I think he located at Philadelphia after 1790 and died there.

WILLIAM REESER.

William Reeser was born in Bern township and carried on farming for a time. He officiated as a county commissioner from 1757 to 1760, and after that time located at Reading. In the beginning of the Revolution, he participated in the public meeting at Reading on July 2, 1774, and he was selected as one of the Committee of Correspondence. In September, 1775, he presided at a meeting of divers inhabitants of the county, held at Reading, who had conscientious scruples against war, but expressed a willingness to contribute towards carrying it on. He also served as one of the Judges of the county courts from 1778 to 1784. During this time, he was busy in preparing last wills, for his name appears as a witness to many of them, indicating that he was a scrivener. His handwriting was very legible and rather bold. He died at Reading in June, 1785. His residence occupied the site of the First National Bank, on Penn Square below Sixth street.

CHRISTOPHER SCHULTZ.

Christopher Schultz was one of the Mennonite family of that name in Hereford township, where they had settled at a very early period in the history of the county. When the Revolution began, he was a man of great prominence in that section, and evidently interested in the popular movement for Independence, for he attended the first public meeting at Reading, on July 2, 1774, and was appointed on the Committee of Correspondence. On December 5th, following, he was placed on the Committee of Observation. He also officiated as a justice of the peace of that district for one term from 1777 to 1784, and died on September 28, 1789.

EDWARD SCULL.

Edward Scull (son of Nicholas Scull, Surveyor-General of Pennsylvania), was born at Philadelphia on October 26, 1716. He was educated to pursue surveying, and was the county surveyor of Northampton County before 1752. He located at Reading shortly after the erection of Berks County, and continued to follow surveying until the breaking out of the Revolution, when he turned his attention to military life. He became a captain and raised several companies at Reading. On May 16, 1778, he was appointed Secretary of the Board of War. He died at Reading, but I could not ascertain the exact time.

PETER SCULL.

Peter Scull, one of the captains from Reading in the Revolution, was born at Philadelphia in December, 1753. He was the eldest son of James Scull, a surveyor, and was educated to be an attorney-at-law. In January, 1776, while residing at Reading, he was commissioned as a captain in the 3rd Pennsylvania Regiment. Subsequently, he was aid-de-camp to Gen'l Washington at the Battle of White Plains, and he showed such a high degree of accomplishment and gallantry that the General recommended him to Congress as a worthy candidate for the office of Secretary of the Board of War. He received the appointment on July 17, 1779. Before this he had served as a major in the regiment commanded by Col. John Patton, his commission having been issued on January 11, 1777. His health failing, he was ordered to go abroad by his physician, and he left Chester for France on October 20, 1779, on the frigate "Confederacy." On the way, he died at sea, December 4, 1779. Shortly before, (November 23), he executed a last will, wherein he made the following bequests: To his friend, Dr. Jonathan Potts, the thanks of a dying man; to Alexander Graydan, his pocket pistols; to George Lux, the sword which was given to him by his honored father-in-law, friend and protector, Edward Biddle; to Col. Morgan Conner, his green-hilted hanger; and to Col. John Patton, of Philadelphia, his silver buckles.

CHARLES SHOEMAKER.

Charles Shoemaker was born at Germantown about the year 1735. His grandfather emigrated to this country with Pastorius and settled in the vicinity of

Charles Shoemaker

Germantown. About the year 1765, he moved to Windsor township, Berks County, and took up a considerable quantity of land. He exerted a large influence in politics and business in the upper section of the county. He represented the county in the Provincial Conference, and also in the Constitutional Convention of 1776. In 1777, he was appointed as one of the justices of the peace of the county for seven years, and at the expiration of his term he was reappointed, serving, doubtless, till the adoption of the Constitution of 1790; and he also officiated as a Judge of the courts from 1785 to 1790. The State Assembly in December, 1777, appointed and empowered him to solicit and take subscriptions for the Continental Loan, this service having required a large measure of ability to conduct the duties of the office with success. He succeeded in obtaining a considerable amount of subscriptions from various citizens of the county. At the close of the war, much loss was suffered by farmers and merchants from nonredemption of these loans. The people exhibited their patriotism to the country by lending their aid in its extremity. In November, 1777, he acted as one of the Commissioners who assembled at New Haven, in Connecticut, to regulate the price of commodities in the Colonies.

He represented the county in the General Assembly for twelve years—1792 to 1801, in 1810 and in 1812; and in the Senate for four years—1813 to 1816. After living a retired life for several years, he died in April, 1820, leaving to survive him five sons, Samuel, Charles, Jacob, Benjamin and John; and three daughters, Sophia (married to Jacob Huy), Catharine (married to Jacob Dunkle), and Mary (married to Benjamin Kepner).

JACOB SHOEMAKER.

Jacob Shoemaker, an elder brother of Charles Shoemaker, was born at Germantown. He became a resident of Reading some time before 1768. In that year, he was elected sheriff of Berks County, and he was commissioned for three years. His residence was on Penn street above Sixth (now No. 607). Being a man

Jacob Shoemaker

of considerable prominence, he was selected in December, 1774, as one of the Committee of Observation. He died at Reading in September, 1783, and left a widow, (afterward married to John Kurtz), and five daughters, Catharine (married to Conrad Foose), Mary (married to Henry Row), Hannah (married to Christopher Nagel), Christiana and Sophia.

JOHN SODER.

John Soder was born in Bern township, Berks County, where his father, Nicholas Soder, had settled in the early history of that district of territory, having emigrated from Berne, Switzerland, in 1735; and he was brought up to farming, which occupation he pursued until his decease.

He served as a captain four different times in the Revolution, each time for a period of sixty days, in different years. The record of his enlistments was obtained from the Pension Office of the United States. His name appears in the Militia Returns of 1777 as a captain of the 5th company in the 3rd Battalion, commanded by Col. Michael Lindemuth; but I could not find it in any other connection with the military affairs of the Revolution. The evidence of his service, however, is unmistakable. Unfortunately, the pension records previous to 1812 were destroyed by the British when they took possession of Washington. From the record of Capt. Soder, I am led to say that there were other enlistments similar to his, but they have not as yet been ascertained.

He died in April, 1817, possessed of a considerable estate, and left to survive him twelve children: four sons, John, Daniel, Jacob and Samuel; and eight daughters, Barbara (married to Peter Noecker), Margaret (married to John Haas), Mary (married to Jacob Zardman), Elizabeth, Sallie, Henrietta, Esther and Hannah. He was married twice, the second wife having been Margaret Eva Angstadt.

JOHN SPOHN.

John Spohn was born in Cumru township, Berks County, on January 19, 1754, a son of John Spohn, an early settler in that township. He was brought up as a farmer, and came to own and carry on for himself at an early age a farm of 156 acres in Exeter township, some distance to the south of Mt. Neversink. At the time of his decease, in 1822, he still owned a farm in that vicinity, exceeding 200 acres.

When the Revolution began, he was a young man. He formed one of the first companies at Reading in April, 1775, and was commissioned as a captain in January, 1776. His company, and also that of Capt. Peter Decker, constituted part of the 5th Pennsylvania Battalion, and participated in the movements of Washington's Army at and about New York. *John Spohn* They were taken prisoners at Fort Washington in November, 1776, and held as such until January following.

He was married to Maria Beidler, a daughter of Conrad Beidler, a prominent miller of Robeson township, who owned and carried on for a time the large mill at the mouth of the Allegheny Creek. Interest in military matters led his son-in-law, Philip Rush (my grandfather), to become identified with the County Militia also at an early age, so that when Berks County was called to supply her quota in the War of 1812–15, he became the fife-major of the 1st Regiment, 2nd Brigade, under the command of Maj.-Gen'l Daniel Udree.

He lived a retired life for some years, and died April 19, 1822. His remains were first interred in the Trinity Lutheran Cemetery, at Sixth and Walnut streets; then transferred to the Neversink Cemetery. He left a widow; three sons, Adam, Solomon and

John ; and four daughters, Catharine (married to John Ingham), Elizabeth (married to Jacob Kerlin), Barbara (married to Philip Rush), and Sarah (married to Daniel Ermold).

When I was a boy, possibly 14 years old, I asked grandfather one day about the early times in a general way, but he stopped all further inquiry abruptly by answering that I was too young to be concerned about such matters. I cannot recall the subject I was then interested in, but the natural bent of my mind displayed itself. Some years after his death in 1871, I began my inquiries in earnest, and I have kept them up unaided ever since.

BENJAMIN SPYKER.

Benjamin Spyker was born in the Palatinate about the year 1723. His father, John Peter Spyker, emigrated to Pennsylvania in 1738, landing at Philadelphia and proceeding thence shortly afterward to Tulpehocken township, where he took up a large tract of

Benjamin Spyker [signature]

land and effected a permanent residence. In 1744, he was licensed to carry on the business of an Indian trader ; and subsequently, he enlisted in the French and Indian War, his business having been destroyed by the rupture between the settlers and the Indians.

During this trying period, he wrote a number of important letters in reference to the cruelties of the Indians and the sufferings of the people. He was a neighbor and intimate associate of Conrad Weiser, and was a saddler by occupation.

At the beginning of the Revolution, he assisted in organizing the Associators of the county and preparing them for active military service. In 1776, he represented the county in the Provincial Conference and also in the Constitutional Convention. He officiated as a justice of the peace for many years in Tulpehocken township, his district comprising the western section of the county; and there he commanded a strong social and political influence. He died in September, 1802, aged nearly 80 years. He was a brother of Peter Spyker, Judge of the County Courts.

PETER SPYKER.

Peter Spyker was a son of John Peter Spyker. He was born in the Palatinate, and emigrated with his

father in 1738, locating in Tulpehocken township shortly after landing at Philadelphia. He carried on farming in that township for many years.

He was appointed one of the Judges of the county in 1763, and he continued to officiate by reappointment until his death in 1789, a period of twenty-six years. He was specially appointed as President of the Courts in 1780, though he had officiated as such since 1767. He was the principal judicial officer of the county during the Revolution. He also served as a justice of the peace of the Tulpehocken district from 1777. He died in August, 1789, in the township named, and left to survive him a widow and five children: John, Peter, Benjamin, Henry and Elizabeth (who was married to Philip Gardner), with a considerable estate for distribution among them under a last will.

HENRY SPYKER.

Henry Spyker was a son of Peter Spyker, Judge of the County Courts. He officiated as Paymaster of the Militia of the county from August, 1777, to the close of the Revolution. In the Militia Returns of 1777, his name appears as the Colonel of the 6th Battalion, which was composed of companies in the western section of the county, and he continued at the head of the militia for that section until 1783. In the Fall of 1777, he commanded the 5th and 6th classes, numbering 400 men, in the campaign about Chestnut Hill and Germantown. He represented the County in the General Assembly for the years 1785 and 1786.

His residence was in Tulpehocken township, where he carried on a general store until 1800, when he removed to Lewistown, Northumberland County.

DANIEL UDREE.

Daniel Udree was born at Philadelphia on August 5, 1751. I was not able to obtain any information about his antecedents; but from the character he displayed in Berks County for a period exceeding fifty years, and the property he acquired and successfully managed, they were evidently of some culture and distinction. The Oldenberg and Odenheimer families were among his prominent relatives.

His uncle, Jacob Winey, a man of large capital, at Philadelphia, became interested in the iron industries of Berks County, particularly in Oley and Richmond townships, about the year 1768, and he acted as clerk under him. While serving in this capacity, he resided on the Moselem Forge property in Richmond township, along the Ontelaunee Creek. In 1778, when only 27 years of age, he was a part owner of the Oley Furnace. Subsequently, he became the sole owner of this prominent industry, and also of the Rockland Forges, with a landed estate altogether embracing 2700 acres in one connected tract.

While still comparatively young, he exerted a large influence in the upper section of the county; and when the Revolution began, his patriotism asserted itself in no uncertain manner. In 1777, he was chosen Colonel of the 2nd Battalion of County Militia, and in the Summer of that year his regiment accompanied the 1st Battalion, commanded by Col. Daniel Hunter, of Oley, to Chester and participated in the Battle of Brandywine, where his horse was shot under him during the engagement. In that year, he was selected as a member of the two committees on forfeited estates, and collecting clothing, etc. He was again elected Colonel of the same battalion in 1778. Subsequently, for many years, he was prominently identified with the militia of the county and State. In the War of 1812-15, he was Major-General of the 6th Division, which included the two battalions that constituted the 2nd Brigade. His military bearing was very attractive, and his horsemanship won for him general admiration.

Col. Udree represented Berks County in the General Assembly from 1799 to 1803, and also in 1805; and while in this body he advocated in an earnest manner legislation relative to the internal improvements of Pennsylvania. He also represented the county in the National Congress for two terms, from 1813 to 1815, and from 1823 to 1825. While at Washington, during the latter term, Adams was elected President by the members of the House. Shortly before the election, he attended a reception that was given by Mrs. Adams, and during the course of the evening he met the distinguished lady, when she, in a quiet, pleasant way, alluded to the probable support which her husband might receive from the Representatives of Pennsylvania. "Yes," said he to her, "we are like the handle of a jug—all on one side," thereby intimating politely that the great majority of them were for General Jackson.

In personal appearance, Col. Udree was of medium height, rather stout but compactly built, and his manner of conversation was quick and nervous. Shortly before his decease, he attended a local celebration of the "Fourth of July" at Pricetown, and, though 76

years old, showed much animation while riding in a superb manner on a favorite bob-tailed sorrel horse.

He died suddenly from a stroke of apoplexy at his home on the Oley Furnace property on July 15, 1828, and left to survive him an only child, a daughter, Maria, who was married to Jacob Udree Snyder, to whom his large and valuable estate descended. His remains were interred in the cemetery connected with the Oley Churches.

HENRY VANDERSLICE.

Henry Vanderslice, son of Anthony Vanderslice and Martha Pannebecker, was born March 9, 1726, in Providence township, then Philadelphia, now Montgomery County, where he was brought up as a miller. About 1760, he removed to Exeter township, in Berks County. In 1774, he was elected sheriff of Berks County, and held that position for three years.

During the Revolutionary War, he bore a prominent part in the military affairs of the county; and when Congress directed the Declaration of Independence to be read publicly in the several counties of each Province on July 8, 1776, he, as the sheriff, performed this distinguished service at the Court House in Reading.

On November 19, 1789, Daniel Brodhead, as Surveyor-General of Pennsylvania, appointed him a deputy surveyor. His sureties were Col. Jacob Morgan and Col. Nicholas Lotz. His surveys were numerous and noted for their accuracy. He died at Reading February 10, 1797, and was buried there.

BENJAMIN WEISER.

Benjamin Weiser, the youngest son of Conrad Weiser, was born in Heidelberg township, Berks County, on August 12, 1744. Upon arriving of age, he conducted a general store in that township, and he carried on this business until 1776, when he was selected as a Captain, by the Executive Council for the German Regiment in the Continental Line. His company was organized out of men from the townships of Heidelberg and Tulpehocken in the western section of the county. It is not known how long they were in service. They participated in the battles of Trenton and Princeton.

During the latter part of 1777, his family, it is believed, removed to Penn township, then in Northumberland County, (now Snyder,) locating in the vicinity of Selinsgrove. On January 21, 1778, he was commissioned as a justice of the peace for the township named, by which it would appear that he had changed his residence.

Among the Representatives from Berks County in the General Assembly for the year 1782, there was one named Benjamin Weiser. This was doubtless another man, for, on the records in the Recorder's Office, one by this name, described as a tinsmith by occupation, lived at Womelsdorf after 1800, and it is probable that he served this position. Notwithstanding this evidence, however, it is possible that Captain

Weiser might have returned to this county and been elected. I could not obtain any facts about him after 1778.

CHRISTOPHER WITMAN.

Christopher Witman was a cordwainer (shoemaker) at Reading in 1756, and continued in this employment until after 1762. In 1774, he was an innkeeper, his public house having been situated on the southwest corner of Penn Square and Fourth street.

In December, 1774, he was selected as one of the Committee on Observation, and he officiated as the county treasurer from 1775 to 1778. He died while holding this position in May, 1778, and left six sons: John, William, George, Abraham, Jacob, Daniel; and a daughter, Catharine.

RETROSPECT.

The foregoing sketches include the names of the most prominent men of Berks County who participated actively in the Revolution. Other men, whose names are mentioned in connection with military and representative positions, committees, &c., are equally deserving of a place in this book, but I found my researches for facts too tedious to extend them without detriment to my regular avocation. I may add that there are still others who have not been mentioned at all. They resided in different parts of the county and contributed their share to the Revolution in various ways, but their names were not given any public prominence during the course of prosecuting the war. Notwithstanding this, they too should be recognized. If sketches of all these men were prepared, it can be readily seen that they would fill a volume of this size. But I did not hope to be able to present so extended a collection, and I trust the reader will consider the numerous disadvantages under which I labored before criticising any imperfections or omissions in this publication.

By the sketches given, it is apparent that Berks County was represented by a class of men who were truly distinguished for their substantial character, and that they, together with similar men elsewhere throughout the Colonies, constituted the foundation of the political movement of the people for free government. My researches in discovering such men afforded me much pleasure, and I take great pride in recording their names in this permanent form for the admiration of their numerous descendants.

In looking back to the time of the Revolution, and appreciating as well the common desire of the people for their welfare, as the sacrifices which they made in that behalf ; and then following the course of human affairs until now, more especially since 1850, as influenced —indeed, I may add, if not controlled—by mechanical progress, we cannot fail to observe that we have been gradually drifting away from the liberal principles which were so boldly announced by the Delegates of 1776, in the Declaration of Independence, and so successfully established in the Constitution of 1787. Equality, fraternity and individuality stood out before our Revolutionary ancestors with prominent, comprehensive and thoroughly appreciated significance ; but it would now seem that success in commerce and manufactures, and in the various enterprises which are largely influenced by steam and electricity, is the principal consideration of financiers, traders, manufacturers, speculators and politicians, howsoever accomplished and with whatsoever sacrifice of local and individual rights.

This common display of character, mostly to gratify selfish purposes, may incline a large proportion of the people to look to the future with distrust and fear. It may apparently weaken the fraternal spirit of populous communities, and cause harmful tendencies to be exhibited in different channels with increasing force until civil strife ensues. But we need not feel unnecessarily alarmed. By the experience of mankind during the past four hundred years, these public mutterings are the certain manifestations of a wonderful and uncontrollable power in the interest of the peace, comfort and contentment of the people.

The natural elements startle us at times, but when the lightnings, storms and floods subside, the air is pure and the sky is clear. It seems that these forces must visit the earth, even if attended with suffering, loss and death; and so it seems that the spirit of social and political agitation must visit a progressive people in the course of their development, even if attended with cruel and destructive warfare. Dictators, rulers and priests, whether in business, politics or religion, may flourish for a time in their vain conceits, and spread extravagant notions in the several affairs of life, and thereby they may obstruct the course of social elevation for a time, just as rocks and cascades impede the flowing waters of winding streams; but they shall pass away like a cloud in the infinite sky, and their influence shall be absorbed by the multitude just as rivulets from the mountains are at last swallowed by the sea.

By speculation and imaginary values, some men may be enabled to reach out hundreds, even thousands, of miles, and affect the labors, the morals, the hopes and the fears of the people; they may build costly temples for various purposes and win temporary applause; they may scatter large gifts here and there with seeming generous hands and awaken great admiration; and they may disturb the social equilibrium by forcing an unnatural and unjust distribution of wealth and power. But they cannot alter the course of free government. It was started centuries ago in the convictions of the people through suffering and bloodshed; and nurtured by succeeding generations until now, particularly through increasing liberality for general education, it has become an indisputable, inalienable and imperishable possession.

The will of the people is expressed in their constant desire for liberty, justice and equality. These principles may again seem weak and presumptuous in the face of concentrating wealth and power. So were they apparently in 1776, but they nevertheless prevailed against a government that was distinguished for its worldly greatness and success. By the course of progress in human affairs, we need not doubt their ultimate triumph, for they are not weak and changing creations from the conception of man, but eternal virtues from the power of God.

INDEX.

ADDRESS of Provincial Conference.................... 45
    For Flying Camp............. 48
Admiralty, Register of Court of... 195
Affairs at Reading, 1777-78........ 198
Allegiance, Oath of Required..... 66
    Oaths Administered in County 69
Appeal for Support in Warfare.... 191
Army Supplies from County...... 174
Army Surgeons from County...... 144
Articles of Association, Preamble to........................ 41
    County Committee Recommends.................... 41
Assembly, Members of, from County..................... 194
Assessors of County.............. 197
Associated Battalions, County Colonels of.................40, 195
Associators, Address to, for Flying Camp..................... 47
    Companies, what to Consist of 40
    County Colonels of............ 40
    County Committee Recommends Articles of........... 41
    Preamble to Articles of........ 41
    Recommendation of Congress as to........................ 39
Attainder, Committee on, of County. 196
Auditing Committee of County... 197

BALDY, Capt. Jacob, Company of in New Jersey........... 133
    Roll of Company.............. 133
    On the Frontier............... 137
Battalions, Companies and Classes, Militia System.............. 67
Berks County, Districts of in 1776, 38
    Population of in 1776.......... 38
    Resolution of Standing Committee to Support Civil Authority..................... 44

Bethlehem, County Troops at..... 92
Biddle Edward, Chairman of Public Meeting in 1774.......... 23
    Delegate to Congress in 1774.. 27
    Member of Assembly.......... 194
    Sketch of..................... 209
Bird, Col. Mark, Battalion of at South Amboy in 1776........ 108
    Letter from, to Council of Safety..................... 108
    Letter About English Prisoners at Reading............... 151
    Sketch of..................... 212
Bower, Capt. Jacob, Company of in Continental Line......... 117
    Roll of Company.............. 118
    Sketch of..................... 214
Bright, Michael, Sketch of........ 215
British Authority, Suppression of Recommended by Congress. 43
    Invasion, not of the County... 126
Brodhead, Col. Daniel, on Committee of Correspondence... 24
    Appointed a Lieutenant....... 35
    Colonel of Associators........ 40
    On Standing Committee....42, 196
    Sketch of..................... 216
Buildings, Pre-Revolutionary at Reading..................... 203
Burd, Edward, at Cambridge..... 80
    At Long Island............... 98
    Sketch of..................... 218

CABAL, Conway................ 200
Canada Campaign, Jones's Company in.................. 80
Captains, Names of, from County in Service 173
    Of County in Continental Line 118
Cause of the Revolution.......... 19
Chester, Two Battalions of County at......................... 119

INDEX.

Christ, Capt. Henry, Company of
    at Long Island in 1776...... 86
    Roll of Company............ 86
    Services of Company........ 87
    Sketch of.................. 219
Churches at Reading Used as
    Hospitals.................. 145
Civil Authority, Support of by the
    County..................... 44
Collectors of Excise............. 196
Colonels, Names of, from County
    in Service.................. 173
    Of Associated Battalions....40, 195
Commissioners of County........ 197
    Of Forage................... 196
Committee on Correspondence................24, 29, 195
    Auditing of County........... 197
    Local....................... 196
    On Attainder and Forfeited
      Estates................... 196
    On Observation..........28, 195
    Standing................42, 196
    To Collect Arms, &c.......... 196
Company Roll of—
    Capt. Jacob Baldy............ 133
    Capt. Jacob Bower............ 118
    Capt. Henry Christ............ 86
    Capt. Peter Decker........... 84
    Capt. Daniel DeTurck........ 94
    Capt. John Diehl.............. 115
    Capt. Michael Furrer.......... 107
    Capt. Conrad Geist.........156, 165
    Capt. Charles Gobin.......... 130
    Capt. Jonathan Jones......... 81
    Capt. Charles Krause......... 164
    Capt. John Lesher............ 105
    Capt. John Ludwig........... 133
    Capt. George Miller........... 106
    Capt. Jacob Moser............ 116
    Capt. George Nagel........... 77
    Capt. Peter Nagel............. 167
    Capt. Ferdinand Ritter........ 131
    Capt. John Robinson......... 139
    Capt. Nicholas Scheffer....... 115
    Capt. Conrad Sherman........ 132
    Capt. John Spohn............ 83
    Capt. Henry Strouch.......... 134
    Capt. Bartholomew Von Heer, 128
    Capt. Benjamin Weiser........ 102
    Capt. George Will............ 114
    Capt. Michael Wolf........... 105

Companies of Associators, what to
    Consist of.................. 40
    From County at New York... 82
    At Newtown................ 113
    In Revolution............... 75
    Militia System............... 67
    Of Ely's Battalion on Frontier, 136
Conference, Provincial, June, 1774, 44
    Address for Convention...... 45
    For Flying Camp........... 47
    Declaration of Independence.. 46
    Deputies from County to....45, 194
    Resolutions of, in 1775........ 31
Congress, Declaration of Independence by................ 49
    Delegate to, from County..... 27
    Deputies to, at Philadelphia,
      1774....................... 27
    Letter to, from Standing Committee..................... 90
    Recommendation of, for Associators..................... 40
    Representatives to, in 1776.... 49
    Resolution by, to Suppress
      British Authority 43
Conscientious Scruples Against
    War....................... 33
    Resolutions Adopted at Public Meeting.................. 33
Constitutional Convention of
    Province in 1776............. 50
    Delegates from County to...50, 194
    Preamble to Constitution..... 51
    Declaration of Rights......... 53
Continental Congress, Delegate to 194
Continental Line, County Men in, 116
    Captains from County in...... 118
    Sundry Enlistments in........ 118
Continental Paper Money........ 187
Conway-Cabal.................. 200
Correspondence, Committee of..29, 195
Councillors, from County........ 195
Counties of Province in 1775...... 39
County Assessors................ 197
    Auditing Committee of........ 197
    Battalions of, at Chester...... 119
    Captains, Names of in Service, 173
    Commissioners............... 197
    Committee Recommends Articles of Association.......... 41

County—(Continued.)
    Colonels of Associators......40, 195
    Committee of Correspondence 24, 29
    Committee of Observation....   28
    Delegates to Constitutional Convention................51, 194
    Delegates to Provincial Conference................29, 45, 194
    Districts of, in 1776............   38
    English People, Location of in,   35
    Enlistments from.............   141
    Forges in......................   183
    Furnaces in....................   183
    Incumbents of Positions—
        National.....................   194
        State........................   194
        County......................   195
    Industries of................183, 184
    Ironmasters of.................   184
    Jail Building...................   204
    Judges of.......................   197
    Lieutenants of.................   196
    Members of Assembly of.......   194
    Militia, Payments for..........   149
    Paymasters of Militia of.......   196
    Quartermaster of   196
    Sub-Lieutenants of............   196
    Support of Civil Authority by,   44
    Surgeons of Army...........144, 194
    Standing Committee,........42, 196
    Troops at Bethlehem..........   92
    Sheriffs........................   197
    Treasurers.....................   197
    Troops at Newtown, 1781......   138
        On Frontier, 1782............   141
        Orders for............146, 147, 148
        At South Amboy.............   103
Court House Building............   204
    Cut of.........................   22
Crumrine, Capt. Stephen, Pay to, for Poor Associators.........   146

DAYS of Drill, Militia System,   68
Decker, Capt. Peter, Company of at New York in 1776   84
    Roll of Company...............   84
    Services of Company..........   84
    One of First Officers Selected from County....................   34
    Sketch of......................   220

Declaration of Independence by Congress....................   49
    Read in Berks County........   50
    By Province..................   46
    Of Rights by Constitutional Convention...................   53
Delegate Continental Congress, 27, 194
    Provincial Conference.......29, 194
    Constitutional Convention...45, 194
DeTurck, Capt. Daniel, Company of at Bethlehem.............   93
    Marching Order to...........   94
    Roll of Company.............   94
    Pay of Men   95
    Order to Organize...........   96
Deputies, Congress of............   27
Diehl, Capt. John, Company of at Newtown.....................   115
    Roll of Company.............   115
Districts of the County in 1776....   38
Douglass, Capt. George, at Long Island......................   90
    Sketch of.....................   220
Drill, Days of, in Militia System..   68
Duel at Reading..................   202
Dundas, Thomas, on Committee of Correspondence..........24, 195
    Sketch of.....................   221

ECKERT, Capt. Conrad, at White Marsh...............   122
    Sketch of.....................   224
Eckert, Valentine. Lieutenant of County...................   196
    Sub-Lieutenant of County....   196
    Sketch of.....................   223
Ege, George, Shot and Shell from to Government..............   177
    Sketch of.....................   225
Ely, Col. Samuel, Battalion of on Frontier Service in 1780.....   136
    Battalion of, at Newtown, 1781,   138
English People, Location of, in County......................   35
English Prisoners at Reading.....   151
    Conduct of...................   152
    Geist's Company as Guard....   156
Enlistments from County.........   141

INDEX.

Estimate of Men in Service......68, 168
Executive Councillors of County.. 195
Excise, Collectors of.............. 196
Exempted Persons from Service in Militia................... 69

F ARMERS' Inn at Reading.... 203
Farmers of Berks County, Letter to as to Wool........ 30
Federal Inn at Reading............ 204
    Cut of.......................... 244
Fines of Militia System............ 69
First Officers Selected from County.................... 34
    George Nagel, Major......... 34
    John Spohn, Captain.......... 34
    Peter Scull,   "   34
    Peter Decker,   "   34
    Daniel Brodhead, Lieutenant, 35
Flying Camp, Address of Conference for.................... 47
    Intentions of Congress Explained................... 91
    Lotz's Battalion in............ 89
Forage, Commissioners of........ 196
Forfeited Estates, Committee on.. 196
Forges of County................ 183
Friends' Meeting House.......... 204
Frontiers, Battalion of Col. Michael Lindemuth on......... 128
    Ely's Battalion on............ 136
    County Troops on in 1782..... 141
Furnaces of County.............. 183
Furrer, Capt. Michael, Company of in Patton's Battalion...... 107
    Roll of Company............. 107

G EEHR, Col. Balser, Battalion of at Bethlehem.............. 93
    Colonel of Associated Battalions...................... 40
    Judge of County Courts....... 197
    Member of Assembly......... 194
    On Observation Committee.. 28, 195
    On Standing Committee.....42, 196
    Sketch of..................... 227
Geist, Capt. Conrad, Company of Guarding English Prisoners, 156
    Roll of Company...........156, 165

Germantown, Reading Officer Wounded at................ 123
German Regiment, Weiser's Company in..................... 101
    Other Men from County in.... 103
German Prisoners at Reading..... 163
Germans to the Rescue............ 35
Graydon Alexander, Extracts from Memoirs.............. 198
    Sketch of..................... 230
Gobin, Capt. Charles, Company of in New Jersey................ 130
    Roll of Company............. 130

H ALLER, Col. Henry, Appointed to Solicit Subscriptions to Loan............... 189
    Battalion near Trenton........ 109
    Desertion of Battalion........ 110
    Conduct Explained 110
    Wagonmaster of County...... 196
    Sketch of.................... 230
Hessian Prisoners at Reading.... 157
    Camp for..................... 158
    Camp Surprised.............. 159
    Letter for Removal of......... 157
    Officer Drowned.............. 162
    Sickness and Burial.......... 163
Hiester, Gabriel, Sketch of........ 232
Hiester, Joseph, Battalion of with Reed's Army in New Jersey, 129
    Company of at Long Island.... 90
    Incidents of Company........ 99
    Sketch of..................... 233
Hospitals at Reading............. 145
Hunter, Col. Daniel, Battalion of in New Jersey in Jan'y, 1777, 111
    At Chester, August, 1777...... 120
    Col Brodhead's Letter........ 111
    Member of Council of Safety.. 51
    Putnam's Letter to Council... 112
    Resolutions of Council........ 112
    Sketch of..................... 235

I NCUMBENTS of Positions from County................ 194
    National..................... 194
    State........................ 194
    County...................... 195

Independence and Peace	205
Independence of the Province	43
Declaration of by Province	46
By Congress	49
Indians, Inhabitants of County Killed by	136
Industries of County	183, 184
Inhabitants of County Killed by Indians	136
Ironmasters of County	184

JAIL Building of County	204
Cut of	155
Jones, Capt. Jonathan, Company of in Canada Campaign	80
Roll of Company	81
Services of Company	81
Jones Thomas, Sketch of	236
Judges of County	197
Justices of the Peace of County	197

KRAUSE, Capt. Charles, Company of Guarding Prisoners at Reading	164
Roll of Company	164
Kutztown, Troops Encamped at	125
Patton's Battalion Marched by Way of	104

LADICH, Capt. Jacob, Company of at Newtown	149
Pay and Bounty of Company	149
Lancaster Committee, Letters to from County Committee	29, 30
Lesher, Capt. John, Company of in Patton's Battalion	105
Roll of Company	105
Letter to Council from, about Supplies Taken	181
Sketch of	237
Letter as to Wool from Committee of Correspondence	30
To James Read from Gen'l Thomas Mifflin	113
To Congress from Standing Committee	90

To Council from Mark Bird	151, 176
From Gen'l Israel Putnam about County Troops	112
From James Read	153
From Jacob Morgan, Jr.	179
From John Lesher	181
Levan, Daniel, Sheriff of County	197
Treasurer of County	197
Sketch of	238
Levan, Sebastian, Sketch of	238
Lexington, Battle at Awakens County	32
Lieutenants of County	196
Lincoln, Abraham, County Commissioner	197
Member of Assembly	194
Sketch of	239
Lindemuth Col. Michael, Battalion of on Frontiers in 1778	128
Letter from on Murder of Inhabitants in 1780	136
One Class of Battalion on Frontiers in 1781	138
On Frontier Service	137, 138
Livingood, Capt. Jacob, Company of in Service in 1781	140
Order for Enlistment	140
Pay of Service	140
Sketch of	241
Local Committees	196
Long Island, Battle of	97
Lotz, Col. Nicholas, Battalion in Flying Camp	89
Notice to Elect Officers of Battalion	89
Committee Letter to Congress	90
Receipt Book of	183
Chairman of Standing Committee	196
Commissioner of Forage	196
Sketch of	242
Lower, Christian, County Commissioner	196
Sub-Lieutenant of County	196
Sketch of	245
Ludwig. Capt. John, Company in New Jersey	133
Roll of Company	133
Justice of Peace	197
Sketch of	246

MANUFACTURED Supplies for Army from County...... 175
Masts for Navy cut in County.. 137, 182
Members of Assembly from County...................... 194
Men, Estimate of in Service....... 168
Men Subject to Military Duty....40, 59
Men Supplied from County, Reports of...................... 145
Mifflin, Gen'l Thomas, Letter about Raising Men at Reading............................ 113
Militia System.................... 56
   County Delegates to Lancaster Convention.................. 58
   County Returns for 1775....... 57
   " " " 1776...... 58
   " " " 1777...... 59
   " " " 1778...... 70
   " " " 1780...... 72
   " " " 1783...... 73
   New System Provided in 1777, Battalions, Companies and Classes.................... 66, 67
   County Districts Established.................... 67
   Days of Drill............... 68
   Fines...................... 69
   Oaths Administered in County................. 69
   Oath of Allegiance......... 66
   Pay and Rations........... 68
   Pensions.................. 69
   Persons Exempted......... 69
   Guard for Prisoners.......... 166
   Payments for, in County...... 149
   Paymasters of County........ 196
   Resolution of Council for..... 167
Miller, Capt. George, Company of in Patton's Battalion........ 106
   Roll of Company............. 106
Money, Continental Paper 187
Morgan, Col. Jacob, Delegate to Constitutional Convention.. 51
   Delegate to Provincial Conference.................... 45
   Judge of County Courts....... 197
   Justice of the Peace.......... 197
   Lieutenant of County......... 196
   Sketch of.................... 247
Morgan, Col. Jacob, Jr., Deputy Quartermaster-General...... 194

   Superintendent of Commissioners of Purchases........ 195
   Quartermaster of County..... 196
   Wagonmaster-General of State...................... 195
   Sketch of.................... 250
Morgan, David, Sketch of......... 253
Moser, Capt. Jacob, Company of in Continental Line......... 116
   Roll of Company............. 116
Murder of Inhabitants by Indians, 136
Musket Barrels, Length of........ 40

NAGEL, Capt. George, Company of at Cambridge in 1775 75
   Form of Enlistment........... 76
   Roll of Company............. 77
   Services of Company..... ... 79
   One of First Officers Selected from County............... 34
   Sketch of.................... 254
Nagel, Capt. Peter, Company of Guarding Prisoners at Reading........................ 167
   Chairman of Meeting of Revolutionary Survivors........ 207
   Roll of Company............. 167
   Sketch of.................... 255
Names of Captains and Colonels from County in Service...... 173
National Incumbents of Positions from County................. 194
Negman John and Children Murdered by Indians in 1780.... 136
Newtown, Companies from County at................... 113
   Mifflin's Letter for, to Read, 113
   County Troops at in 1781...... 113
New York, Companies at from County in 1776.............. 82

OATH of Allegiance Required in 1777................... 66
   Administered in County...... 69
Observation, County Committee of,......................28, 195
Old, Capt. John, Company of in Lotz's Battalion............ 90
   At Bethlehem................ 93
Oley, Supplies Taken from in 1778, 181
Otto, Dr. John A., Sketch of..... 261

Otto, Dr. Bodo, Delegate to Provincial Conference.......... 45
   National Surgeon.............. 194
   Surgeon of Army............. 144
   Sketch of........ 258

PATTON, Col. John, Battalion of at Bethlehem............. 93
   At South Amboy.... 103
   Appointed to Sign Currency.. 189
   Judge of County Courts....... 197
   Member of Assembly......... 194
   Pay to for Cannon Shot....... 178
   Sketch of..................... 262
Paper Money, Continental........ 187
Patriotic Spirit of the County..... 23
Pay and Rations of Militia....... 68
Payments for County Militia...... 149
Paymasters of County Militia..... 196
Pay of Men in Service........76, 95, 186
Pennybacker, Capt. Dirck, Pay to 149
Pennsylvania, Counties of in 1775. 39
   Men from, in service in 1776.. 145
   In 1777...........:........... 147
   Population of in 1776......... 38
Peace, Independence and......... 205
Pensions of Militia System........ 69
Persons Exempted from Service in Militia 69
Philadelphia, Public Papers Removed from, to Reading.... 198
Population of County in 1776...... 38
   Pennsylvania in 1776 38
Potts, Dr. Jonathan, Army Surgeon from County.......... 144
   Delegate to Provincial Convention..................... 29
   Letters to Lancaster Committee 29
   Letter to Farmers as to Wool, 30
   National Surgeon............. 194
   On Committee of Observation, 28
   Sketch of..................... 263
Prayer, First Recommendation for 190
Pre-Revolutionary Buildings at Reading..................... 203
Prices During Revolution.... 185, 186
Prisoners of War at Reading...... 151
   English........ 151
   Hessian..................... 157

German...................... 163
Militia Guarding..156, 164, 165, 167
Proclamation for Favor of God... 190
Prominent Industries of County... 183
   Furnaces..................... 183
   Forges....................... 183
Prothonotary of Supreme Court.. 195
Province, Counties of in 1775..... 39
   Independence of............,.. 43
Provincial Conference at Philadelphia, July, 1774.............. 26
   Notice issued for............. 26
   Conference, June, 1776........ 44
   Address for Flying Camp by 47
   Address Issued by.......... 45
   Declaration of Independence 46
   Deputies from County to..45, 194
   Resolutions of in 1775......... 31
Provincial Convention, Notice for on January 23, 1775......... 28
   County Delegates to.......... 29
   Resolutions of.............. 31
Provost Guard, Dragoons of County in.................... 127
Public Meeting at Reading, 1774... 23
Public Papers Removed from Philadelphia to Reading.... 198
Purchases, Superintendent of Commissioners of........... 195
   Superintendent of............ 196
Putnam, Gen'l Israel, Letter of about Berks County Troops, 112

QUAKER Prisoners at Reading...................... 154
Quartermaster of County.......... 196
Quartermaster-General, Deputy, from County................. 194

RATIONS of Militia........... 68
Read, Collinson, Secretary of Standing Committee, 42, 44, 196
   Sketch of..................... 264
Read, James, Appointed to Sign Continental Notes.......... 189
   Committee on Correspondence......................24, 195
   Executive Councillor.... :..... 195
   Justice of the Peace........... 197

INDEX.

James Read—(Continued.)
   Letter from About English Prisoners.................... 153
   Member of Assembly.......... 194
   Register of Court of Admiralty........................ 195
   Sketch of................... 265
Reading, Affairs at............... 198
   Centre of Trade............... 25
   Churches at, used as Hopitals, 145
   Duel at....................... 202
   Federal Inn at................ 204
   First Companies at............ 33
   Hospitals at.................. 145
   Militia to Guard Stores at.... 148
   Patriotic Feeling at in 1775.... 33
   Pre-Revolutionary Buildings.. 203
   Prisoners of War at........... 151
   Public Meeting at in 1774..... 23
      Committee Appointed by.... 24
      Resolutions Adopted by.... 23
   Public Papers removed to, from Philadelphia.................. 198
   Social Condition in 1777....... 198
   Storekeeper at................ 196
Receipt Book of Col. Nicholas Lotz......................... 183
Reeser, William, Chairman of Meeting....................... 33
   On Committee of Observation.......................28, 198
   Sketch of..................... 266
Reformed Church Building....... 204
   Cut of........................ 144
Register of Court of Admiralty... 195
Reports of Men Supplied from County........................ 145
Return of the Soldiers........... 206
Revolution, Cause of............. 19
Revolutionary Survivors.......207, 208
Riehm, Capt. George, Company of at Newtown............138, 149
   Pay of Company for Services.. 149
Ritter, Capt. Ferdinand, Company of in New Jersey............. 131
   Roll of Company.............. 131
Robinson, Capt. John, Company of at Newtown in 1781...... 139
   On Frontiers in 1782.......... 141
   Roll of Company.............. 139

SCHEFFER, Capt. Nicholas, Company of at Newtown.... 115
   Roll of Company.............. 115
Schultz, Christopher, Justice of the Peace.................... 197
   On Committee of Correspondence...................... 24
   On Committee of Observation, 28
   Sketch of..................... 267
Scull, Edward, Secretary of Board of War...................... 194
   Ordered on Recruiting Service, 1778.................... 147
   Sketch of..................... 268
Scull, Peter, one of First Officers Selected from County....... 34
   Sketch of..................... 268
Secretary of Board of War from County....................... 194
Service, Estimate of Men in from County....................... 168
Sherman, Capt. Conrad, Company of in New Jersey...... 132
   Roll of Company.............. 132
Sheriffs of County............... 197
Shoemaker, Charles, Delegate to Constitutional Convention, 51
   Delegate to Provincial Conference...................... 45
   Justice of the Peace........... 197
   Sketch of..................... 269
Shoemaker, Jacob, on Committee of Observation............28, 195
   Sketch of..................... 271
Shot and Shell from George Ege to the Government.......... 177
Snell, Dr. Nicholas, Surgeon at Newtown..................... 149
South Amboy, County Troops at in 1776....................... 103
Social Condition at Reading in 1777 and 1778................ 198
Soder, Capt. John, Sketch of...... 271
Soldiers, Return of the........... 206
Spohn, Capt. John, Company of at New York in 1776........... 83
   Roll of Company.............. 83
   Services of Company.......... 84
   One of First Officers Selected from County................. 34
   Sketch of..................... 272

Spyker, Benjamin, Delegate to
  Constitutional Convention............................51, 194
  Delegate to Provincial Conference..................45, 194
  Sketch of 274
Spyker, Col. Henry, Battalion of
  at White Marsh............. 122
  Orders to for Pay of Militia... 150
  Paymaster of County Militia, 196,
  Sketch of....................... 276
Spyker, Peter, Judge of County
  Courts...................... 197
  Justice of the Peace........... 197
  Sketch of..................... 275
Standing Committee......42, 44, 91, 196
  Letter of to Congress......... 90
State Incumbents of positions from
  County...................... 194
Strouch, Capt. Henry, Company
  of in New Jersey............ 134
  Roll of Company.............. 134
Storekeeper at Reading.......... 196
Sub-Lieutenants of County....... 196
Supplies for Army from County.. 174
  Manufactured................. 175
  Collected.................... 177
  At Reading................... 180
Suppression of British Authority
  Recommended by Congress, 43
Surgeon of Army from County.... 144
  National from County......... 194
Supreme Court, Prothonotary of.. 195
Survivors of Revolution........207, 208

TORIES, who Designated.....21, 37
  Trinity Lutheran Church
    Building................... 204
    School Building............ 204
Tulpehocken, Companies from at
  Bethlehem................... 93

UDREE, Daniel, Colonel of
  Militia....................61, 70
  Commanded Battalion at
    Chester..................... 120
  Sub-Lieutenant of County.... 196
  Sketch of..................... 277

VON HEER, Capt. Bartholomew, Company of Dragoons
  in Provost Guard............. 128
  Roll of Company.............. 128

WAR, Conscientious Scruples against............... 33
Wagonmaster of County.......... 196
Wagonmaster-Generals of the
  County...................... 195
Warfare, Appeal for Support in... 191
Washington's Army near the
  County...................... 124
Weiser, Capt. Benjamin, Company in German Regiment.. 101
  Roll of Company.............. 102
  Services of Company.......... 102
  Sketch of..................... 281
Weiser Store Building............ 204
Whigs, who Designated.......... 21
White Marsh, Battalion of Col.
  Henry Spyker at............. 122
Whitman, Lieut., Wounded at
  Germantown................. 123
Will, Capt. George, Company of
  at Bethlehem................ 93
  At Newtown.................. 114
  Roll of Company.............. 114
Wilson, Capt. James, Recommended for Recruiting Service in 1778.................. 148
Wolf, Capt. Michael, Company of
  in Patton's Battalion........ 105
  Roll of Company.............. 105
Wool, Committee Letter as to.... 30